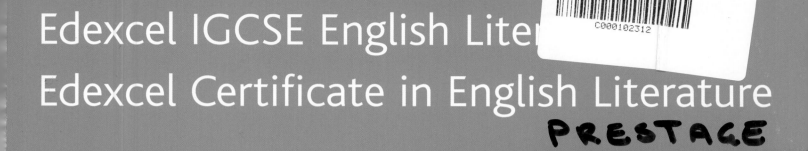

Edexcel IGCSE English Lite...
Edexcel Certificate in English Literature

Student Book

Pam Taylor

A PEARSON COMPANY

Published by Pearson Education Limited, a company incorporated in England and Wales, having its registered office at Edinburgh Gate, Harlow, Essex, CM20 2JE. Registered company number: 872828.

www.pearsonschoolsandfecolleges.co.uk

Edexcel is a registered trademark of Edexcel Limited

Text © Pearson Education Ltd 2011

First published 2011

15 14 13 12 11

IMP 10 9 8 7 6 5 4 3 2 1

ISBN 978 0 435046 75 0

Copyright notice

Original design by Richard Ponsford and Creative Monkey
Typeset by TechType
Original illustrations © Pearson Education Ltd 2011
Cover design by Creative Monkey
Cover photo © Alamy Images: Lisa Moore
Printed in the UK by Scotprint

Acknowledgements

The author and publisher would like to thank the following individuals and organisations for permission to reproduce photographs:

(Key: b-bottom; c-centre; l-left; r-right; t-top)

Alamy Images: 66tl, Black Star 87cr, Classic Image 55tr; **Bridgeman Art Library Ltd:** 121tr; **Corbis:** Bettmann 76tl; **Dreamstime.com:** Lu2006 131tr; **Fotolia.com:** 149tr, 154cl, 157tr, 149tr, 154cl, 157tr, air 23tr, alex 60tl, Andrey Kiselev 148tr, Ashwin 63tr, beawolf 26cl, Bill Perry 31tr, chameleonseye.com 129tr, chiyacat 12tl, cilin 125tr, Evgeny Dubinchuk 69tr, FlemishDreams 99tr, Glenda Powers 117tr, iofoto 1t, James Thew 81tr, Jason Stitt vi, Kablonk Micro 109tr, Laurence Gough 150tl, maksymowicz 45tr, Marek Kosmal 145br, Martin Garnham 39cr, Martin Mullen 135tr, Michael Felix 147tr, micro monkey 123cr, newa 142cr, Oleg Kozlov 115tr, quayside 6cl, Robert Elias 139tr, Sandra Cunningham 111cr, Star Jumper 18tl, Stefan Andronache 71br, Steve Byland 84tl, Tein 42bl, Tomislav Forgo 119tr, vintn 113tr, Vukas 107br, Waldemar 144t, Yuri Arcurs 105tr, 127cr, Zacarias da Mata 143tr; **iStockphoto:** 9tr, Peter Spiro 15tr; **Pearson Education Ltd:** title-pagec; **Shutterstock.com:** ARENA Creative 2cl, David Hughes 28bl, Dmitriy Shironosov 92tl, Gemenacom 49cr, Grin Maria 53tr, Monkey Business Images ix, Nathan Kresge 36, OtnaYdur 140tl

All other images © Pearson Education

The author and publisher would also like to thank the following for permission to reproduce copyright material:

p.98 from 'The Bacillus' by H.G. Wells. Reproduced by permission of A P Watt Ltd on behalf of The Literary Executors of the Estate of H G Wells; p.110 from 'Prayer Before Birth' by Louis MacNeice from *Selected Poems* 2007, reproduced with permission of David Higham Associates; p.112 from 'Half Past Two – Neck Verse' by U. A. Fanthorpe. First published in *Neck-Verse* (Peterloo Poets, 1992), reproduced by permission of Dr R.V. Bailey; p.116 from 'Hide and Seek' from *The Collected Poems of Vernon Scannell*, Faber Finds (Vernon Scannell, 2010). Reproduced by permission of The Estate of Vernon Scannell; p.122 from 'Poem at Thirty Nine' from *Horses Make a Landscape Look More Beautiful*, Orion (Alice Walker, 1985). Reproduced by permission of David Higham Associates; p.128 from The poem 'War Photographer' taken from *Standing Female Nude* by Carol Ann Duffy, published by Anvil Press Poetry in 1985, reproduced by permission of Anvil Press; p.134 from 'Refugee Mother and Child' by Chinua Achebe taken from *Collected Poems* copyright © 1971, 1973, 2004, 2005 Chinua Achebe. Reproduced by permission of The Wylie Agency (UK) Ltd. All Rights Reserved; p.136 from 'Do not go gentle into that good night' by Dylan Thomas from *Collected Poems/The Poems of Dylan Thomas*, Orion, copyright © 1952 Dylan Thomas. Reproduced by permission of David Higham Associates and New Directions Publishing Corp; p.142 from 'Blackberry Picking' from *Opened Ground: Selected Poems 1966–1996* by Seamus Heaney, copyright © 1998 by Seamus Heaney. Reproduced with permission from Faber & Faber Ltd and Farrar, Straus and Giroux, LLC; p.144 from 'Afternoons' by Philip Larkin. Reproduced with permission from Faber & Faber Ltd; CD: from 'Warning' by Jenny Joseph from *Selected Poems*, Bloodaxe, 1992. Copyright © Jenny Joseph. Reproduced with permission of Johnson & Alcock Ltd; CD: from 'Incendiary' by Vernon Scannell, from *The Collected Poems of Vernon Scannell* (Faber Finds, 2010). Reproduced by permission of The Estate of Vernon Scannell; CD: from 'I Shall Return' by Claude McKay. Reproduced by courtesy of the Literary Representatives for the Works of Claude McKay, Schomburg Center for Research in Black Culture, The New York Public Library, Astor, Lenox and Tilden Foundations; CD: from *The Woman In Black*, published by Vintage (Susan Hill, 1983) copyright © Susan Hill. Reproduced by permission of Sheil Land Associates Ltd.

Every effort has been made to contact copyright holders of material reproduced in this book. Any omissions will be rectified in subsequent printings if notice is given to the publishers.

Websites

The websites used in this book were correct and up to date at the time of publication. It is essential for tutors to preview each website before using it in class so as to ensure that the URL is still accurate, relevant and appropriate. We suggest that tutors bookmark useful websites and consider enabling students to access them through the school/college intranet.

Disclaimer

This material has been published on behalf of Edexcel and offers high-quality support for the delivery of Edexcel qualifications.

This does not mean that the material is essential to achieve any Edexcel qualification, nor does it mean that it is the only suitable material available to support any Edexcel qualification. Edexcel material will not be used verbatim in setting any Edexcel examination or assessment. Any resource lists produced by Edexcel shall include this and other appropriate resources.

Copies of official specifications for all Edexcel qualifications may be found on the Edexcel website: www.edexcel.com.

Contents

Contents

This book has several features to help you with IGCSE English Literature and Certificate in English Literature.

Characters

For each drama and prose text, a list of characters is provided. These boxes include a list of key facts about each character and are useful for revision.

Top tips

The boxes in the margin give you extra help or information. They might explain something in a little more detail or guide you to linked topics in other parts of the book.

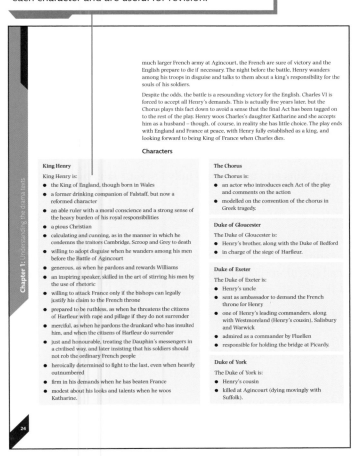

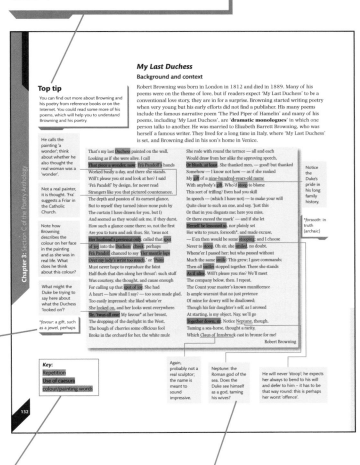

Footnotes

For difficult words or phrases, the footnotes explain what they mean.

Key

The key explains what the highlighted, bold or underlined words in the poem show.

Callouts

The callout boxes give extra information, draw your attention to important lines or themes in the poem and ask questions for you to consider.

Introduction

This book has been written to support both the updated Edexcel IGCSE English Literature (first examination June 2012) and the new Edexcel Certificate in English Literature (first examination June 2012). It is written for students and teachers and aims to help all students achieve their full potential during the course and in each of the assessments. One specification covers both the IGCSE and the Certificate. The IGCSE has two routes: one that is assessed entirely through examination at the end of the course and one that includes coursework. The Certificate is assessed entirely through examination at the end of the course. This book will prepare students for all aspects of both the qualifications.

Students

How will this book help you? We hope you will find it:

● useful in developing your skills and techniques fully for your Edexcel examinations

● provides valuable assistance with preparing the prose and drama prescribed texts

● a helpful aid to your reading of the selected Section C poems from the *Edexcel Anthology for IGCSE and Certificate qualifications in English Language and English Literature* (Route 1 of the IGCSE and the Certificate)

● a support in preparing for unseen texts (Route 1 of the IGCSE and the Certificate)

● useful in working on the Poetry Coursework (Route 2 – IGCSE only).

It should be:

● an aid to developing ideas and responses

● a basis for discussion

● a clear guide for revision.

Getting to know the different routes

This book and the ActiveBook that accompanies it deal with all the requirements for the two IGCSE routes and the Certificate in English Literature, with explanations, suggestions and questions. It also includes a number of practical activities and examples to practise and to see what really good answers look like.

If you are an IGCSE student, when using this book you need to check that you are focused on the route you are following. There are important differences between Route 1 and Route 2.

If you are a Certificate student, you will follow Route 1 of the IGCSE. However, the following points apply to both routes except where indicated.

Figure 0.1 *You know you can succeed.*

Top tip

Remember to plan your work: the sooner you organise yourself and your ideas, the easier you will find your preparation for every section of the examination! This book aims to give you confidence by improving your skills and techniques.

Know your texts

It is very important to make sure that you have a really good grasp of the selected Drama and Prose texts (both routes and qualifications), and Anthology poems (both routes and qualifications). Every year, examiners read answers where the candidates write in a way that shows that they do not understand, or have not prepared carefully, the texts that are set. Use the sections from this book to strengthen your knowledge of the texts.

Use your sources

A key part of the examination is testing your ability to apply what you have learned about poetry and prose when confronted with an unfamiliar poem or prose extract (Route 1 and Certificate), and to show both that you have understood and responded to what you have learned and that you can base your own writing on the ideas you have met.

Know and apply properly your technical terms

As with other subjects, English Literature has a number of technical terms that you may need to use. It is important that you can use the correct term and that you can spell it as well as understand how and why it has been used by the writer. Refer to the Glossary on pages 159–161 to help you. Note that terms in the Glossary are often printed in bold type in the text, so that you can check their meaning.

Explore how to improve the structure and organisation of your answers

You should look closely at the model answers given in the ActiveBook. This will help you to write detailed, successful responses that answer the question.

Presenting your work effectively

How you set out your own writing is important for various reasons. Get into the habit of producing writing that is:

- neat and regular
- spelled accurately
- correctly punctuated
- set out in clear paragraphs
- presented well.

Such strengths in your writing will bring many advantages, both in the examination and in later life:

- Examiners will be able to read your answer easily; they will not be able to if your handwriting is poor and if it is not written in proper sentences.

- How you organise your response, as well as what you write, will be considered when your work is marked.

- Good writing skills are useful for applications for jobs or college courses.

- Many jobs need people who can write clearly, accurately and precisely.

Knowing your own strengths and weaknesses

Even though this is an English Literature course, it is still very important to write clearly and accurately. It will help you to get your points across better to the reader. Keep a checklist of your most common errors in spelling, punctuation and grammar.

During your English Literature course

The following hints may seem obvious, but every year many students fail to do as well as they could because they did not keep to these basic points.

Remember:

- Concentrate during class or group discussions.
- Make sure you know what you have to do in class.
- Be sure you understand what the homework is asking you to do.
- For Route 2: check what your coursework assignment is and remember that you must write about three poems from Section C of the Anthology in detail, and make brief but relevant reference to three others to show your wider reading.

Take part:

- Ask questions in class.
- Answer questions in class.
- Contribute to discussion.
- Be fully involved in group work.

Make notes!

- Write down key points from: teachers; books you read; class work; articles or worksheets.
- Annotate your copy of the Anthology poems in Section C carefully (both routes).
- Add points missed onto the end of your homework or practice questions when they are returned to you.

Keep up!

- Hand work in on time.
- Keep files or exercise books up to date.
- Make sure you do not get behind with your homework.
- Do not leave work unfinished. It is always difficult to remember what has been missed unless you amend it at the time.
- Check off completed work in your records.

Seek help!

- Ask teachers to explain what you have to do if you are unsure.
- Discuss the work with friends.
- Look things up by using dictionaries, encyclopedias and the Internet.

Top tip

Use a system such as different-coloured cards or sticky notes to remind yourself of the key points on each text.

Be organised! Organise yourself as you go through the course, as this is much better than trying to catch up at the last minute.

- Present work neatly.

- Set yourself targets.

- Stick to deadlines.

- Keep your files neat and your notes together.

- Make a note of key words or very short phrases from your texts that you can use in Paper 1 for your Drama and Prose texts.

The following table gives a brief outline of each route and how to use this book to improve your knowledge and skills:

Assessment details	Where to find guidance	IGCSE Route 1/Route 2/both	Edexcel Certificate
Paper 1 Drama texts	Chapter 1	Both routes	✓
Paper 1 Prose texts	Chapter 2	Both routes	✓
Paper 2 Anthology poems	Chapter 3	Route 1	✓
Paper 2 Unseen poem	Chapter 4	Route 1	✓
Paper 2 Unseen prose	Chapter 5	Route 1	✓
Paper 3 Coursework option	Chapter 6	Route 2	

Assessment overview – guidance for teachers

The table below gives an overview of the assessment for this course.

We recommend that you make this information available to students to help ensure that they are fully prepared and know exactly what to expect in each assessment.

This section summarises the alternative routes that can be taken: Paper 1 is the compulsory unit for both the IGCSE and the Certificate; Paper 2 is taken by those opting for the 100 per cent examination route for the IGCSE (Route 1) and ALL Certificate students. Those IGCSE students who opt for coursework take Paper 3 instead of Paper 2. N.B. This option is available only to IGCSE students, and cannot be taken by Certificate students.

Route 1 – 100 per cent written examination paper (Paper 1 and Paper 2)

Route 2 – 60 per cent written examination paper and 40 per cent internally assessed coursework (Paper 1 and Paper 3)

Route 1

Paper 1	Percentage	Marks	Time	Availability
Written paper Drama and Prose	60%	60	One hour and 45 minutes	January and June examination series

First assessment June 2012 |

Figure 0.2 *It's important to organise yourself as you go through the course.*

Paper 2	Percentage	Marks	Time	Availability
Written paper Unseen texts and Poetry Anthology	40%	40	One hour and 30 minutes	January and June examination series First assessment June 2012

Route 2

Paper 1	Percentage	Marks	Time	Availability
Written paper Drama and prose	60%	60	One hour and 45 minutes	January and June examination series First assessment June 2012

Paper 3	Percentage	Marks	Time	Availability
Coursework Poetry	40%	30	n/a	June examination series First submission June 2012

Assessment Objectives and weightings

AO	Description	Percentage
AO1	a close knowledge and understanding of prose, poetry and drama texts and their contexts	20%
AO2	understanding and appreciation of writers' uses of the following as appropriate: characterisation, theme, plot and setting	20%
AO3	understanding of the writers' use of language, structure and form to create literary effects	30%
AO4	a focused, sensitive, lively and informed personal engagement with literary texts	30%

Notes on the Assessment Objectives

AO1

'**Close knowledge and understanding**' of the set texts are essential, especially as the examinations are largely 'closed text'. Students are not permitted to bring copies of the set texts into the examination with them. This is to ensure fairness as every student will have to use the same version of the text.

Close knowledge and understanding may be demonstrated in the way the students range across the text in their answers, showing understanding of the whole as well as the significance of specific incidents or speeches. Students should support their points either by referring to particular moments in the text ('*this is clearly shown when Juliet tells Romeo that...*'), or by memorised quotations. Examiners look for well-chosen details from the texts, but these need not take the form of direct quotations. In Paper 2, all the poems from Section C of the *Edexcel Anthology* will be printed as a poetry booklet additional to the examination paper. Students may not take their copies of the Poetry Anthology into the examination.

'**Contexts**' may be examined through questions that ask about the society in which a text is set. The answer should always be rooted in the text and how the text reveals the social or cultural setting; it should not be a historical or sociological essay, divorced from the text.

AO2

'**Characterisation, theme, plot and setting**' refers to the techniques used by the writer to achieve effects. These may be specific to prose or drama; for example, in prose texts, how characters and themes are developed and presented to the reader. In drama texts, the emphasis will be on dramatic techniques: how words and actions reveal character; how dialogue is used in the interaction between characters; how dramatic contrast is used to highlight differences between characters, moods and actions.

'**Understanding**' implies that the student shows a grasp of the techniques.

'**Appreciation**' suggests an ability to explore the effects of those techniques, and an evaluation of their use in the text.

AO3

'**Language, structure and form**' refers to the way in which a writer constructs a poem or piece of prose, through such matters as the selection of vocabulary and imagery, the use of particular genres (for example, the sonnet or short story), or of sound, rhyme or rhythm, and the organisation of the material, including narrative devices such as whether there is a third or first person narrator, or use of dialogue.

AO4

'**Personal engagement**' is shown when a student engages with a text in an individual way. The questions are designed to allow students to explore, in detail, a specific point or technique, which provide a focus for the student's response. Successful answers will be clearly structured around the key words of the question; less successful answers will tend to be coached, over-prepared responses that are not focused on the question. There is nothing to be gained from students learning stock answers to imaginary questions by heart. The outcome of such an approach will be the opposite of the 'focused, sensitive, lively and informed personal engagement' required by the Assessment Objective.

Assessment summary

Paper 1	Description
Paper 1 Written paper Drama and Prose	**Taken by all students.**
	Assessment of this paper is through a one hour and 45 minute examination, set and marked by Edexcel.
	The examination is untiered and will be targeted at students across the ability range A* – G.
	The paper is divided into two sections: drama and prose. Students must answer one question from each section.
	There is a choice of two questions for each text in both sections.
	This is a closed book examination – texts may not be taken into the examination.

Paper 2	Description
Paper 2 Written paper Unseen Texts and Poetry Anthology	**Available to students following Route 1 of IGCSE assessment (100% examination) and compulsory for Certificate students**
	Assessment of this paper is through a one hour and 30 minute examination, set and marked by Edexcel.
	The examination is untiered and will be targeted at students across the ability range A* – G.
	The paper is divided into two sections: unseen texts and Poetry Anthology. Students must answer one question from each section.
	There is a choice of two questions in each section.
	Section A: Students answer on either an unprepared poem or unprepared prose text.
	Section B: Students answer one of two questions set on poems from Section C of the *Edexcel Anthology.*
	All the poems from the Anthology will be printed in a poetry booklet as an insert to the examination paper.
	Students are not permitted to take copies of the Anthology into the examination with them.

Paper 3	Description
Paper 3 Coursework Poetry	**Available only to IGCSE students following Route 2 of assessment (40% coursework)**
	The coursework option is open to centres who have been approved by Edexcel to conduct coursework.
	The assessment of this paper is through one coursework assignment, internally set and assessed and externally moderated by Edexcel.
	Coursework assignments must be based on a selection of at least three poems in depth from Section C of the *Edexcel Anthology* with reference to at least three further poems, which may be drawn from outside of Section C of the Anthology.
	Typically, assignments may be between 1,000 and 1,500 words but there are no penalties for exceeding this guidance.

Chapter 1: Understanding the drama texts

Introduction

The word 'drama' comes from a Greek word meaning 'do' or 'perform'. Dramas (plays) are meant to be acted out in a theatre (or on film, radio or television) for people to hear and see (except for radio plays). It is sometimes easy to forget this when you are reading the text of a play on a printed page. In a live performance, you can tell how well a particular production is achieving the playwright's effects. If it is meant to be funny, is the **audience** laughing? If it is meant to be moving, does it affect the audience?

For this reason, seeing actual performances of the plays you are studying is a really valuable part of helping your understanding. The other thing about seeing the play acted out is that you can watch it all the way through. When studying a drama text in school or college, it often has to be broken up into quite small chunks, so it is much harder to feel the flow of the action. Watching a play on stage, or in a filmed or televised performance, helps you to see how the **characters** and relationships are presented and developed and enables you to focus on the **themes**.

Figure 1.1 *Actor holding masks of Comedy and Tragedy.*

Comparing productions is therefore another good way of increasing your understanding of a play. There are many ways of using modern technology to see the differences between different directors' ideas . This need not involve watching an entire production. For example, a common source is YouTube, where it is possible to find many short video and audio clips of many different plays. Or there are CD-ROMs that have wide-ranging photographs and stills from different productions. The Resources section (page 162) has a number of suggestions.

For the IGCSE and Certificate English Literature examinations, you will not be allowed to take a copy of the text with you into the examination room. Therefore, you will need to know the text very well so that you can draw on it for your examination answer. You will also need to remember a small number of brief quotations that you can call on as relevant for your answer.

Before analysing the play in more detail, you may find it helpful to read through the play once quickly by yourself, so that you have an idea of what happens and who is who – plot, theme and characters. Make some brief notes when you first read the play, so that you can go back to any passages that had a particularly strong effect on you.

For each play studied for Paper 1, there are sections on:

- background and context
- plot
- characters
- themes

- stagecraft and setting
- language and symbolism
- activities
- some questions to consider.

Arthur Miller: *A View from the Bridge*

Background and context

Arthur Miller was born in New York in 1915 and died in 2005. Many people think of him as the greatest playwright in the 20th century, certainly from the United States and possibly in the world. His family had arrived in the United States from Poland and moved to the district of Brooklyn, the setting for *A View from the Bridge*, which refers to the famous Brooklyn Bridge (pictured on the left). He graduated from the University of Michigan in 1938 and started to work as a journalist, but also wrote plays, some of which were extremely successful, such as *All My Sons*, *Death of a Salesman* and *The Crucible*. (You may wish to read or watch on video a production of one of his other plays.)

A View from the Bridge was inspired by his time working in the Brooklyn shipyards and getting to know the Italian community. It was a very tough time, as jobs were extremely hard to come by. He listened to their stories about coming to the United States to escape from the poverty that afflicted much of Italy in the post-war period, and based the story on something he heard about an Italian family.

Figure 1.2 *Brooklyn Bridge.*

Plot

The play is set in Brooklyn, New York. Two of Beatrice's Italian cousins, Marco and Rodolpho, arrive as illegal immigrants and stay in the Carbone household with Beatrice, her husband Eddie and their 17-year-old niece Catherine. Eddie becomes disturbed by the developing relationship between Rodolpho, the younger cousin, and Catherine as he has begun to feel a strong attraction to his niece. Eddie always finds fault with Rodolpho and his actions and behaviour. Unable to control his hidden desire, Eddie decides to inform the Immigration Bureau about Marco and Rodolpho's illegal status and the two brothers are arrested.

There is suspicion that Eddie was the one who informed on them, and Beatrice and Catherine become sure that Eddie's jealousy made him do it. Eddie is also accused by Marco, who spits in Eddie's face during his arrest. Eddie does not succeed in getting rid of both cousins; Rodolpho will still be able to marry Catherine and will then be able to apply to become an American citizen. This does not apply to Marco, who finds out that he will have to go back to Italy. He is let out on bail and then kills Eddie, turning Eddie's own knife on him.

Characters

The play is centred on the Carbone family, who are part of the poor Italian community that live in Brooklyn, one of the districts of New York.

Eddie Carbone

Eddie is:

- the husband of Beatrice
- a Sicilian American, aged 40: 'a husky, slightly overweight longshoreman'
- a traditional Italian master of the house
- happy to offer the cousins a home and to be generous towards them
- not someone who trusts people easily; suspicious of people's motives: 'the less you trust, the less you be sorry'
- someone who believes in the importance of his good name and of honour
- protective towards women, especially his niece Catherine
- obsessive in his love for Catherine
- in a marriage with a lack of warmth and intimacy
- jealous of Rodolpho, implying that he may have homosexual tendencies
- so desperate to get Rodolpho out of the way that he is prepared to inform the Immigration Bureau
- killed in a fight with Marco
- the 'tragic hero' of this 'Greek tragedy', ruined by his fatal weakness: the obsessive and improper love for his niece.

Beatrice Carbone

Beatrice is:

- the loyal and dependable wife of Eddie
- devoted to her niece Catherine, the daughter she never had
- a caring person, anxious to do the right thing by the cousins
- obedient to Eddie's desire to run everything in the home
- worried about her marriage and lack of intimacy
- aware of Eddie's feelings for Catherine and prepared to confront him about them
- an advisor to Catherine about Eddie and growing up
- someone who, to the very end, stands by Eddie, who recognises this by saying 'My B!' as he dies.

Catherine

Catherine is:

- the 17-year-old daughter of Beatrice's dead sister Nancy
- a lively, attractive and happy person
- naïve and innocent
- a young woman who has little experience of the outside world, having been very much confined to the Carbone household
- someone who has always seen Eddie as a father figure whom she loves
- unable at first to understand that things need to change now she is an adult
- excited by the arrival of the cousins – so it is not surprising that she quickly falls for one of them
- torn because she still respects Eddie and feels at first she cannot marry Rodolpho if he disapproves, though eventually she does choose Rodolpho over Eddie.

Marco

Marco is:

- the older of the cousins and brother of Rodolpho
- poor, desperate and grateful to the Carbones
- an illegal immigrant to the USA; he has left behind at home in Sicily his wife and three children whom he loves (one is a baby who is ill with tuberculosis)
- desperate to earn some money in the USA to look after the family as things are so bad in Sicily
- always polite, understanding his position in the Carbone household
- calm and peaceful in Act One
- angry and frustrated in Act Two
- well known as a strong man, and described as 'a bull'
- straightforward and direct, and speaks clearly and simply
- responsible and protective towards Rodolpho, with a strong sense of family honour.

Rodolpho

Rodolpho is:

- the younger of the cousins and brother of Marco
- unmarried and unattached; someone whose good looks and blond hair make an immediate impression on women, especially Catherine
- calm and polite throughout the play
- popular, intelligent, with a good sense of humour
- someone who takes to the American way of life and wants to enjoy all that New York has to offer
- very different from the Italian male stereotype, as he has interests such as cooking and sewing and is not afraid to express his 'feminine side'
- keen to calm things down between Eddie and Marco, but cannot stop the fight that leads to Eddie's death.

Alfieri

Alfieri is:

- an Italian-born lawyer; a character in the play but also the play's narrator
- part of the immigrant community in Brooklyn
- important in the play as commentator on the events, similar to the role the Chorus played in a Greek tragedy
- the one who introduces the characters, discusses the events, talks to the audience and reasons with the other characters
- powerless in the end to stop the tragedy, although he is a kind and sensitive man who would do anything to be able to do so
- a reliable friend, who is honest and firm when he warns Eddie
- a voice for Arthur Miller and his views.

Themes

Love

The many different aspects of love are explored in the play: family love, parent/ child love, brotherly love, romantic love, love between friends and love for your country. Miller shows that love can have both positive and negative effects. Love becomes twisted in the mind of Eddie in particular and is therefore the source of the battles that then occur. Look at Activity 2 (on page 7), which asks you to think in more detail about the different forms of love and their effect in the play.

Jealousy

Jealousy, particularly that of men over a woman they love, is a common subject for playwrights to explore: Shakespeare used it in the play *Othello*, for example. Here it is what makes Eddie turn against Rodolpho as he does, and it is strong enough to make him even abandon the principle of family honour, which is so important in his community.

Justice and the law

The importance of this theme is set out at the start of the play by Alfieri who, significantly, is himself a lawyer. This is something that immediately establishes a link to Greek tragedy, which was often about different ideas of justice: 'In Sicily, from where their fathers came, the law has not been a friendly idea since the Greeks were beaten.' This opening speech shows how there can be a conflict between the law and a deeper unwritten law, that is sometimes called 'natural justice', or the 'Divine law'. Alfieri refers to this near the end of the play when he says 'Only God makes justice'. Eddie also has strong views on justice and what he feels is right. The differences between American and Sicilian law are highlighted. So the play asks the question: what is *really* just; it is a question about who judges and what is right and wrong. The play does not answer such questions, but it asks them in a powerful way.

Honour

Codes of honour are very important in many societies, but they are particularly connected with Italian and Sicilian society. Sicily has long been a noted centre for the Mafia, whose activities are often illegal, but also influenced by a strong sense of family honour. This is shown particularly in the *Godfather* films and the television series *The Sopranos*. Family honour is often seen as more important than the law, as demonstrated in this play by the story of Vinny Bolzano at the start of the play. Betraying the family in any way is something that should be punished. This story sets the scene for Eddie's betraying of Rodolpho and Marco.

Anger and violence

This theme is linked to the themes of justice and honour, but it also reveals itself through the frustration Eddie feels and the tensions that grow through the play, resulting from the effect of the cousins' arrival.

Sexuality

The play touches on several aspects of people's sexuality, including the question 'What makes a man a man?'. It was written at a time when old stereotypes and attitudes were beginning to be questioned, and in Eddie, Marco and Rodolpho there are three different 'types' of man. Two of them are influenced strongly by Mediterranean 'machismo' (excessive or exaggerated masculinity) and one, Rodolpho, represents what we might call the 'new man' – challenging the traditional assumptions and hence posing a threat to the traditionalists. In addition, the play looks at what happens when a man, whose marriage has become rather distant, is overcome with desire for a much younger woman, who is also his niece.

While the focus is mainly on male sexuality, we are also very aware of how Beatrice wishes again to have a full marriage – which is made much more difficult by her husband's desires for Catherine. The play also looks at the awakening of sexual feelings in Catherine and the confusion about her feelings for Eddie and Rodolpho.

Fate

Another important theme that Arthur Miller takes from Greek tragedy is that of fate, in which things are just 'meant to happen', and human beings are seen as almost like pawns in a cosmic chess game where the result is known in advance and cannot be changed, whatever moves are made. It is Alfieri who reveals the final destiny, just as he is the one who gave warning of it at the start of the play when he introduces the storyline of the play.

Stagecraft and setting

Setting

The play takes place mainly in the Carbones' apartment and this gives it something of a claustrophobic feel. This is again characteristic of Greek tragedy, which was always set in a single location, with references to events elsewhere communicated (as in this play) through the words of the characters. The streets outside the apartment and the strong presence of Brooklyn Bridge also give the feeling of a close community.

Structure/form

The play has just two Acts, which are very closely connected, with certain parallel events, such as the Immigration Bureau situation. The role of Alfieri is central to the way in which these events are linked together, and he himself suggests that the play runs a course, which he, and to some extent the audience, know will lead to a 'bloody' end. This foreknowledge relates to the theme of fate and also contributes to the idea of **dramatic irony**, which is when the audience knows or can sense what will happen in the play, even when this is unknown to the characters.

Language and symbolism

Colloquial speech

The Carbones, including to some extent the cousins, speak in a **colloquial** way, one that Miller has clearly based on the actual speech patterns of the Italian Brooklyn community. This speech uses abbreviations and forms that are not standard American English. The strong New York dialect and accent help make the **dialogue** seem very realistic, as shown by the following: 'That's a hit-and-run guy baby...Them guys don't think of nobody but theirself.'

Professional language

In contrast to the speech of the Carbone family, Alfieri speaks in a more 'correct' way, using formal language, including examples of the ways in which a professional lawyer might speak ('every few years there is still a case...in some Caesar's year... Another lawyer... sat there as powerless as I.').

Euphemism

One example of the use of euphemism (which finds a more delicate or indirect way of saying something that might otherwise appear blunt or uncomfortable) is when Beatrice asks 'When am I gonna be a wife again, Eddie?', rather than saying 'When are we going to have sex again?', which in 1955 would have been far too direct a question to have said on stage.

Brooklyn Bridge

Brooklyn Bridge is the link between the poor areas of Brooklyn, Red Hook, and the material success of Manhattan. Crossing the bridge symbolises people's aspirations for prosperity.

High heels

Catherine's love of high heels shows her femininity and growing womanhood. She likes wearing them and attracting admirers. Eddie hates the 'clack clack' they make, as he becomes aware that Catherine will appear desirable, and that this could lead to her marrying and leaving home.

The chair

The chair used in the contest of strength between Marco and Eddie at the end of Act One becomes a **symbol** of masculinity and power.

Figure 1.3 *High heels are used to symbolise Catherine's femininity in the play.*

Activity 1: Understanding the text

1. Check through the places in the play where characters use the words *just, justice, law, right, wrong, illegal, crime, criminal* and any other connected words you can find. (Look particularly closely at everything said by Alfieri.)

2. From this, see what different ideas about justice and the law you can find in the play and work out your ideas on what you, as a viewer or reader of this play, are meant to think about these subjects.

3. Imagine you are a lawyer defending Marco. What would you say in his defence? If possible, work in a group of three – one could be the defence lawyer, one the prosecutor and the third could be a judge – and conduct a trial of Marco. Write your points in the table below. Think about how such a 'weighing of the evidence' could help your understanding of the play.

Role	Points to be made	Evidence
Defence lawyer		
Prosecutor		
Judge		

Activity 2: Thinking about the characters

Which characters tell us about the different sorts of love in the play? Look at the subject of love from the point of view of all of the characters, taking account of the different types of relationship. Complete the table below, which shows which type of relationship applies to which characters and add a comment on how this is portrayed both positively and negatively in the play. You could add brief quotations to support your points.

Type of love	Characters	How the relationships are portrayed:	
		Positive features	Negative features
Family love			
Parent/child love			
Brotherly love			
Young love/romance			
Love between friends			
Love of country			

Activity 3: Thinking about the characters

Write down what you think the audience expects to happen after the play to Catherine and Rodolpho and to Beatrice. If possible, compare your ideas with a partner or in a group. You may wish to consider whether they are destined to be happy and how the ending of the play leaves you feeling about them and their future.

Some questions to consider

Thinking about these questions (and perhaps writing notes or timed short answers) will be helpful when you revise for the exam, as they will help you to focus on some of the key aspects of the text:

1. Why do you think Miller chose the title he gave this play?

2. Do you feel that Miller wanted us to feel any sympathy for Eddie? Why?

3. How does the play make you feel that there is a higher law than the country's law? Explain your thoughts. Think about different views on law and justice.

4. Does the theme of fate suggest that in this play the characters are helpless pawns who cannot control their actions? Explain your thoughts.

J B Priestley: *An Inspector Calls*

Background and context

John Boynton (J B) Priestley was born in Yorkshire in 1894 and died in 1984. He left school aged 16 and worked in an office as a clerk, then joined up to fight in the First World War, where he narrowly escaped being killed. After the war, he went to Cambridge University, before working in London as a writer. His first play was followed by another 50. He was very active in politics and supported the development of the Welfare State; he was opposed to war and supported the Campaign for Nuclear Disarmament. The play *An Inspector Calls* was very influenced by the subject of war, as it was set in 1912, the year the *Titanic* sank, and just two years before the outbreak of the First World War, which the characters discuss. It was a time of increasing industrialisation, with more and more people moving from the country into the cities to take jobs in factories. This period, from the death of Queen Victoria in 1901 until the start of the First World War, was known as the Edwardian Era (after King Edward VII) and was seen by many people as a fairly untroubled and peaceful time. The two World Wars that followed changed things completely, so those who saw *An Inspector Calls* when it first came out in 1946 would have recognised it as being set in a very different era, not least for the wealthy, who lived in luxury and employed plenty of servants.

Figure 1.4 *An Edwardian couple.*

Plot

In Act 1, the characters and setting are introduced in the dining room of the Birling family during an engagement party for Sheila, the daughter of Mr and Mrs Birling, and Gerald Croft. This is followed by the arrival of the Inspector, which then changes the whole course of events. He announces the very recent suicide of Eva Smith and starts to question Mr Birling, after showing him the photograph of the girl, who turns out to have worked for Mr Birling's firm and to have been dismissed for trying to obtain a pay rise and going on strike. The Inspector goes on to question Sheila, who admits her jealousy of Eva because of the way she looked in a dress Sheila had liked. Her complaints about the girl's rudeness also contributed to Eva losing her job. After this, it emerges that Gerald had an affair with Eva during the last summer.

In Act 2, Gerald talks about his relationship with Eva Smith (who was also known as Daisy Renton). When Gerald leaves, the Inspector turns his questioning on Mrs Birling, and the audience learns that she had refused Eva's pleading for help when she was pregnant and had no money to survive. Mrs Birling also states that the man who got Eva pregnant should admit his guilt and take responsibility for his actions.

In Act 3, Eric returns from a walk and becomes the next to be questioned by Inspector Goole; he also confesses to a relationship with Eva, which had led to her pregnancy. He admits that he gave her money at first, but that she refused to take it when she learned that it was stolen from Mr Birling's office. At this point, Inspector Goole leaves, and there is a bitter family argument, with all of the family blaming one another. Gerald returns and announces that the Inspector is a fake. They check with the local hospital, and are told that no girl has committed suicide that night. There is a great sense of relief, and the family concludes that the whole story was a bluff. Sheila and Eric quarrel with their parents. At this point, the phone rings. It is the police, who are ringing because a girl has committed suicide. It seems that an inspector is on his way to ask them some questions about this suicide.

Characters

Mr Arthur Birling

Arthur Birling is:

- a 'heavy-looking, rather portentous man in his middle fifties but rather provincial in his speech'
- proud of what he has achieved, such as having been mayor
- keen to impress the Inspector about his friends and position in society
- equally keen to impress those whom he considers above him in society (such as Gerald's parents)
- delighted about the engagement party, but not just for the sake of his daughter – it is a good business opportunity for him as well, as Gerald is the son of his competitor
- not good at assessing current issues – he is sure that there will not be a war and that the *Titanic* is unsinkable
- a very selfish man, who wants to look after himself and his family above everything else
- pompous; he tries to use his connections to frighten the Inspector
- worried that his knighthood may not be given to him if there is any scandal over the girl
- determined to protect his reputation
- opposed to new ideas, such as socialism
- unable to learn to accept responsibility, complacent, set in his ways.

Mrs Sybil Birling

Sybil Birling is:

- 'about fifty, a rather cold woman and her husband's social superior'
- rather a snob
- lacking in respect for the Inspector and arrogant in her attitudes to him
- inclined to regard Sheila and Eric as still being children rather than adults
- in denial over Eric's drinking problems; dismisses the fact that Gerald had an affair with Eva/Daisy
- capable of acting in a prejudiced way because of her strict principles
- still refusing at the end of the play to accept that she has done anything wrong.

Sheila Birling

Sheila Birling is:

- 'a pretty girl in her early twenties, very pleased with life and rather excited'
- perceptive, intelligent and curious; quick to realise the truth about people, for example when it is revealed that Gerald knew Daisy Renton/Eva Smith
- very sympathetic to Eva when she hears how her father treated her
- horrified to discover that she has played a part in Eva Smith's downward spiral
- the first to express doubts as to whether the Inspector is a real inspector
- growing in maturity as the play progresses and in many ways is much wiser by the end of it
- angry with her parents because they 'pretend that nothing much has happened'
- able to accept fully her own responsibility and that of others in the family for what happened to Eva.

Eric Birling

Eric Birling is:

- 'in his early twenties, not quite at ease, half shy, half assertive'
- embarrassed and rather awkward
- a heavy drinker
- feeling guilty about how he treated Eva and, by the end of the play, prepared to accept his responsibility
- ashamed of what his actions had led to
- more concerned about what happened to the girl than the fact that he had stolen from the firm
- able to stand up to his father in the end and tell him he disagrees with his attitudes
- prepared to stand with Sheila in opposing his parents' wishes to cover up the events.

Inspector Goole

Inspector Goole is:

- a man who creates 'an impression of massiveness, solidity and purposefulness. He is a man in his fifties, dressed in a plain darkish suit. He speaks carefully, weightily, and has a disconcerting habit of looking hard at the person he addresses before actually speaking'
- someone who works in a very methodical way, facing suspects with facts to make them speak
- a figure of great authority and firmness
- someone with a great amount of knowledge about Eva Smith/Daisy Renton and the Birling family; is clearly perceptive
- able to tell seemingly what is going to happen; appears **omniscient**
- a man with a strong message for the characters and audience – provides a voice for Priestley and his views
- a mystery figure. Is he real? Is he an inspector? Is he a ghost? How does he know so much?

Gerald Croft

Gerald Croft is:

- 'an attractive chap about thirty, rather too manly to be a dandy but very much the easy well-bred man-about-town'
- very well born, from an aristocratic family, son of Sir George and Lady Croft, socially superior to the Birling family
- unwilling at first to admit anything, as he pretends not to have known the girl; is very moved when he hears of her death
- suspicious that the Inspector is not genuine
- someone who, at the end of the play, has learned very little, much like Mr and Mrs Birling.

Eva Smith/Daisy Renton

Eva Smith is:

- not strictly speaking a character in the play, as she is dead and never appears on stage
- described as 'very pretty'
- said to be the daughter of parents who had died
- a working-class girl from the country
- something of a mystery, who keeps the characters guessing
- brave – unafraid to ask for a rise
- someone with principles – would not accept stolen money
- representative of people who are treated unfairly by upper/middle classes.

Themes

Responsibility

From his first appearance, the Inspector introduces the idea of our being responsible for helping others, and taking responsibility for our actions. This is central to the whole play, with this compassionate view contrasted with a self-interested view, which is represented particularly by the capitalist Mr Birling. Everyone has a collective responsibility within society. Priestley presents each character as having a different attitude to responsibility, but also makes the audience question their own views.

Social class

The play is set in a period when the divisions between the upper, middle and working classes were very marked. The play looks closely at the way the class system worked, with some people who did very well out of it, like Mr Birling, and others who suffered great hardships because of it, like Eva Smith. This is one of Priestley's great personal concerns.

Love and marriage

The position of women is explored with the only option suggested for Sheila as being a suitable marriage. This is contrasted with the plight of lower-class women, who have no status and who may be forced through hardship into becoming mistresses or even prostitutes. Marriage is seen by Mr Birling as an alliance to further his business and social ambitions.

Youth and age

While the older Birlings remain fixed in their views, Eric and Sheila are open to change. This suggests that older people may be more set in their ways and resistant to changing their points of view. This is also highlighted by Mr Birling's refusal to accept that a war may be coming or that a ship like the *Titanic* might sink.

The supernatural

Inspector Goole's name makes us ask whether he is a 'ghoul' and whether there is a divine purpose.

Stagecraft and setting

The play is not exactly like a conventional detective thriller, but it does have elements of a 'whodunnit?'. Of course, as none of the cast has committed any actual crime, it is really an attempt to answer the moral question of 'who was responsible for it?'

Other people have seen the play as being like the morality plays of the Middle Ages, which often looked at the seven deadly sins: wrath, sloth, greed, pride, lust, envy and gluttony. It is certainly possible to see elements of these moral weaknesses in the characters, and this may have been Priestley's intention.

Language and symbolism

Colloquial language

'Posh' **slang** of the period is used – for example when Eric is described as 'squiffy' (meaning drunk).

Puns

There seems to be a **pun** at the heart of the play: the name of the Inspector – 'Goole' – is a pun on 'ghoul', meaning ghost. How you interpret this is very important to your view of the play.

Didactic language

The Inspector is the main character who uses **didactic language**, which is meant to teach someone a lesson, or point out the rights and wrongs in the Birling family and in our society.

Figure 1.5 *Sheila and Gerald's engagement: symbols of their proposed union.*

Activity 1: Understanding the text

Part of the mystery of the play is created by questions about the character of the Inspector himself. It seems clear that he is not really an inspector from the local police force, because the characters have this checked out.

- Is he meant to be a ghost? Remember the pun on Goole and 'ghoul'.
- Is he the playwright's own voice?
- Is he a voice of a powerful God offering a warning?
- Is he a voice that acts as the conscience of all of the characters?

What other ideas do you have? If possible, share these with a partner or in a group.

Activity 2: Understanding the text

Read carefully through the stage directions at the beginning of Act 1. List the main features of the room and the furnishings and note the way in which the author describes the room. These details are meant to help the director and producer of the play to reproduce the right setting for *An Inspector Calls*. *(*Note: all three Acts take place in the same room.)

Activity 3: Understanding the text

If you are able to watch the scene from a video, CD or YouTube version, compare this with the play as Priestley wrote it. Do you see any important differences?

Activity 4: Thinking about the characters

Look through the following list of words that have been used to describe characters in the play. Fill in the table below, matching the words with the characters. You may find that some **adjectives** describe more than one character.

manipulative   controlling   masterful   stern   perceptive   mature   determined
courageous   untruthful   relieved   kind   unfaithful   arrogant   superior   cruel
unfeeling   self-important   pompous   prejudiced   snobbish
heartless   unrepentant

Character	Qualities
The Inspector	
Mr Birling	
Mrs Birling	
Sheila	
Eric	
Gerald	

Some questions to consider

1. What difference does it make to your understanding of the play if you decide there was no real Inspector?

2. Why do you think Priestley makes Sheila the character who accepts responsibility more than the others? Which character do you find (i) most interesting and (ii) most sympathetic; and why?

3. Of the play's themes (see pages 11–12), which do you think is the most important, and why?

4. How effective do you find the play's ending, and why?

William Shakespeare: *Romeo and Juliet*

Background and context

William Shakespeare was born in 1564 in Stratford-upon-Avon in England and died in 1616. When he was 18, he married Anne Hathaway and some time later moved to London to write and act. There was a famous theatre company at the time called The Lord Chamberlain's Men, of which he became one of the leading actors. Shakespeare was writing during the last part of Queen Elizabeth I's reign, at the end of the 16th century, and the early part of the reign of King James I. Both rulers admired his work and The Lord Chamberlain's Men became known as 'The King's Men'.

Shakespeare wrote over 30 plays, most of which are still often performed all over the world today, having been translated into many languages. *Romeo and Juliet*, with its 'young love' interest, is one of the most popular of his plays. Its story has been used in several operas and films, including the very popular Franco Zeffirelli and Baz Luhrmann versions, as well as in animated versions. It also led to the famous musical adaptation *West Side Story*.

Figure 1.6 *William Shakespeare.*

Plot

The play centres on the love between Romeo, a Montague, and Juliet, a Capulet, both from the Italian town of Verona. These families have a long-running feud, which is shown by the fighting at the very start of the play between the servants of the two families. When Prince Escalus intervenes to try to restore peace, Romeo meets his friend Benvolio and tells him of his feelings for Rosaline (which it seems may be infatuation, rather than real love); as it appears she does not return his affections, Benvolio advises him to look for someone else. Meanwhile, Juliet's hand in marriage is sought by the nobleman Paris, which causes her father to invite many people to a feast, including Paris. Romeo and Benvolio decide to 'gatecrash' in the knowledge that Rosaline will be there. At the feast, Romeo catches sight of Juliet and immediately forgets all about Rosaline. There is a strong instant attraction, and Romeo and Juliet kiss within minutes of seeing each other. Only afterwards does Juliet learn that Romeo is a Montague.

Romeo refuses to leave with his friends and creeps round the garden to call out to Juliet from outside her window, and they swear their love to each other. This is the famous 'balcony scene' where Juliet 'stands aloft'. When Romeo leaves, he realises that their new-found love causes problems because the family feud makes it seem impossible for them to marry. He visits a priest, Friar Laurence, who agrees to marry them secretly, hoping that this will bring the two families together and put an end to their feud. However, in the marketplace, at the height of the day's heat, Romeo's friend Mercutio is killed by the Capulet Tybalt, Juliet's cousin, who is then killed by Romeo in return. This causes Juliet great pain because of her divided loyalties. After their wedding night, Romeo has to flee, as he knows that if he returns he will himself be killed.

Juliet's father is now determined that she should marry Paris, not knowing of her marriage to Romeo. She at first refuses, despite the Nurse's advice, but then agrees to do so because of the plan she and Friar Laurence have put together. This involves her in taking a special potion to put her to sleep so that she appears to be dead, and her parents duly bury her in the family tomb. However, the message to Romeo from the Friar does not reach him, so he is unaware of the plot. He returns to Verona and visits the tomb. He is therefore convinced that she really is dead.

Romeo sees Paris, who has been scattering flowers in memory of Juliet. He fights and kills Paris; then, seeing the 'dead' body of his love, kills himself with the poison he has brought with him for the purpose. After his death, Juliet comes out of her deep sleep and finds that Romeo has killed himself. She kisses his lips, hoping the poison will kill her. When it fails to do so, she takes his dagger and stabs herself in the chest, falling on his body and then dying. Their death does, however, achieve one thing: an end to the feud between the two families.

Characters

Romeo

Romeo is:

- the son of Lord and Lady Montague
- supposedly romantically in love with Rosaline, although he is really in love with the idea of being in love; he is able to forget her quickly and fall immediately in love with Juliet
- passionately in love with Juliet from the moment he sees her and prepared to die if he cannot have her
- a man of honour and principle, refusing to fight Tybalt
- capable of extreme and violent emotions and reactions, including anger and the desire for revenge
- fond of friends' company, among whom he appears intelligent and capable of enjoying witty exchanges.

Friar Laurence:

The Friar is:

- a religious figure who acts out of concern for Romeo
- able to offer Romeo advice because he knows him very well
- someone who seems wise and knowledgeable and is trusted
- brave, as he is prepared to suggest a very risky plan that does not work out well; he could be blamed by some for the deaths of Romeo and Juliet
- a schemer, who has a plan to end the feud between the families, based on the plan he offers Juliet.

Juliet

Juliet is:

- the daughter of Lord and Lady Capulet
- allowed by her father to be wooed by Paris, although she is not yet 14
- someone who matures rapidly from girl to woman over the course of the play
- brave and independent – she is prepared to marry Romeo, despite the family feud and her parents' wishes
- headstrong and confident, as she is happy to kiss Romeo when she hardly knows him and to comment on his kissing
- the first to suggest marriage
- capable of falling in love very quickly and then of being loyal and committed
- willing to go ahead with a dangerous plan and then to take her own life.

The Nurse

The Nurse is:

- like a mother in her protective attitudes to Juliet
- devoted to the Capulet family but prepared to take risks to help Juliet
- inclined to chatter a great deal and the source of many comical exchanges
- prepared to go against her own views in the advice she gives her about marrying Paris
- happy to tease Juliet initially by withholding information from Romeo.

Lord Capulet

Lord Capulet is:

- Juliet's father
- always prepared to fight against the Montagues; lacking self-control
- an apparently kind and friendly host
- able to prevent a fight between Tybalt and Romeo at his house
- the one who makes the arrangements for Juliet to marry Paris
- angry with Juliet for her disobedience
- regretful about his actions after her death.

Lady Capulet

Lady Capulet is:

- a slightly distant figure for her daughter Juliet, who is much closer to her Nurse
- on the side of her husband, not of Juliet.

Lord Montague

Lord Montague is:

- the father of Romeo
- head of the Montague family
- the one who reports his wife's death from grief about Romeo.

Lady Montague

Lady Montague is:

- the mother of Romeo
- so grief-stricken by Romeo's banishment that she dies.

Tybalt

Tybalt is:

- the cousin of Juliet
- a very aggressive character: 'fiery Tybalt'
- interested in picking fights with the Montagues
- full of hatred and anger.

Benvolio

Benvolio is:

- a good friend of Romeo and his cousin
- a different kind of young man from Mercutio and Tybalt – neutral and fair
- keen to stop the fighting between the families; a peace-maker
- someone who, as his Italian name suggests ('wishing well'), wants the best outcome
- a reliable go-between for the Montagues and Escalus.

Mercutio

Mercutio is:

- Romeo's best friend, to whom he is very loyal
- intelligent, quick and clever; a 'character' with strong **opinions**
- someone who likes a joke and to make fun of people, including Romeo
- always spoiling for a fight, which leads to his death.

Themes

Love

Many plays, including those of Shakespeare, look at different types of love: this is a major theme of Shakespeare's *Much Ado About Nothing*, for example. We are introduced to Romeo as someone whose feelings for Rosaline might be called 'puppy love' or infatuation; he is immediately shown as completely 'love-struck', but the superficiality of his feelings is underlined by the speed with which he abandons them at the sight of Juliet.

The play gives several examples of close friendship as a form of love, particularly the protective love shown by the Nurse to Juliet and the Friar to Romeo; as well as the 'laddish' friendships of the young men, which is still instantly recognisable in

Figure 1.7 *The Romeo and Juliet balcony in Verona, Italy.*

any street in Italy today, and marked by what the Italians themselves call braggadocio (a kind of boastful swagger). However, such friendship can generate fierce loyalty, to the point of being willing to die for one's friend, as happens with Mercutio.

There is also the view that marriage is above all a business contract, in which love is not a very important consideration: Paris wishes to marry Juliet, but admits that he has 'little talked of love', and even Juliet, when asked how she feels about the idea of marriage to Paris, only says 'I'll look to like'. Capulet says to Juliet: 'I give you to my friend'.

Part of the overall treatment of love is that of sexual love. Although, clearly, the marriage of Romeo and Juliet is happily consummated, many of the references to sex are not directly linked to their love. Instead they are there to provide an endless source of complicated puns and **witticisms**, particularly for the young men – but they are even indulged in by the Nurse. Such jesting treats love in an altogether more basic way than the idealism of the central relationship.

The theme of true love is explored mainly through the rapidly developing relationship between Romeo and Juliet. Some cynics think it is all too fast to be true, denying the idea of 'love at first sight' and saying that their instant falling for each other is not based on true appreciation of each other's qualities. (For readers of Jane Austen's *Pride and Prejudice*, for example, it lacks the value of Elizabeth and Darcy's learning process.) Romantics, on the other hand, love this love born of immediate attraction that rapidly blossoms into a close and unbreakable relationship. The couple will do anything for each other.

The opposite of love, of course, is hatred, and this is explored in particular in the theme of families and their feuding. Shakespeare sees these opposites, which he places together as **oxymorons**, as being closely connected, as in the lines from the very first scene (lines 169–170):

> Here's much to do with hate but more with love.
> Why then, O brawling love, O loving hate.

Violence and death

Like many other plays written around Shakespeare's time, there is a strong atmosphere of violence, connected with hatred, which leads to death upon death. Revenge was often associated with families and their feuds or **vendettas**. Death of several characters and the theme of revenge itself occur in other plays by Shakespeare, notably *Hamlet*, and in *Romeo and Juliet* a number of young lives are cut short in consequence. Note how Shakespeare uses violence and the end of violence to alter the mood of the play: from broad comic scenes to dark, tragic ones.

Fate

The Prologue of the play, in **sonnet form**, is striking because it tells us what is going to happen and that nothing can change it because it is decreed by fate: Romeo and Juliet are described as 'death-marked'; they are a 'pair of star-crossed lovers'. Romeo and Juliet cannot stop the family feuds or the effect these will have on their own and others' lives.

They themselves are very conscious that their lives may be fated. The idea of 'fate' was an important one in Greek tragedy, which had a strong influence on Shakespeare's thinking. We learn from such plays as Sophocles' *Oedipus the King* that characters cannot avoid their destiny, even if desperate measures are taken to try to prevent it happening. In *Romeo and Juliet*, it is the failure of the message from Friar Laurence to reach Romeo that leads to Romeo not realising the situation. But fate means that the tragedy would have occurred no matter what any of the characters do: thus Romeo and Juliet are the innocent victims of a fate that has already been worked out, and their helplessness in the face of fate is one of many causes of the audience's feelings of sympathy towards the lovers.

Families

As we have seen, the long-running dispute between two of Verona's leading families, which are both strongly patriarchal (ruled by the father), is central to the play. This quarrel is brought into sharp focus by the idea of a marriage that is, in this sense, a union of opposites, however well matched the young couple may be personally. Inevitably, therefore, the couple's actions will have an effect on their families: the prospect of a marriage with Paris, with his connections to the Prince, was seen by Capulet as so attractive that Juliet's feelings hardly seem to matter. The final union between the families gives the play more of a 'happy ending', though the deaths of the younger members of the family will continue to cast a long shadow.

Stagecraft and setting

Stagecraft

Shakespeare's use of the Prologue is important because, much more so than in other of his plays, the speaker gives a great deal of information about what is to come. This permits an element of **dramatic irony** because the audience is well aware that the love of the young couple will not end happily.

In addition, Shakespeare keeps the action moving swiftly and distracts the audience's attention by the frequent changes of scene – there are 24 scenes in all. This often has the effect of altering the mood and atmosphere, as when we 'cut' from Romeo running for his life after the deaths of Tybalt and Mercutio to the very different scene where, with more dramatic irony, Juliet is waiting for Romeo to arrive, ignorant of these events. Light relief is provided after scenes of great tension, such as the appearance of the musicians.

Setting

The play is set in Verona and, for the scene in which Romeo flees (Act 5, Scene 1), Mantua. These two northern Italian cities are not that far apart and it is possible to work out that the action occupies four days – the beginnings and ends of days give important links to the events.

On Sunday, the first day of the play and the week, there is the servants' fight. Romeo and Juliet meet at the feast and declare their love. The hasty and secret marriage takes place on Monday, and on the same day Romeo kills Tybalt and is banished. He does, however, spend his honeymoon night with Juliet. On Tuesday, at dawn, Romeo leaves for Mantua and Juliet is told she is to marry Paris. Juliet, therefore, makes her plans with Friar Laurence. Capulet then brings forward the wedding to Paris from Thursday to Wednesday. Juliet decides she must drink the sleeping potion that night.

On Wednesday, the servant Balthasar is supposed to go to Mantua to inform Romeo of Juliet's death but because of an outbreak of plague he cannot get there. Because Romeo does not hear about the plan, he rides immediately to the Capulet's tomb, kills Paris and drinks the poison, after which Juliet also kills herself. Late the same night, the bodies are found by the Friar, the families and Prince Escalus.

Most of the play takes place outside the house, the orchard of the Capulets being associated with life, hope and blossoming fruitfulness, and the graveyard with its family tombs being a scene of death and gloom. The fight scene at the start takes place in a public setting – the streets of Verona – for all to see. We learn that fights between members of the families have taken place in public places before. The scene in which Tybalt confronts Mercutio at the start of Act 3 is also set in one of Verona's public squares, linking it closely with the opening of the play. The action takes place in July, and the heat of the weather may be linked to the heat of the characters' passions, whether anger or desire.

Language and symbolism

Opposites

We saw above how Shakespeare often puts together opposite ideas (or antitheses), of which 'love and hate' are the obvious example in this play. Sometimes these are combined in a single idea, called an **oxymoron**, in which words with opposite meanings are placed together, forming a **paradox** of apparently opposed ideas. 'Loving hate' in a good example of an oxymoron, as is one of the play's most-quoted (or misquoted) lines: 'Parting is such sweet sorrow'. Look also at the antithesis in the line: 'More light and light, more dark and dark our woes!' The striking linking contrast is made between the dawn breaking and their troubles breaking: light and dark are important ideas in the play, often linked to life and death.

Puns

Another technique Shakespeare uses is the pun. A lot of jokes are puns – word-play using words that sound similar but have different meanings. When Mercutio is dying he says that tomorrow he will be a 'grave man' – 'grave' as in 'serious', but also as in 'dead and buried'. Puns can be used like this to make fun of characters and situations, like the two servants at the start who link everything they do and think about with sex.

Shakespeare's verse

For much of the play Shakespeare uses his favourite **rhythm** of **blank verse**, basically consisting of ten syllables, in five metric feet, the so-called **iambic pentameter**. You will meet this rhythm in the Poetry Anthology. In this, a stressed syllable follows an unstressed: te-tum, te-tum, te-tum, te-tum, te-tum.

You should note when the characters speak in verse and the difference when they speak in normal speech rhythms in prose, in which the pace is often more rapid and the length of lines varies.

Another notable feature is that, in places, complete **sonnets** are woven into the play. These follow the pattern of rhythm and rhyme set out in the comments on 'Sonnet 116' in Section C of the *Edexcel Anthology*. This use of sonnets is unusual and perhaps Shakespeare chooses it because he sees it as particularly fitting for a play dealing with love as its central theme.

Activity 1: Understanding the text

Study carefully Mercutio's 'Queen Mab' speech (Act 1, Scene 4). Go through it closely to check your understanding of the meaning, and make notes of points you find interesting. What do you make of this speech and what, if anything, do you think it adds to the play? Think particularly about the nature of the **imagery** and how this changes during the speech.

O, then, I see Queen Mab hath been with you.
She is the fairies' midwife, and she comes
In shape no bigger than an agate-stone
On the fore-finger of an alderman,
Drawn with a team of little atomies
Athwart men's noses as they lie asleep;
Her wagon-spokes made of long spiders' legs,
The cover of the wings of grasshoppers,
The traces of the smallest spider's web,
The collars of the moonshine's watery beams,
Her whip of cricket's bone, the lash of film,
Her wagoner a small grey-coated gnat,
Not so big as a round little worm
Prick'd from the lazy finger of a maid;
Her chariot is an empty hazel-nut
Made by the joiner squirrel or old grub,
Time out o' mind the fairies' coachmakers.
And in this state she gallops night by night
Through lovers' brains, and then they dream of love;
O'er courtiers' knees, that dream on court'sies straight,
O'er lawyers' fingers, who straight dream on fees,
O'er ladies ' lips, who straight on kisses dream,
Which oft the angry Mab with blisters plagues,
Because their breaths with sweetmeats tainted are:
Sometime she gallops o'er a courtier's nose,
And then dreams he of smelling out a suit;
And sometime comes she with a tithe-pig's tail
Tickling a parson's nose as a' lies asleep,
Then dreams, he of another benefice:
Sometime she driveth o'er a soldier's neck,
And then dreams he of cutting foreign throats,
Of breaches, ambuscadoes, Spanish blades,
Of healths five-fathom deep; and then anon
Drums in his ear, at which he starts and wakes,
And being thus frighted swears a prayer or two
And sleeps again. This is that very Mab
That plats the manes of horses in the night,
And bakes the elflocks in foul sluttish hairs,
Which once untangled, much misfortune bodes:
This is the hag, when maids lie on their backs,
That presses them and learns them first to bear,
Making them women of good carriage:
This is she –

Activity 2: Understanding the text

Write a very short summary of each scene in the play, noting down just the basic points – time of day, location, mood, action. From this, build up your picture of how the changes of scene work to create dramatic effect in the play.

Activity 3: Thinking about the characters

You can learn a great deal about the different characters by studying a particular scene in detail. A good example of such a scene is the central scene (Act 3, Scene 1) in which Romeo kills Tybalt.

Working with a partner, in a group or by yourself, note down the following points:

- What happened in the previous scene, and therefore what mood is set for the audience.

- The signs that a fight is brewing.

- Whether the fighting and killing are presented as inevitable.

- Links with the fight at the start of the play.

- How the audience feels about Romeo at the end of the scene.

- How the scene paves the way for the next scene. (Does it seem to be sandwiched between the preceding and following scene?)

- How the end of the scene relates to the earlier fight and the warning from the Prince in Act 1.

Some questions to consider

1. Think about the advice that is offered by the Nurse and by Father Laurence. Who do you think gives better advice and why? Which other characters act as advisers, and how successfully do they do so?

2. Does love triumph over hatred in this play?

3. Is Juliet a more convincing representative of true love than Romeo? Why do you think this?

4. How important are fate and destiny in *Romeo and Juliet*?

William Shakespeare: *Henry V*

Background and context

Henry V is one of Shakespeare's history plays, and is based loosely on historical events recorded in Hall's *Union of the Two Noble Houses of Lancaster and York* (1548) and Holinshed's *Chronicles* (1587). The historical Henry V was born in Monmouth in 1387. While his father was still King, he campaigned against the Welsh. On gaining the throne in 1413, he demanded the return of several French territories to England, and waged three campaigns in support of this claim. The first ended with the English victory at Agincourt in 1415, the climax of Shakespeare's play. It was Henry's second campaign, five years later, that made him heir to the French throne and the French king's son-in-law. Shakespeare glosses over this time lapse. Nor does the play mention that the real Henry died of dysentery on his third campaign, before he was able to succeed to the French throne.

A Shakespearean audience would expect a patriotic play focusing on the role of the King. There was also widespread belief in the doctrine of the Divine Right of Kings – the idea that kings were appointed by God, and that to betray a king was therefore to betray God. In *Henry V*, Shakespeare explores the idea of 'the ideal king' and what a monarch's responsibilities were. It is therefore significant that, in his earlier plays, *Henry IV, Parts 1 and 2*, Henry V is portrayed as a wild and dissolute youth, although even then he does realise he will have to change his ways. He has now become responsible, moral, and a supporter of the Church – although the play's opening shows that he does not bow down to the Church as an institution, despite its power and wealth.

Plot

Henry has recently come to the throne after the death of his father Henry IV. He has impressed all by his conversion from wild, hard-drinking young prince to responsible monarch. The Archbishop of Canterbury and Bishop of Ely are worried that a new law will deprive the Church of much of its wealth. Henry consults them on the legality of his claim to the French throne. In much complicated detail, they justify his claim. They promise to back his campaign financially and the proposed law is dropped.

A messenger arrives with an insulting gift of tennis balls for Henry from the Dauphin (the French king's eldest son). The message is clear: the Dauphin thinks that Henry is still an irresponsible playboy, not a king to be taken seriously. Henry sends back a message that the Dauphin will regret his joke when the English invade France. We cut to Henry's former tavern friends, Pistol, Nym and Bardolph, who plan to go to the war in France. The action then quickly moves to Southampton, where Henry's army is about to embark. Henry springs some bad news on Scroop, Cambridge and Grey: their plot to assassinate him in return for a French bribe has been exposed, and they are to be executed. We also hear that Henry's old drinking companion Sir John Falstaff has died.

Henry lands in France. The French consider their situation. Henry sends Exeter to King Charles VI to demand his crown. Charles' offer of his daughter and some dukedoms is not enough: Henry lays siege to the town of Harfleur, which surrenders rather than be overrun by Henry's army. However, Henry's army is weakened by disease, lack of food, and hard marching. When it is halted by the

Top tip

For details about Shakespeare, please see the start of the section on *Romeo and Juliet* (page 15).

Figure 1.8 *King Henry V.*

much larger French army at Agincourt, the French are sure of victory and the English prepare to die if necessary. The night before the battle, Henry wanders among his troops in disguise and talks to them about a king's responsibility for the souls of his soldiers.

Despite the odds, the battle is a resounding victory for the English. Charles VI is forced to accept all Henry's demands. This is actually five years later, but the Chorus plays this fact down to avoid a sense that the final Act has been tagged on to the rest of the play. Henry woos Charles's daughter Katharine and she accepts him as a husband – though, of course, in reality she has little choice. The play ends with England and France at peace, with Henry fully established as a king, and looking forward to being King of France when Charles dies.

Characters

King Henry

King Henry is:

- the King of England, though born in Wales
- a former drinking companion of Falstaff, but now a reformed character
- an able ruler with a moral conscience and a strong sense of the heavy burden of his royal responsibilities
- a pious Christian
- calculating and cunning, as in the manner in which he condemns the traitors Cambridge, Scroop and Grey to death
- willing to adopt disguise when he wanders among his men before the Battle of Agincourt
- generous, as when he pardons and rewards Williams
- an inspiring speaker, skilled in the art of stirring his men by the use of rhetoric
- willing to attack France only if the bishops can legally justify his claim to the French throne
- prepared to be ruthless, as when he threatens the citizens of Harfleur with rape and pillage if they do not surrender
- merciful, as when he pardons the drunkard who has insulted him, and when the citizens of Harfleur do surrender
- just and honourable, treating the Dauphin's messengers in a civilised way, and later insisting that his soldiers should not rob the ordinary French people
- heroically determined to fight to the last, even when heavily outnumbered
- firm in his demands when he has beaten France
- modest about his looks and talents when he woos Katharine.

The Chorus

The Chorus is:

- an actor who introduces each Act of the play and comments on the action
- modelled on the convention of the chorus in Greek tragedy.

Duke of Gloucester

The Duke of Gloucester is:

- Henry's brother, along with the Duke of Bedford
- in charge of the siege of Harfleur.

Duke of Exeter

The Duke of Exeter is:

- Henry's uncle
- sent as ambassador to demand the French throne for Henry
- one of Henry's leading commanders, along with Westmoreland (Henry's cousin), Salisbury and Warwick
- admired as a commander by Fluellen
- responsible for holding the bridge at Picardy.

Duke of York

The Duke of York is:

- Henry's cousin
- killed at Agincourt (dying movingly with Suffolk).

Archbishop of Canterbury

The Archbishop is:

- worried that a bill before Parliament will deprive the Church of some of the wealth it uses to finance the Crown and support the poor and sick
- prepared to give the Church's financial backing to the war against France if the bill is dropped
- impressed by how responsible and pious Henry has become since his father's death
- an expert in international law
- backed up by the Bishop of Ely.

Gower

Gower is:

- an English captain
- a 'dear friend' of Fluellen
- a good soldier
- scornful of self-serving men like Pistol
- fully in approval of Henry's order for the French prisoners to be killed.

Pistol

Pistol is:

- a former drinking companion of Falstaff
- a friend of Bardolph (hanged for stealing from a church, despite Pistol's efforts)
- recently married to the Hostess, to the dismay of Nym
- a standard-bearer in the war
- an admirer of the King
- keen to line his own pocket in France
- full of empty boasts, but reported by Fluellen to have done valiant service in defending the bridge at Picardy
- an opportunist, as when he captures a French lord so that he can claim a ransom
- beaten and forced to eat a leek by Fluellen for insulting him
- left downcast after hearing that his wife has died.

Cambridge, Scroop and Grey

Cambridge, Scroop and Grey are:

- high-ranking conspirators who have accepted money from France in return for killing Henry
- exposed and condemned to death by Henry in Act 2, Scene 2.

Fluellen

Fluellen is:

- proud of being Welsh – and easily identified by his accent
- a loyal supporter of Henry
- rather verbose
- a fighter when roused
- fond of talking about Roman and Greek generals
- intelligent and knowledgeable in the arts of war
- a good captain and a good man
- a friend of Gower
- critical of Captain MacMorris
- unmoved by Pistol's plea to intervene to save Bardolph from execution by Exeter
- outraged at how the French kill the luggage boys, against 'the law of arms'
- good-humoured about being used in the trick the King plays on Williams.

MacMorris

MacMorris is:

- a captain directing the siege of Harfleur
- Irish and fiercely patriotic
- oversensitive to possible slights against his country
- quarrelsome.

Sir Thomas Erpingham

Sir Thomas Erpingham is:

- a loyal and dignified old knight who commands a regiment
- asked to lend his cloak to Henry.

The Dauphin

The Dauphin is:

- son and heir of the King of France ('Dauphin' is a title, not a name)
- arrogant and too sure of France's power, as shown by his mocking present of tennis balls to Henry
- rather foolishly proud of his horse, which he praises at length to the French lords
- melodramatically ashamed of the French defeat at Agincourt.

Katharine

Katharine is:

- the French princess, daughter of Charles VI
- learning English from her maid Alice
- married to Henry late in the play to cement his claim to the French throne.

Jamy

Jamy is:

- a brave and experienced Scottish captain.

Themes

Kingship

Figure 1.9 *Kingship.*

Many critics believe that in *Henry V* Shakespeare wanted to portray the ideal king. A number of authors before him had tried to compile a list of the ideal king's attributes, and he was probably influenced by Erasmus in his *Institutio Principis* (1516) and later writers using the ideas of Erasmus. The ideal king was meant to be a good Christian; a scholar; just; firm but merciful; concerned to protect the state from its enemies but without desire for personal revenge; self-controlled; attentive to wise counsel but immune to flattery; deeply aware of his responsibilities, including the welfare of the common people. He should be aware of the evils of war and should therefore not enter into it lightly. Finally, he should marry – and not merely to make a political alliance.

Henry meets every one of these requirements, a point that we should bear in mind when trying to analyse him. His virtues definitely outweigh his possible faults, but every fault of which he could be accused can equally be justified in terms of these ideals. He could be seen as cynically using the bishops to justify his intended aggression against France, buying them off with the promise of dropping the law that threatens their wealth. We might even think that he is making sure that, if the war goes badly, he can blame them for encouraging him to start it. However, if we assume that he is an ideal king, we must see his consulting them as showing a concern for international law and for his duty to pursue a rightful claim. We can also say he is not entering into a war without considering the loss of life and destruction that it will cause – which also occupies his mind the night before Agincourt.

Similarly, we might see Henry's treatment of the three conspirators as playfully cruel, but he is showing his intelligence and self-control, and protecting the state rather than exacting personal revenge. Likewise at Harfleur he appears ruthless, but he is in fact abiding strictly by the code of war, and shows mercy once the town surrenders. On a more personal scale, it is perhaps unfair that he tricks the common soldier Williams into agreeing to fight him if they both survive the battle, but then he shows mercy in pardoning him and generosity in rewarding him. We also see his mercy earlier, in his pardoning the drunkard who has insulted him. This also serves further to condemn the three conspirators, who urge him to show no such mercy.

Above all, Henry is an inspiring figurehead, nobly lifting the spirits of his men before Agincourt, prepared to die himself rather than be ransomed, respected by nobles and commoners alike. Moreover, he is a man of many parts, in battle fierce and brave, but also able to woo Katharine with tenderness, modesty and humour. He is, for Shakespeare, not just the ideal king but the ideal Englishman.

Loyalty and betrayal

There are a number of betrayals in the play, but also significant displays of loyalty. A major betrayal, of course, is that of Cambridge, Scroop and Grey, exposed and condemned to death for plotting to assassinate Henry. The King is especially disappointed in Scroop, who had been his close friend. He calls him a 'cruel, ingrateful, savage and inhuman creature', in a speech that expresses his bitter regret that a man who seemed so good could have been so thoroughly corrupted.

We see a different sort of betrayal in the way the French disregard the rules of law when they kill the luggage boys in the English tents. Although this is recorded as an actual occurrence by the historian Holinshed, Shakespeare is perhaps using the incident to imply that this sort of treacherous behaviour was to be expected from the French, whereas the English were just and trustworthy. Apart from the three conspirators, all the English characters are loyal to the King and prepared to follow him to the last, even when outnumbered five to one. Westmoreland even wishes that he and Henry alone could take on the French together. Only the soldier Williams openly doubts that the King would actually die rather than let himself be ransomed.

Friendship

Closely related to loyalty is friendship. Henry is wounded by his friend Scroop's betrayal. However, it could be argued that Henry himself has in a less obvious way betrayed his old drinking friends from *Henry IV (Parts 1 and 2)*, especially Falstaff, who does not appear in *Henry V* but who is said to be dying from Henry's neglect. In Henry's defence, he could hardly remain friends with such characters and be fully respected as a king. However, Pistol does not seem to hold this against him, as we see when the disguised Henry meets him when walking among his troops. Pistol is a rogue, but he still tries to prevent his old friend Bardolph from being hanged.

Henry feels that friendship is very important, often addressing his commanders affectionately. He calls Exeter 'good uncle', and says that Sir Thomas Erpingham deserves 'a soft pillow for his good white head'. He even extends this bond of friendship to his troops, addressing them as 'dear friends' and 'good yeomen'. At Agincourt, he asserts that he would not want to die with anyone 'that fears his fellowship to die with us'. They are not just an army, they are 'a band of brothers'.

Other friendships in the play are that between Fluellen and Gower, two brave and good-hearted captains, and between York and Suffolk, who die in each other's arms.

Patriotism

Henry regards it as his patriotic duty to lay claim to the French throne. Once on French soil he frequently appeals to his men's sense of patriotism – most notably in his 'Crispian's Day' speech in which he shows he regards it as an honour to fight on behalf of his country, and that the honour of his 'happy few' is all the greater for the heavy odds stacked against them. The common men are patriotic, though realistic about the prospect of death, seeing it as a necessity more than an honour.

Henry's patriotic belief in the determination of the English is such that he tells Montjoy that, even if the English die at Agincourt, their rotting bodies will cause a plague that will infect and kill the French.

The French nobles seem more concerned with boasting and squabbling than with patriotism, though Burgundy seems genuinely concerned for his country's welfare after the defeat at Agincourt, in Act 5.

Stagecraft and setting

Stagecraft

A strong feature of the play is the way it compresses action on an epic scale into the space of a few hours on stage. The Chorus helps to achieve this, filling in gaps in the action and giving the audience an overall view of it, asking them to imagine the battlefields while they are in the 'wooden O' of the theatre. Shakespeare also uses a number of relatively short scenes that form snapshots of the whole campaign. By switching between different scenes – from the nobles to the common soldiers, and from one part of the battle to another – he gives an impression of scale. This also helps to sustain the pace. The play seems to move slowly, with lengthy, considered speeches when the Archbishop advises Henry on the legality of his claim and when Henry is moving among his troops the night before Agincourt. In the former, the slowness perhaps gives a sense of the weightiness of the question and how seriously Henry takes it; in the latter, Henry's soliloquy about the responsibilities of kingship again shows him as a moral and deeply thoughtful man. It also provides a calm before the storm of the battle itself, when we see him in a much more active and inspiring mood.

Another feature of Shakespeare's stagecraft is the way he interweaves scenes involving Henry and his nobles with those featuring the lower-class characters Pistol, Bardolph and Nym. This provides a variety of moods, and offers comic relief. Fluellen acts as a link between the two types of character, having a conversation – and an argument – with Pistol, but also speaking to the King.

There are also moments of great suspense and corresponding dramatic impact, as when we wait for the traitors to be accused, and then see them turn pale as they read the charges against them. More light-heartedly, we wait for Williams to discover that he has agreed to fight the King, and are then gratified by Williams' dignity and Henry's graciousness when the truth emerges.

The final Act, focusing on Henry's wooing of Katharine, seems very different from the earlier ones, and perhaps it is intended to show Henry's softer side, and to give a sense of a new union between the two countries, promising social stability and peace through a happy marriage.

Figure 1.10 *The reconstructed Globe Theatre in London.*

Setting

The play swings briskly between far-flung settings, giving us a sense of it operating in a wide arena. We begin in the King's Palace, possibly in London, though according to Holinshed the events actually took place in Kenilworth and Leicester. We then move to Southampton, to the French court at Rouen, to Harfleur, to Agincourt, and finally to the French court at Troyes. Shakespeare compares the French unfavourably with the English, at least until Act 5, when perhaps a sense of reconciliation is required. We have a charming sense of place in the scene involving Katharine and her maid Alice. Shakespeare uses enough French language to give a flavour of the country, but not so much as to alienate members of his audience who did not know French.

Language and symbolism

Rhetoric

The play is written partly in blank verse (lines of unrhymed **iambic pentameter**), and partly in prose. The lower-class characters speak in prose, and even Henry does so occasionally, as when he speaks in disguise to the common soldiers. The play features some highly emotive and effective verse speeches, mostly given by Henry. The first of these is his condemnation of his former friend Scroop. Typical rhetorical devices are his use of: groups of three, in his accusations; **rhetorical questions**; **personification** – for example, of treason and murder as twin devils; **alliteration** – as in 'botch and bungle'; and questions with the repeated answer, 'Why, so didst thou'. Equally effective, but inspiring rather than damning, is his use of repetition with rhythm in 'Once more unto the breach, dear friends, once more' and 'We few, we happy few, we band of brothers'. He can also use repetition to bitter effect, as when he warns the French messenger that the Dauphin's 'mock' will 'mock mothers from their sons, mock castles down'.

Imagery

Henry V is rich in **imagery**, of two kinds in particular. There are many images relating to gardening, suggesting that England is a garden and Henry the gardener who ensures its healthy, well-ordered growth, and that Henry himself is a product of England's garden. For example, the Bishop of Ely compares Henry to a strawberry that 'grows underneath the nettle'. Cambridge flatteringly speaks of Henry's subjects sitting 'under the sweet shade of your government'. The French king uses another gardening image in calling Henry 'a stem of that victorious stock', indicating his lineage. Burgundy notes sadly that France, the 'best garden of the world', has long been neglected and overgrown with weeds. A related image is that in which the Archbishop portrays the state as a beehive in which the different types of bee all perform their individual tasks for the greater harmony of the whole.

The play is also full of animal imagery, befitting the savagery of war. For example, the Bishop of Ely compares the Scots to a weasel that 'comes sneaking' to suck the English eagle's 'princely eggs'. Henry urges his men to 'imitate the action of the tiger' and compares them to greyhounds straining to be unleashed to hunt.

Activity 1: Understanding the text

Read aloud Henry's speech at the start of Act 3, Scene 1, 'Once more unto the breach, dear friends, once more'. Then discuss and write about the following:

- how the speech shows Henry's attitude towards his men
- how it reflects the theme of patriotism
- how it portrays peace and war
- how he uses language, including imagery and rhythm, to inspire.

Activity 2: Understanding the text

Imagine you are Williams, the soldier who challenges Henry in Act 4, Scene 1, talking to your grandchildren years later. Write the account that you might tell them of the night before Agincourt, the battle itself, and how you came to be pardoned and rewarded by the King. Remember to say what you think of it all now, as you look back.

Activity 3: Thinking about the characters

Read aloud Henry's soliloquy in Act 4, Scene 1, from 'Upon the king!' to Sir Thomas Erpingham's entry. Write a summary of it in your own words. Then write a paragraph about what it reveals about Henry and his attitude towards kingship.

Activity 4: Thinking about the characters

In groups of four or five, one person should take the role of Fluellen, another that of Pistol. The rest of the group should question them about their dealings with each other at Agincourt, trying to get each man's version of events, and how each feels about what has happened.

Some questions to consider

1. What does the subplot involving Pistol, Nym and Bardolph add to the play?
2. How convinced are you that Henry truly regards his soldiers as 'brothers'?
3. What character, apart from Henry, do you find the most interesting, and why?
4. What do you think the final scene adds to the play? Does it really help to round off the events, or is it just tagged on?

William Shakespeare: *Much Ado About Nothing*

Background and context

Much Ado About Nothing is a comedy, but a strange one because it almost turns into a tragedy. Its basic story, that of a lover deceived by an enemy into believing that the woman he loves has betrayed him, was used by many writers before Shakespeare, for example the 5th-century Greek author Chariton, in *Chaereas and Kallirrhoe*. Later versions of the story to which Shakespeare was indebted are Ariosto's *Orlando Furioso* (1516, translated into English in 1591) and Bandello's *La Prima Parte de le Novelle* (1554). *Much Ado About Nothing* is closer to the latter, though there are significant changes in plot that show Shakespeare's own dramatic intentions.

The play is part of a dramatic tradition. As an Elizabethan comedy, it features amusing misunderstandings and confusions, disguise, love, and plenty of witty banter. Don John, too, is a version of an Elizabethan type, the melancholic, who takes little pleasure in the world around him. In this, he shares some traits with Jaques in *As You Like It* and Malvolio in *Twelfth Night*. However, he is more evil than either of them. In the pleasure he seems to take in making other people suffer, with very slight cause, he resembles Iago in *Othello*, though he lacks Iago's deceitful cleverness.

We must also bear in mind the play's social context. There was a strict hierarchy of status in Shakespeare's time. All the main characters are nobles: only the conniving Borachio, the foolish Dogberry and the rest of the Watch are commoners. Don Pedro, the Prince, is respected and obeyed by the other characters – except the illegitimate Don John, who is probably bitter about not being recognised as his half-brother's equal. Women, though important as love objects, have no power and must obey their fathers, then their husbands. It is also vital for them to be virgins before marriage.

Plot

Don Pedro, the Prince of Aragon, arrives in Messina from the wars, which have gone well for him. With him are his friends Benedick and Claudio, and his brother, Don John, who has recently regained his favour. They visit Leonato, Governor of Messina, and Claudio quickly falls in love with Leonato's daughter Hero. Benedick is amused, being a confirmed bachelor himself – at least as appears to be the case from his humorous banter with Beatrice. Leonato and his older brother Antonio are planning a masked ball. Don Pedro promises to woo Hero posing as Claudio, win her, then get her father's permission for Claudio to marry her. The villainous Don John hears of the marriage plans from Borachio and sees an opportunity to cause trouble for his brother and get his own back on Claudio, whose success and favour with Don Pedro he resents. First, he persuades Claudio that Don Pedro is wooing Hero for himself. When Don Pedro reassures Claudio, Don John hatches a plot with Borachio to convince Claudio that his bride-to-be has already slept with other men.

A romantic subplot now develops: Don Pedro, Leonato and Claudio trick Benedick into believing that Beatrice is in love with him; Hero and Ursula trick Beatrice into believing that Benedick is in love with her. The mood of the play darkens as Don John puts his second plan into action. Borachio will woo Margaret at Hero's

Top tip

For details about Shakespeare, please see the start of the section on Romeo and Juliet (page 15).

Figure 1.11 *A masked Don Pedro tries to win Hero for Claudio.*

bedroom window, with Margaret posing as Hero. Don John will arrange for Claudio and Don Pedro to witness this, so that they believe his accusations about Hero. We then cut to Dogberry and the Watch, who overhear Borachio telling Conrade how well this ploy worked. The Watch arrest the pair, but fail to get Leonato's attention long enough to explain the matter to him before he goes off to plan his daughter's marriage to Claudio. The congregation assemble for the wedding, at which Claudio now intends to shame Hero. He accuses her publicly, and she faints.

The Friar carrying out the wedding believes Hero to be innocent, as does Beatrice. He tells Leonato to let people think that Hero is dead. Despite the grim mood, Benedick and Beatrice reveal their mutual love. Urged by Beatrice to 'kill Claudio', Benedick promises to challenge him. Fortunately, it is discovered that Don John has fled the city, and that he had orchestrated the plot against Hero. The Friar gets Claudio to promise to marry Hero's 'cousin', who looks just like her. Of course it is actually Hero, and Claudio is overjoyed. Meanwhile, Don John is captured and Benedick looks forward to devising 'brave punishments' for him, as well as to marrying Beatrice.

Characters

Don Pedro

Don Pedro is:

- the Prince of Aragon
- the most powerful figure in the play
- the brother of Don John
- a close friend of Benedick and Claudio
- a bachelor
- something of a schemer, albeit for good ends
- good-humoured
- an appreciator of witty banter.

Don John

Don John is:

- Don Pedro's illegitimate brother ('the Bastard')
- a melancholic whose only pleasure seems to be in destroying the pleasure of others (something like the serpent in the Garden of Eden)
- resentful of his brother, and of Claudio
- a bare-faced liar
- cruelly indifferent to the extreme suffering he causes to Hero
- another bachelor, convinced that only fools marry.

Claudio

Claudio is:

- a handsome young man
- a friend of Benedick who enjoys his wit
- ready to fight Benedick when challenged
- a favourite of Don Pedro
- convinced that Hero is the woman for him
- prepared to let Don Pedro woo her on his behalf
- easily persuaded that Don Pedro is wooing Hero for himself
- equally convinced that she is promiscuous the minute Don John says so
- cruel and calculating in his public shaming of Hero in church
- not particularly upset when he learns of her 'death'
- devastated when he learns that he was tricked and Hero was in fact virtuous
- unable to see that he has betrayed Hero in believing in her guilt so quickly
- moved to tears of gratitude when Leonato asks him to marry Hero's cousin
- apparently overjoyed to find that Hero is still alive.

Hero

Hero is:

- the daughter of Leonato
- cousin and good friend to Beatrice
- a model of Elizabethan feminine virtue, quiet and obedient
- happy to be marrying Claudio
- devastated by Claudio's accusing and shaming her
- not very effective in her own defence when accused
- prepared to forgive and marry Claudio without accusing him of wronging her.

Beatrice

Beatrice is:

- an orphaned cousin of Hero, and her great friend
- a lover of witty word-play who uses words to duel with Benedick
- never going to marry – according to her
- tricked into believing that Benedick loves her
- fairly quick to declare her love for Benedick
- the first person to declare Hero's innocence
- passionate in Hero's defence.

Borachio

Borachio is:

- a commoner
- a follower of Don John
- the man who thinks of the scheme to trick Claudio and Don Pedro into believing in Hero's guilt, and carries it out with Margaret
- pleased to have earned a thousand ducats by tricking Don Pedro and Claudio
- quick to confess his guilt when challenged.

Conrade

Conrade is:

- a villainous gentleman and follower of Don John
- captured by the Watch, along with Borachio.

Benedick

Benedick is:

- a good friend of Don Pedro
- a bachelor
- cheerful most of the time
- a wit who enjoys word-play
- a rival in mutually insulting witty banter with Beatrice
- easily tricked into believing that Beatrice is in love with him
- quick to declare his own love to Beatrice
- prepared to challenge Claudio, and possibly kill him, when Beatrice asks him to
- not very good at writing poetry
- engaged to marry Beatrice by the end of the play
- the character who has the last word in the play.

Leonato

Leonato is:

- Governor of Messina
- father of Hero
- uncle and guardian of Beatrice
- surprisingly quick to doubt Hero's virtue
- shamed himself by her apparent guilt
- prepared to go along with the Friar's scheme to tell people that Hero is dead
- furious with Claudio and Don Pedro when he realises that Hero is innocent
- not quite as furious as his brother Antonio, whom he has to calm down for fear that he will attack Don Pedro and Claudio
- content for Claudio to marry Hero in the end.

Antonio

Antonio is:

- the elderly brother of Leonato and therefore uncle to Hero and Beatrice
- furious with Claudio and Don Pedro for wronging Hero.

Friar Francis

Friar Francis is:

- meant to marry Claudio to Hero, and eventually does so
- convinced of Hero's innocence
- the originator of the plan to pretend that Hero is dead, then get Claudio to marry her while thinking he is marrying her cousin.

Dogberry

Dogberry is:

- the Master Constable, head of the Watch
- a well-meaning buffoon.

Margaret

Margaret is:

- Hero's lady-in-waiting and companion
- in love with Borachio
- a pawn in Borachio's ploy to trick Don Pedro and Claudio.

Themes

Love and marriage

Both plots, that focusing on Claudio and Hero and that on Benedick and Beatrice, revolve around love, and in Shakespearean comedy this almost always leads to marriage. We first see the playful war of words between Benedick and Beatrice, which seems to hide an established mutual affection that neither will openly acknowledge; then Claudio quickly falls in love with Hero and decides that he must marry her. The love between Benedick and Beatrice is based on long acquaintance and on equality – Beatrice gives as good as she gets in their witty exchanges – whereas Claudio and Hero barely know each other, and the power in their relationship rests with him. The conventionally virtuous and obedient Hero agrees to marry Claudio because he, the Prince and her father want her to do so. The trickery of Don John, himself loveless and scornful of marriage, sorely tests Claudio's love. Significantly, the trick depends on Margaret's undeserved love for Borachio. Claudio fails the test, too readily believing in Hero's guilt. We may wonder if he really did love her, or merely idealised her. Beatrice tests Benedick's love by telling him to 'kill Claudio', something he reluctantly agrees to do. The problems of the play are resolved by the marriage of Claudio and Hero, and the promised marriage of Benedick and Beatrice.

Loyalty and betrayal

The main action of the play is triggered by Don John's disloyalty to Don Pedro, which according to Shakespearean convention is linked to his illegitimacy (compare this with the illegitimate Edmund in *King Lear*). He has only just been reconciled with Don Pedro, yet is already plotting against him and against his favourite Claudio. His disloyalty can be compared with the fierce loyalty of Antonio, who backs his brother Leonato to the hilt in his quarrel with Don Pedro and Claudio after the 'death' of Hero. Ironically, it is Borachio's loyalty to Don John, together with Margaret's to Borachio, that makes Don John's deception possible – although it could be argued that Borachio's loyalty has to be bought with a thousand ducats.

The central crisis of the play comes when Claudio accuses Hero of betrayal. So far is she from this that her shock and disbelief prevent her from defending herself properly. It could be argued that it is Claudio who betrays Hero, in so readily believing in her guilt. Initially her father Leonato can be said to betray her too, before he is persuaded of her innocence. Only Beatrice steadfastly stands by her from the outset. Indeed, she challenges Benedick to prove his new-found love for her by killing his friend Claudio, which presents Benedick with a dilemma of divided loyalties, in which his loyalty to Beatrice wins. This can be resolved only when Don John's betrayal is discovered and Hero's reputation is restored.

Appearance and reality

Don John's deception of his brother and Claudio is central to the play, as is Claudio's mistaken belief that Hero only appears to be virtuous, and is in fact like a 'rotten orange'. However, the theme of appearance and reality can also be found in the playful dialogue that is based on puns – where a word or phrase can appear to mean one thing while hinting at something else. The speeches of Dogberry and Verges have something of the same play on appearances, in that they simply get words wrong. The conversations of Benedick and Beatrice are full of deliberate word-play, and give the appearance of their being at odds, when in fact they are secretly fond of each other. Their friends perhaps play on this when they trick them into mutual declarations of love. There is benign deception at a more profound level when the Friar, backed by Leonato, deceives Claudio into believing that he is marrying Hero's cousin. Deception, it seems, can have good results as well as bad.

Guilt and redemption

When Hero faints in church, her father hopes she is actually dead. For him, her guilt is too great for possible redemption. Arguably, however, the real guilty party is Claudio. It is a dramatic problem that he seems to feel no remorse on hearing that Hero is dead: he continues to joke with Don Pedro. However, he feels at least a sense of great loss when he hears Borachio's confession – given freely and penitently – and discovers her innocence. Claudio still claims that he sinned only 'in mistaking', but to his credit he invites Leonato to name his 'penance'. His redemption comes when he gives himself up to this penance, which proves to be nothing worse than marrying the still-living Hero.

Stagecraft and setting

Stagecraft

Overall, the play, like other Shakespeare comedies, moves from a settled social situation to a chaotic one characterised by confusion, concealment and misunderstandings, and is finally resolved when these are revealed and explained to all concerned. Don Pedro and his followers return from the pursuit of conflict and social division – the wars – and naturally turn their thoughts to what the Elizabethans saw as the source of social harmony: love and marriage. Claudio himself says that before going off to fight he saw Hero only with a soldier's eye, but now he sees her as the woman he must marry. However, it would be a dull plot if he simply proposed and married her. Hence the social harmony is turned to chaos by Don John's antisocial malevolence.

A major feature of Shakespeare's stagecraft, then, lies in the interweaving of the scenes of harmonious social ritual with those of malignant plotting. Sometimes, too, Shakespeare makes these overlap in time. For example, in Act 2, Scene 1, while Leonato is planning his daughter's wedding, and Don Pedro and his friends are playfully planning to trick Benedick and Beatrice into falling in love, Don John is making his own treacherous plans with Borachio. This ensures changes of mood from one scene to the next, involves the audience in that they know what's going on, while the characters do not (an example of dramatic irony), and heightens the suspense.

The plot involving Benedick and Beatrice neatly occupies our interest during the time leading up to the intended wedding of Claudio and Hero. Moreover, their mutual declarations of love allow for a new source of dramatic tension – the question of whether Benedick will indeed kill Claudio. A third strand of the plot, the discovery of Don John's treachery when Dogberry and the Watch overhear Borachio and Conrade, is also cleverly handled. On the one hand it reassures the audience that the truth will probably emerge to prevent the play tipping over into tragedy; on the other it creates keen comic suspense, because Leonato has neither the time nor patience to listen to Dogberry's long-winded account of the villains he has arrested, and therefore does not find out the truth in time to prevent Hero being shamed.

Setting

All the action of the play takes place in or near the house of Leonato in Messina, Sicily. His house is seen as a place of courtly, civilised behaviour and conversation. Benedick and Beatrice are tricked by their friends in the garden, which might symbolically be seen as 'the garden of love'. Claudio's denunciation of Hero takes place in the church, which gives it a special dramatic power. Similarly, there is a ritualistic power in the setting of his eventual marriage to her, at what is meant to be her tomb. This implies that she is in effect reborn for Claudio, or perhaps that their relationship can be reborn.

Language and symbolism

Eloquence and word-play

Unusually for Shakespeare, most of the play is in prose, not verse. This is in order to give free rein to the verbal dexterity of the courtly characters, who take delight in witty, elaborately imaginative language, and in playful contests of wit. Typically they pick up on each other's words, deliberately seeming to mistake their meanings, and extending their **metaphors** – for example, when the Messenger says that Benedick is 'stuffed with all honourable virtues', Beatrice chooses to take this negatively: 'It is so indeed, he is no less than a stuffed man' (Act 1, Scene 1), or when in the same scene Benedick calls Beatrice 'a rare parrot-teacher', she retorts, 'A bird of my tongue is better than a beast of yours.' (She means he is a dumb animal!)

Despite the 'war' between Beatrice and Benedick, most of the language in the play is positive, appreciative and complimentary, though this is often playfully undercut, as in Beatrice's reply to the Messenger, above. There is also a joyful use of exaggeration, even in a superficially negative context, as when Benedick pleads with Don Pedro to send him on a mission 'to the Antipodes' or to fetch 'a toothpicker now from the furthest inch of Asia' so that he can get away from Beatrice.

Figure 1.12 *Messina in Sicily.*

Imagery

The play abounds in **imagery**, much of it wittily exaggerated, as when Benedick complains about Beatrice to Don Pedro: 'She speaks poniards [daggers], and every word stabs' (Act 2, Scene 1). At other times there are amusing images, as when Hero compares Beatrice to a lapwing running close to the ground to escape notice (Act 3, Scene 1). Don John's language contrasts with this, showing his bitterness and evil intent in images of disease, constraint and repressed violence: 'I had rather be a canker in a hedge than a rose in his grace... I am trusted with a muzzle... I have decreed not to sing in my cage' (Act 1, Scene 3). His language also contrasts with the sheer eloquence of other characters. Claudio seems to descend into the same kind of imagery as Don John when he refers to Hero as 'this rotten orange' (Act 4, Scene 1).

Although most of the play is in prose, there are some passages of lyrical verse containing effective imagery, especially **personification**. See, for example, Claudio's 'How still the evening is, / As hush'd on purpose to grace harmony! (Act 2, Scene 3) or Don Pedro's description of dawn dappling 'the drowsy east with spots of grey' (Act 5, Scene 3).

Activity 1: Understanding the text

Study carefully Benedick's soliloquy below (Act 2, Scene 3).

> I do much wonder that one man, seeing how much another man is a fool when he dedicates his behaviours to love, will, after he hath laughed at such shallow follies in others, become the argument of his own scorn by failing in love: and such a man is Claudio. I have known when there was no music with him but the drum and the fife; and now had he rather hear the tabour and the pipe: I have known when he would have walked ten mile a-foot to see a good armour; and now will he lie ten nights awake, carving the fashion of a new doublet. He was wont to speak plain and to the purpose, like an honest man and a soldier; and now is he turned orthography; his words are a very fantastical banquet, just so many strange dishes. May I be so converted and see with these eyes? I cannot tell; I think not: I will not be sworn, but love may transform me to an oyster; but I'll take my oath on it, till he have made an oyster of me, he shall never make me such a fool. One woman is fair, yet I am well; another is wise, yet I am well; another virtuous, yet I am well; but till all graces be in one woman, one woman shall not come in my grace. Rich she shall be, that's certain; wise, or I'll none; virtuous, or I'll never cheapen her; fair, or I'll never look on her; mild, or come not near me; noble, or not I for an angel; of good discourse, an excellent musician, and her hair shall be of what colour it please God. Ha! the prince and Monsieur Love! I will hide me in the arbour.

Check your understanding of the meaning. Then explain in your own words:

- why Benedick is criticising Claudio

- what the speech shows about Benedick's character and his attitude to marriage

- why the speech is ironic, given what is about to happen

- how this speech relates to the themes of the play.

Activity 2: Understanding the text

Divide a sheet of paper into three columns, as below. Then write a short summary of each scene – who does/says what – adding your summary beneath the heading that best describes the scene's overall mood. (One has been done for you.) Use Column 3 for scenes in which the mood is mixed, or which are comic but have serious implications. Add each summary on a new table row. There are 20 scenes, so you may need more than one page.

When you have completed the table, discuss and/or write about how Shakespeare varies the mood.

1. Light-hearted, happy, comic	2. Serious, foreboding	3. Uncertain
Act 1, Scene 1: Leonato hears Don Pedro is returning; Beatrice asks about Benedick; Don Pedro and friends arrive (with Don John); Benedick and Beatrice bandy words; Claudio falls for Hero; Benedick says he'll never marry; Don Pedro says he will woo Hero for Claudio.		

Activity 3: Thinking about the characters

Reread Act 4, Scene 1, Act 5 Scenes 1 and 3–4. Then write two accounts of Claudio's behaviour, one 'prosecuting' him, showing him in as negative a light as possible, and one 'defending' him, showing him in as positive a light as possible. Be sure to refer to the evidence of the text. Alternatively, you could do this in pairs, each person tackling one account.

On balance, how do you really judge Claudio's behaviour? Write a summary of your views.

Activity 4: Thinking about the characters

Write a comparison of the characters of Beatrice and Hero, referring to evidence from the play.

Some questions to consider

1. What do you think of the behaviour of Don Pedro? Consider his wooing of Hero on Claudio's behalf, his trust in his brother – especially relating to Hero – and his position at the end of the play.

2. Friar Francis' plan works out well, but how wise was it? Consider what might have gone wrong. If you know *Romeo and Juliet*, consider how badly wrong the Friar's plan to bring the two lovers back together goes in that play.

3. Do you think either Benedick or Beatrice has the upper hand in their wars of words, or are they equally matched? Consider Act 1, Scene 1, Act 2, Scenes 1 and 3.

4. How do you think the villainous Don John and his two followers, Borachio and Conrade, add to the dramatic interest of the play?

Oscar Wilde: *The Importance of Being Earnest*

Background and context

The playwright and poet Oscar Wilde was born in 1854 in Dublin and studied in both Ireland and England. He became very well known in London society, but his life was full of controversy. In 1897, he was imprisoned in Reading Gaol because of his relationship with Lord Alfred Douglas, which had become a scandal as homosexual relationships were illegal in Britain at that time and remained so until the 1960s. After his release in 1897, he decided to move to France. The time he spent in gaol had affected his health and he died in 1900, a year before Queen Victoria. His plays have always been extremely popular, none more so than *The Importance of Being Earnest*, which was produced in 1895. He poked much fun at Victorian society, particularly the upper classes.

Plot

This can be a little confusing, and was meant to be, with questions of identity and names, including the pun on Ernest/earnest, hanging over the whole play. The central character is Jack Worthing, who has houses both in the country and in London. In London he is known as Ernest, but in the country as Jack. To his household in the country (in particular, his ward, the young and pretty Cecily Cardew) he also pretends that 'Ernest Worthing' is his rascal of a brother, who gives him a reason to travel frequently to London.

In Act 1, Jack is intending to propose to Gwendolen, and calls on her cousin, Algernon Moncrieff. Algernon has found Jack's cigarette case, with an inscription to 'Uncle Jack', and he forces Jack to confess his double life. In return, he tells him about his fictitious friend, called Bunbury, and accuses Jack of being a 'Bunburyist' himself. Algernon also finds out about the 'excessively pretty' Cecily. When Jack proposes, Gwendolen accepts, yet also admits she had always wanted to marry a man named Ernest and would not marry anyone with any other name. Additionally, Gwendolen's mother is the formidable Lady Bracknell, a woman obsessed with social standing. Because Jack was found, abandoned, in a handbag in a railway station, he does not know who his parents are. Lady Bracknell refuses permission for the marriage unless Jack discovers his parentage.

In Act 2, Algernon turns up at Jack's country estate (with Jack still in London), pretending to be the notorious Ernest, and introduces himself to Cecily. Unfortunately for both, Jack then returns, dressed in mourning clothes, having finally decided to 'kill Ernest off'. Finding Algernon posing as Ernest does not amuse him and neither does the fact that he is now apparently madly in love with Cecily. Algernon, meanwhile, is surprised to discover that Cecily had invented a romance with the imagined brother Ernest – a name that she too finds irresistible – but takes advantage of the situation to propose 'officially'. When Gwendolen arrives at the country house to see Jack/Ernest, a huge argument follows because Gwendolen and Cecily both think they are engaged to Ernest Worthing and Jack has to confess that he is not truly named Ernest. Both Jack and Algernon try to be re-christened Ernest, by Dr Chasuble, to save their marriages.

The final Act, Act 3, also takes place in Jack's country house, but in the drawing room, not the garden. Lady Bracknell, who has also come down from London, has decided that as Cecily is very rich she may be a good match for her nephew,

Figure 1.13 *Afternoon tea with Algernon Moncrieff.*

Algernon. However, as guardian of Cecily, Jack has strong bargaining power and will not allow the marriage unless Lady Bracknell lets him marry Gwendolen. Lady Bracknell still refuses, but the mention of a Miss Prism, Cecily's governess, attracts her interest. We discover that Miss Prism had previously worked for Lady Bracknell's sister but vanished suddenly, to everyone's surprise. This prompts Miss Prism's confession that, in error, she had placed the text of her novel into the baby's pram, and placed the baby into her handbag. On discovering this, she abandoned the handbag at Victoria railway station in London. We thus discover that Jack is Lady Bracknell's nephew and Algernon's older brother who was originally christened Ernest. This enables the happy ending, with both couples marrying and the blossoming of the feelings of Miss Prism and Dr Chasuble for each other.

Characters

John (Jack/Ernest) Worthing, JP

Jack is:

- an apparently responsible, respectable young man, but one who leads a double life
- known as Jack in the country, where he has an estate and pretends to have a brother called Ernest who lives in London
- known as Ernest in town
- a mystery, because of his discovery in a handbag in the cloakroom of Victoria Station (the Brighton line)
- the guardian of Cecily Cardew, the granddaughter of the man who found him as a baby
- able to produce comic statements at times
- in love with his friend Algernon's cousin, Gwendolen Fairfax, whom he wants to marry.

Gwendolen Fairfax

Gwendolen is:

- Algernon's cousin and the daughter of Lady Bracknell
- in love with Jack, whom she thinks of as Ernest, a name she loves
- a rather sophisticated and fashionable young lady.

Dr Chasuble

Dr Chasuble is:

- the rector on Jack's estate
- approached by both Jack and Algernon to be christened 'Ernest'
- romantically inclined towards Miss Prism.

Algernon Moncrieff

Algernon is:

- a charming young bachelor who is rather lazy and not very useful
- the nephew of the ferocious Lady Bracknell, his 'Aunt Augusta'
- a cousin of Gwendolen Fairfax, whom Jack wants to marry
- the best friend of Jack, who he thinks is called Ernest
- somewhat greedy and self-centred, and inclined to make witty remarks
- the inventor of the fictional 'Bunbury', who is supposed to be his invalid friend – 'Bunbury' provides an escape mechanism to avoid unwelcome invitations.

Cecily Cardew

Cecily is:

- the ward of Jack, who as her guardian has to look after her till she comes of age
- the granddaughter of the old gentleman who found and adopted Jack when Jack was a baby
- also mysteriously obsessed with the name Ernest
- a highly imaginative romantic, who keeps a vivid diary
- rather attracted to the idea of being in love with a disreputable person such as Jack's imaginary brother Ernest, so falls for Algernon.

Lady Bracknell

Lady Bracknell is

- Algernon's Aunt Augusta and Gwendolen's mother
- determined that her daughter should also marry 'well' (i.e. someone rich)
- someone who says exactly what she thinks, which is often extremely amusing, usually unintentionally so
- a snob, whose attitudes are made fun of by Wilde.

Miss Letitia Prism

Miss Prism is:

- Cecily's governess
- clearly rather scatterbrained and absent-minded at times
- a would-be novelist in her youth, only she was parted from the text of her novel in unusual circumstances
- rather romantically inclined towards Dr Chasuble.

Lane

Lane is:

- Algernon's manservant.

Merriman

Merriman is:

- the butler at Jack's estate in the country.

Themes

Love and marriage

Although almost everyone in the play is married or wants to be, Wilde is happy to make fun of the institution of marriage, and of people's attitudes towards it and towards love. In particular, he sees aristocratic families as motivated by a mixture of money and snobbery. Several characters make comments about marriage that seem very cynical, and the speed of Algernon's engagement to Cecily does not suggest that marriage is a relationship necessarily based on deep knowledge of the other person.

Society

The play focuses on the lives of the 'upper classes', and looks at some aspects of how London 'society' in the late Victorian era is presented. Wilde suggests that 'society' tended to be very superficial and concerned with trivial things. He makes fun of people's manners, which are often seen as a mask for insincerity and hypocrisy – until, as in the case of Gwendolen and Cecily, the pretence becomes too hard to keep up and the discussion over tea in the garden becomes overheated at one point. The upper classes are also often depicted as ignorant and uninformed, with Gwendolen's surprise at the 'flowers in the country' typical of urban 'sophistication'.

Morality and sincerity

The play has many references to moral attitudes and to a worldly lack of concern for ordinary morality on the part of some characters. This is closely linked with questions about whether one should be sincere, and the place of hypocrisy in Victorian society, which Wilde suggests means that some people's moral declarations should not be taken seriously. Of course, Victorian morality was often very 'earnest', and so the play questions whether people really should be earnest (as well as 'Ernest'). The play was subtitled 'A Trivial Comedy for Serious People': Wilde does not seem to have felt that serious people should take themselves too seriously and uses his wit to expose these weaknesses.

Stagecraft and setting

Setting and stage directions

Productions of this play often literally 'go to town' (but also go to the country) with the sets and furniture, with the elegant Mayfair townhouse and a splendid country manor house – Wilde wishes us to be clear that these are very rich, upper-class people, who live most elegantly, with servants, stunning outfits and fine food. Note the wording of the stage directions: 'luxuriously and artistically furnished'.

Structure

The two settings, one in the town and one in the country, show the two sides of Jack's and Algernon's lives, and present important visual contrasts that relate to the themes. By keeping the action in the same place for the final Act, the speed of the play's narrative structure is maintained: everything seems to happen in a great rush. Another way in which Wilde has a strong sense of balance between two elements is the fact that the two young couples move forward in parallel and arrive finally at the same destination.

Humour

Wilde uses a variety of forms of humour to great effect throughout the play, which, when performed well, is quite as funny today as when it was written, which is certainly not the case with all 'comedies' from a hundred or more years ago. Much of the humour is in the actual words spoken, which give a striking sense of what the characters are like. There are also several farcical elements: misunderstandings and mistakes create situations that are hilarious: for example, Jack's thinking Miss Prism is his mother; or his announcement of the pretend Ernest's death followed shortly by the sight of a very real Algernon, pretending to be a very much alive Ernest.

Language and symbolism

The language of the play is a key means for Wilde to employ his **wit** and **irony**. Wilde was famous for his skill at creating **epigrams** – short, witty sayings that often twist a familiar idea into a new and often unexpected one (a paradox). Of all Wilde's plays, this one perhaps has the greatest number of quotable epigrams, some of which have passed into the English language: 'a *handbag?*' 'to lose one parent...'. And as we have seen already, the whole play centres on a pun between the name Ernest and the adjective 'earnest' (meaning 'serious and sincere'), neither of which either of the two 'Ernests' can really be said to be; and if they had been, their fiancées would probably never have fallen for them. There is also the use of **clichés**, or **platitudes**: Miss Prism is particularly inclined to use such phrases, sometimes Biblical in their inspiration ('as a man soweth, so may he reap').

Figure 1.14 *'A handbag?'*

Activity 1: Understanding the text

Understanding Wilde's use of **verbal humour**:

Look at what is said opposite about humour and language, and check that you can see how Wilde achieves his comic effects through his words. A good place to start is to look through the lines of Lady Bracknell (Aunt Augusta) and comment on the humour. Complete the table below, in which the first two have been done for you. If you are working with others, compare your lists and comments: you may be surprised at how many different examples there are.

Lady Bracknell's lines	The effect of these
'A *handbag?*'	Her astonishment at such an outrageous way for a baby to behave is shown by her tone of voice.
'To lose one parent, Mr Worthing, may be regarded as a misfortune. To lose both looks like carelessness.'	The humour comes partly from the neat use of repetition ('to lose...'), but also by the unexpected use of the word 'carelessness' as though losing parents was rather like leaving umbrellas on the bus.

Activity 2: Understanding the text

Study the tea-time scene between Gwendolen and Cecily. You can see how important a part 'good manners' play in this scene. However, you should be able also to find places where what each character says seems insincere. Pick out examples of this, and also note how it becomes harder for the two young ladies to behave in the manner expected of them. Why does this happen, and what is the effect?

Activity 3: Thinking about the characters

Choose any one of the characters and write notes to help an actor who has been selected to play that character understand how to play the part – think about such aspects as what the person is like, appearance, way of speaking and tone of voice, gestures and movements.

Activity 4: Thinking about the characters

Look closely at the characters of Jack and Algernon. Which do you prefer and why? Write down some of your favourite lines, those that give an idea of why you like the character.

Activity 5: Understanding the text

Keep a log as you read the play, noting down brief but important quotations for the major characters, themes and context of the play. Remember always to include a comment on *why* a particular quotation is important. Also, you may need to limit yourself to quotations that really *are* important, because Wilde is so quotable.

Some questions to consider

1. Think about the fictional character Bunbury. How does his creation shed light on the plot and characters, and why in the end is it necessary for him to 'die'?

2. Look closely at the relationship between Miss Prism and Dr Chasuble. What is *their* importance in relation to 'being earnest'? Why do you think Wilde finally brings them together at the end?

3. Aunt Augusta has been regarded as one of the great comic creations of all time. Why do you think this claim is or is not justified? Think of evidence to support your view.

4. Has Wilde anything earnest (sincere and serious) to say in this play or is it just a trivial comedy?

Thornton Wilder: *Our Town*

Background and context

Thornton Wilder was born in 1897 in the United States, in Madison, Wisconsin. He died in 1975. After graduating from university, he became a teacher who wrote in his spare time, until the success of his novel *The Bridge of San Luis Rey*, which won the Pulitzer Prize in 1927, meant that he was able to become a full-time writer. He wrote several novels, but in the 1930s he switched to writing plays, and *Our Town* was produced in New York's famous Broadway in 1938, where it was very successful, winning him a second Pulitzer Prize. He fought in the Second World War and afterwards resumed his writing career.

The 1930s were a difficult time both in Europe and the United States: a depression caused widespread poverty and unemployment, combined with the threat of a second major war, with the rise of Hitler and Germany's desire to expand its power in Europe. The audiences who watched *Our Town* were attracted by its 'small-town' setting, with ordinary people getting on with their day-to-day lives in the quieter times at the beginning of the 20th century. It was produced only a year before the outbreak of the Second World War in Europe, even though the USA did not enter the war for another two years, after the Japanese bombing on the American fleet at Pearl Harbor.

Figure 1.15 *Church in a small American town.*

Plot

The Stage Manager is both the narrator and takes on the role of various characters in the course of the play. He is very important throughout, and begins by introducing the audience to Grover's Corners, its background and the people living there. The audience is told that this is a town in one of the states of New England, New Hampshire. The action takes place in 1901. The Gibbs and the Webbs are the two central families, and the play focuses strongly on the relationship between George Gibbs and Emily Webb. The stage directions indicate that the small amount of furniture belongs to their houses. The fact that even this amount of furniture is placed on stage at the start by the Stage Manager is a sign of his controlling influence.

The action starts with the beginning of the day, and Act 1 takes us through the day's activities. As could happen anywhere, there are milk rounds and newspaper deliveries, the families have breakfast and the children are sent off to school. The wives meet for a chat about their lives and what they would like to do.

At this point, the Stage Manager invites Professor Willard and Mr Webb to come to tell the audience about Grover's Corners. Mr Webb is also questioned by some 'members of the audience'. These have actually been written in by the playwright and are really characters from the play.

In the afternoon, the children come out of school and George meets Emily. The Stage Manager mentions the idea of putting a time capsule under a new bank building in town, with a copy of the play *Our Town*.

In the evening, the choir meets to sing the hymn 'Blessed Be the Tie That Binds'. After choir, some members return home talking about the choirmaster's drinking problem. As the day ends, so does Act 1.

In Act 2 we learn that three years have passed. It is the day of George and Emily's wedding. George is not allowed to visit Emily, because this is supposed to be bad luck, so he chats to Mr Webb about marriage and being a husband.

Wilder then decides to use a **flashback**, introduced by the Stage Manager, to explore the courtship of George and Emily. This fills in some of the three-year gap, by explaining how the couple admitted their feelings for each other over ice-cream sodas, after Emily has warned George that his sporting success was making him conceited. George then decides to stay in Grover's Corners to be with Emily, rather than going away to agricultural college.

After the flashback, we are back on the wedding day, and the parents are calming the nerves of the bride and groom. The wedding takes place, with the Stage Manager taking on the role of the clergyman – more evidence of his power to make things happen. He then announces to the audience that it is time for another break.

There is another gap, this time of nine years, to Act 3. This Act takes place in a cemetery that looks down onto the town, just as the audience does. We find out that Emily has died while giving birth and it is her funeral. The funeral party is at the back of the stage, and in front are some dead souls from the cemetery, who are seated on chairs at the front, facing the audience, which represent the graves in the cemetery. They include several characters who were alive as characters in the earlier Acts, such as Mrs Gibbs, Mrs Soames and the choirmaster Mr Stimson. During the funeral the dead souls speak, commenting on life and events. The soul of Emily joins the other souls; she would like to go back to her life, much to the disapproval of the other souls.

The Stage Manager helps Emily to go back to the morning of her twelfth birthday, a flashback to several years before the start of the play, with the milk and paper rounds going on just as in the other two Acts. Emily watches the scene in which at the same time she is one of the characters. (Dickens uses this idea in *A Christmas Carol*, when Scrooge is taken back by the spirit to observe his past life.) Emily decides to rejoin the dead souls, while George stays, grief-stricken, by the grave. Emily's return to the living world shows her that people do not appreciate every second of the life they have and how soon it will pass. Day turns into night as the play, like the day, ends at Grover's Corners.

Characters

There is a fairly large cast of characters, some more prominent than others.

Stage Manager

The Stage Manager is:

- the play's host, or 'master of ceremonies'
- the supreme controller of the action, like the **omniscient narrator** in a novel
- able to take part in the action, taking on the roles of characters in the town
- also able to interrupt the action to talk to the audience, breaking out of the action of the play.

George Gibbs

George is:

- the son of Dr and Mrs Gibbs
- the older brother of Rebecca
- a star in the high school baseball team
- intending at first to go to agricultural college but keen to marry Emily Webb, so decides to stay
- presented as a very respectable young man.

Emily Webb

Emily is:

- the daughter of Mr and Mrs Webb and the older sister of Wally
- at first the school friend and next-door neighbour of George and later his fiancée and wife
- a very bright student and a dutiful daughter
- one of the dead souls (she dies while giving birth) who wishes to come back to life.

Mrs Gibbs

Mrs Gibbs is:

- the mother of George
- the wife of Dr Gibbs
- keen to visit Paris, but never gets there
- a dutiful, hard-working wife.

Mrs Webb

Mrs Webb is:

- the mother of Emily
- the wife of Mr Webb
- quite calm and practical about her daughter's wedding day
- worried that she has not given her enough advice about married life.

Simon Stimson

Mr Stimson is:

- the choirmaster
- an alcoholic, about whom people gossip
- one of the dead souls in Act 3, after committing suicide.

Minor characters include the following.

Rebecca Gibbs

Rebecca is:

- the younger sister of George
- interested in how Grover's Corners relates to the rest of the universe.

Dr Gibbs

Dr Gibbs is:

- the father of George
- the town doctor
- an expert on the American Civil War, which had happened within living memory of many of the characters
- the next-door neighbour to the Webbs.

Mr Webb

Mr Webb is:

- the father of Emily
- the husband of Mrs Webb
- editor and publisher of the local paper, the *Grover's Corners Sentinel*
- a character who draws the audience into the action by asking questions.

Mrs Soames

Mrs Soames is:

- a local gossip
- a member of the town choir, as are Mrs Webb and Mrs Gibbs
- one of the dead souls in Act 3.

Wally Webb

Wally is:

- the younger brother of Emily
- one of the group of dead souls, after dying young of a burst appendix.

Howie Newsome

Howie is:

- the local milkman
- someone who appears once in each Act, in the morning, doing his daily rounds.

Professor Willard

Professor Willard is:

- a professor at the State University
- a 'reporter' to the audience about Grover's Corners
- aware of the importance of the Native Indians in the USA's history, as they were there before the Europeans arrived.

Constable Warren

Constable Warren is:

- a local policeman
- a guardian of the community
- someone who knows the people of the town well.

Joe Crowell, Jr

Joe is:

- the boy who delivers the papers every day
- someone who chats with other characters
- the older brother of Si Crowell, who takes over the round.

Sam Craig

Sam is:

- the cousin of Emily Webb
- a former resident of Grover's Corners who has left to travel west
- something of an outsider, who does not understand what has been going on in the town since he left.

Joe Stoddard

Joe is:

- the town's undertaker
- sad about the death of the young, such as Emily.

Themes

'Seizing the day'

Time passes fast for the characters in the play, and opportunities are not always fully grasped or understood. Wilder reflects that for this reason we need to make the most of what time we have: it is sometimes referred to as the '*carpe diem*' philosophy, from the Latin phrase meaning 'seize the day'. There is less time than we think, so we should not keep putting off doing what we really want, as Mrs Gibbs does. Even simple, everyday actions need to be appreciated and made the most of.

This theme is particularly emphasised by the scene with the souls of the dead, who have the ability to see how easy it is to waste time and opportunities through 'ignorance' and 'blindness'. Even showing grief over the dead is seen as preventing people getting on with their lives. Wilder focuses on the 'big events' of life – birth, marriage and death ('hatch, match and dispatch', as it is sometimes known), and by compressing the time between them he creates the sense that things move on very fast.

Marriage and friendship – the importance of relationships and community

Wilder looks at a spectrum of relationships from casual exchanges with passers-by, or with the milkman or paper boy, to deeply romantic or passionate relationships and marriages of different kinds. The most important relationship in the play is that between George and Emily, which develops and changes over the course of the play until her untimely death. Wilder seems to suggest that lasting love is one way to fight against the rapid passing of time.

Other kinds of relationship are also present and there is perhaps a suggestion that 'everybody needs somebody'. There is even a much closer direct link between people in the audience and those on the stage, because the Stage Manager in particular makes this relationship happen. It is 'our' (not 'my' or 'their') town in the title, and this strengthens the sense of the importance of community: people often act in groups – in the choir or the dead souls, for example.

Real life and the theatre

Many plays invite their audience to 'suspend their disbelief' and be so absorbed in the events that they do not think that what they are seeing is 'unreal'. Following a tradition becoming established between the two World Wars, especially through the work of the playwright Brecht, some writers deliberately moved away from this. This is sometimes referred to as breaking down the 'fourth wall' (a phrase developed by another theatrical innovator, Stanislavski, to suggest that the stage is like three sides of a box, with the audience looking through the open side). The Stage Manager is Wilder's way of doing this. So Wilder, mainly through the Stage Manager, but not exclusively, reminds the audience that the theatre is not the same as real life: we are watching something that has been made up to show us some aspects of 'real life' but to do so in a way which we know is not 'really real'. The Stage Manager comments on the events as well as taking part in them and creates a simple set, with, for example, chairs and tables – where needed.

Time

Wilder is interested in the passage of time and the never-ending cycle of life, as has been seen above, but he also plays around with time, in particular using the device of the **flashback** (for example, the soda fountain and the return to the day of Emily's twelfth birthday). Moving out of real time into the past (or flashing forward, in some cases) is common in books and some films or television programmes. It helps disturb our sense of what is 'real' because it is not 'real time'. It is perhaps harder to do on stage because it can be confusing for an audience, which is where the device of the Stage Manager comes in: he leads and guides the audience.

The three scenes that include the hymn 'Blessed Be the Tie That Binds' also prominently feature Emily and George, highlighting the 'tie that binds' the two of them. The first instance of the song comes during a choir practice, which occurs simultaneously with George and Emily's conversation through their open windows in Act 1. The second instance comes during the wedding ceremony in Act 2. The third instance comes during Emily's funeral, as her body is buried and she joins the dead in the cemetery, leaving George behind. By associating this particular song with the play's critical moments, Wilder foregrounds the idea of companionship as an essential, even divine, feature of human life. The hymn may add some degree of

Figure 1.16 *The audience watching the stage is often asked to suspend their disbelief.*

Christian symbolism to the play but Wilder, for the most part, downplays any discussion of specifically Christian symbols. He concentrates on the hymn because of what it says about human beings in general.

Stagecraft and setting

The setting of the play in a small town is emphasised by the stage directions, which keep everything on a small scale, without elaborate set designs. As in the plays of Shakespeare, the audience needs to use its imagination to turn the stage into a real world. While Shakespeare tells his audience in *Henry V* that he wishes he could make it more 'real', and asks people to use their imagination to conjure up the battlefields and royal characters, Wilder uses the staging deliberately to create a sense of unreality and a world of ordinary people. This is underlined by the simple props, such as the ladder, which represents another storey and the trellis, which stands in for a garden.

The use of the Stage Manager as narrator, commentator and manipulator, as well as actor of several parts, is the most striking way in which Wilder creates a play that departs from traditional conventions and follows the ideas of Bertolt Brecht. However, the role of the Stage Manager is also derived from the leader of the Chorus in ancient Greek plays, who could address the audience and comment on the action.

Another important example of the stagecraft is that the characters do not have props to support the actions they are meant to be carrying out. This lack of props again goes back to the origins of the theatre, and in particular the traditions of **mime** and **pantomime**, in which actors rely on movement and gesture to enable the audience to tell what is meant to be happening. This again makes the members of the audience use their imaginations. In this play, for example, Howie the milkman does not have any bottles of milk in his hands, but he mimes the carrying of the bottles of milk, accompanied by the sound of milk bottles off stage. He also talks to his horse, but there is no horse.

The audience is also directly involved in the action through the 'question and answer' session, which plays with the idea of 'realism' in a different sense, as the audience may well think at first that the person asking the questions is a 'real' member of the audience, although it is a member of the cast who takes this 'role'. This is another way in which the usual distance between audience and cast is crossed.

At various points in the play, therefore, Wilder teases and plays with the audience's expectations. These devices make the audience think not only about the ideas in the play but also about the nature of the experience they are having. They are not just watching a representation of 'real' events, but questioning the nature of reality.

Language and symbolism

Language

Wilder's language is mostly fairly simple and direct, to reflect the everyday conversations of the characters. Sometimes he uses very short sentences that give a rather abrupt effect, almost like writing a short telegram (in those days) or a

Tweet/text in ours. Look at the following example, in which the Stage Manager is speaking to the audience:

> Stage Manager: (To audience) I've married two hundred couples in my day. Do I believe in it? I don't know. I suppose I do. M marries N. Millions of them. The cottage, the go-cart, the Sunday afternoon drives in the Ford—the first rheumatism—the grandchildren—the second rheumatism—the deathbed—the reading of the will—Once in a thousand times it's interesting.

Look at Activity 1 below, which asks for your response to this example.

The time capsule

It is the Stage Manager who refers to the burial of a time capsule underneath a new bank that is being built in the town. Apart from obvious suggestions, the Stage Manager suggests including a copy of the play *Our Town*. The symbol of a capsule that freezes the normally fast-flowing events of the town links to the play's main themes.

The daily deliveries

The deliveries of milk and newspapers are important in the play partly because they are not important or unusual but represent everyday events. They stand for the sense of routine and highlight the fact that some things do not change. It does not even matter who is carrying out the delivery: the individual may change, but the activity continues. However, there is also another form of delivery – Dr Gibbs' delivery of babies into the world. There is, therefore, a parallel between deliveries that start the day and those that start life: both are symbols of the continuity of human life. This symbol is given a twist by the fact that Emily dies while giving birth: both ends of the natural cycle come together.

The singing of the choir

The choir may be seen as the town in miniature: just as the town is a microcosm (literally 'small world'), so the choir is a small world within a small world. But it is also a symbol of a community coming together for a common purpose, and the hymn that it sings, which is about the 'tie that binds', contributes to that symbolic message. It also represents the Christian view of life, as it is a hymn used in the local church.

Activity 1: Understanding the text

Go back to the quotation above from the Stage Manager's address to the audience. Think about the effect of these very short comments, and, in particular, suggest how the phrases separated by long dashes might help our understanding of some of Wilder's ideas. What themes are presented in this section?

Activity 2: Understanding the text

Some of the play's characters, especially the Stage Manager, have a strong sense of history – both American and that of the ancient civilisations of Greece and Rome. Pick out as many examples of references to history or historical events as you can find, and write comments suggesting why these are introduced. Think especially about the theme of 'time'. An example has been given to start you off.

Historical reference	Comment on why it is used
Mrs Webb, of Dr Gibbs: 'Mr Webb just admires the way Dr Gibbs knows everything about the Civil War.'	This presents a strong sense of history and the security that can come from a deep knowledge of the past.

Activity 3: Thinking about the characters

Write a brief summary of the character of Emily based on what you find out about her in Act 1. Think how she comes across and what qualities you would wish to emphasise.

Now look closely at the following short extract of her words, just before the marriage. Are you surprised or even shocked to hear her speaking like this? Why do you think Wilder gives her such words to say? What does it tell us about her that adds to our earlier impressions?

> Emily: I never felt so alone in my whole life. And George, over there – I hate him – I wish I were dead. Papa! Papa!

Activity 4: Thinking about the characters

Think about any one of the souls of the dead, except Emily. Look closely not only at what this character says and does but also at what other characters say and think about him or her. How is this important in the play?

Some questions to consider

1. Commentators on the play have often suggested that although it is set a hundred years ago, it is just as relevant today. Do you agree? If you were the director and chose to set the play in the early 21st century and not the early 20th century, what changes would you make and why? (Think, for example, about the routines of daily life.)

2. Why do you think Wilder introduced the 'dead souls'? Do you think they add to the play?

3. What do you feel Wilder wanted us to think about the relationship between George and Emily?

4. To what extent do characters in this play achieve what they want from life? How does their success or lack of it contribute to the effect of the play?

Chapter 2: Understanding the prose texts

Introduction

In many respects, there are close similarities between the 'ingredients' of a prose text, such as a novel or short story, and a drama text, which, after all, is a story acted out. The common elements of plot – character, theme, a fixed period of time and language, for example – can be found in any of the texts read in this section in preparation for Paper 1. In addition, any fiction text will have a setting: it may have several. It is less restricted than a play because, instead of having to paint scenes and bring in furniture and other props, the description can be done by word-painting, a particular skill of many writers. Good writers enable you to picture the scene. Just as it has been said that listening to drama on the radio 'creates the best pictures', the reader can conjure up vivid pictures of places or people through the writer's craft.

Readers approach the reading of a novel or short story in different ways. They choose the approaches that suit them as individuals. For example, there are some people who are 'aural' readers, and who therefore love to hear a book read aloud. This preference is now very well catered for by the existence of 'talking books'. Many people listen to these on their MP3 players or computers. This is not perhaps surprising, as so many people learn to love stories through being read to as children. There are others who like to read a book through in one sitting, quite quickly, and then read it again more slowly. Others read a chapter at a time, and then come back to it the following day. Whatever your approach, rereading a text is always important, because you will notice more and more each time you return to it. Some use a pencil (if it is possible to make notes in the copy) or highlight a photocopy, so that they can mark the passages that they really enjoy or find interesting. Others may use different 'codes' for theme, character or language points. None of these approaches is necessarily better than another: it depends on what works for you. One good method is to use your pencil notes (or sticky notes) in the copy for particular quotations or passages, and to keep a notepad beside you for your own thoughts or summaries, including page numbers for particular references. Chapter summaries are particularly useful where the plot is complicated.

Your reading will need to focus on a number of features of the text. These include:

- Characters: check that you note any indication of:
  - name
  - age
  - appearance
  - links to other characters (for example, their relatives or loved ones).

Remember that the section on each novel has bullet-point summaries of the main characters.

Figure 2.1 *Different prose texts.*

- The sequence of events (with any indication of seasons, dates or times of the day, to make sure that you get things in the right order – look out for any flashbacks).
- Themes.
- Features of language, such as:
  - o vocabulary (check out the meaning of unfamiliar words using a dictionary)
  - o imagery
  - o tone
  - o dialogue
  - o irony, including dramatic irony
  - o humour
  - o dialect
  - o colloquial language
  - o symbolism.
- Narrative voice.

For the IGCSE English Literature and the Certificate examinations, you will not be allowed to take a copy of the text with you into the examination room, so you will need to know the text very well in order to draw on it in your examination answer. You will also need to remember a small number of quotations that you can call on as relevant for your answer.

For each prose text studied for Paper 1, there are sections on:

- background and context
- plot
- characters
- themes
- author's craft
- language
- activities
- some questions to consider.

Jane Austen: *Pride and Prejudice*

Background and context

Jane Austen was born in 1775 and died in 1817. It was a period with wars against Napoleon following the French Revolution, including both the Battle of Trafalgar in 1805 and the Battle of Waterloo in 1815. These were not the subject of Jane Austen's work, although officers often appear in her novels, including *Pride and Prejudice*, in which the arrival of the regiment causes a huge social stir. Jane Austen focuses on the social classes with which she was most familiar, the middle and upper classes, and on how people from these classes behave – their vanities and snobberies, love matches and family sagas.

Plot

The fact that the novel has a plot that centres on marriage is set out from its famous opening lines:

Figure 2.2 *Jane Austen.*

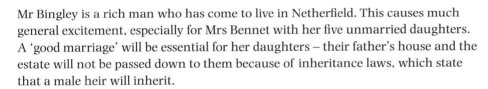

It is a truth universally acknowledged, that a single man in possession of a good fortune must be in want of a wife.

Mr Bingley is a rich man who has come to live in Netherfield. This causes much general excitement, especially for Mrs Bennet with her five unmarried daughters. A 'good marriage' will be essential for her daughters – their father's house and the estate will not be passed down to them because of inheritance laws, which state that a male heir will inherit.

Mrs Bennet is keen for her eldest daughter, Jane, to meet Mr Bingley, and Jane dances with him at a village ball. Bingley's friend, Mr Darcy, is seen by others to be very proud and arrogant. He meets Elizabeth, the next eldest daughter, but is not impressed with the lower social status of the Bennets and is rather rude about Elizabeth. Later, Elizabeth learns (mistakenly, as it turns out) that Mr Darcy has acted dishonourably to Mr Wickham, a handsome and pleasant young officer stationed at Meryton, and so she forms an equally low opinion of Darcy. However, Darcy gradually changes his mind about Elizabeth, valuing her intelligent conversation and her 'bright eyes', to the extent that, while they are at Rosings, he declares his love. To his surprise, he is rejected, partly because of his involvement in separating Jane and Bingley and partly because of Elizabeth's beliefs about his behaviour towards Wickham. Elizabeth has very different ideas about marriage from many of those around her. Her friend, Charlotte Lucas, marries the unpleasant Mr Collins (who proposed to her only because Elizabeth turned him down too) for practical and financial reasons.

Darcy realises that he must behave differently if he is to win Elizabeth, and writes to her explaining why he acted as he did with regard to Jane and Mr Wickham. He sets out the story of Mr Wickham in full, in particular how he had almost seduced Georgiana Darcy (his younger sister) in an attempt to take possession of her money. Elizabeth now begins to question whether she has misjudged Darcy. On a holiday with her aunt and uncle in Derbyshire, she meets Darcy at his splendid estate of Pemberley and finds his manner very altered. She later becomes even more grateful to him for rescuing the situation after Wickham and Lydia, her youngest sister, have eloped, by arranging, anonymously, for them to marry and for Wickham's debts to be paid. Elizabeth assumes she will never see Darcy again, but Darcy, in guilt, admits to Mr Bingley that he was wrong to intervene in Bingley's relationship with Jane and brings about Bingley's renewed hopes for Jane.

Mr Bingley returns to Netherfield Hall, with the intention of proposing to Jane, who delightedly accepts. Darcy returns with him. By this time, both Elizabeth and Darcy have overcome their prejudice against each other, and abandoned the pride which had stopped them expressing their true feelings. The novel, therefore, ends with the marriage of Elizabeth and Darcy and of Jane and Bingley, much to the joy of all, not least of Mrs Bennet: the opening words seem to have come true.

Characters

Mr Fitzwilliam Darcy

Mr Darcy is:

- romantically inclined towards Elizabeth Bennet
- proud, prejudiced, arrogant and at times even rude
- loyal
- stubborn
- handsome, intelligent, rich and exceptionally well connected
- a kind master
- often awkward
- a loving brother
- prepared to admit he has been wrong and to change
- the owner of Pemberley, reportedly one of the most beautiful estates in England.

Mr Bingley

Mr Bingley is:

- romantically inclined towards Jane Bennet
- good-natured and affable
- easily led
- eager to please
- Darcy's oldest friend
- the wealthy occupant of Netherfield Hall
- someone who always sees the best in people.

Elizabeth Bennet

Elizabeth is:

- the next eldest daughter of the Bennets
- romantically inclined towards Mr Darcy
- impulsive
- intelligent, spirited and witty
- her father's favourite daughter
- loving and loyal
- stubborn and at times proud and prejudiced
- idealistic about love and marriage
- independent in her views.

Jane Bennet

Jane is:

- the eldest daughter of the Bennets
- romantically inclined towards Mr Bingley
- calm and collected
- someone who wants the best for everyone and sees the best in everyone
- the most beautiful of the Bennet sisters
- incapable of nastiness or deception
- very close to Elizabeth
- someone who does not readily show her feelings.

Mr Bennet

Mr Bennet is:

- the father of five daughters
- sharp-witted but capable of being sarcastic
- closest to Elizabeth out of all his daughters
- intolerant of foolishness and childishness
- quiet and studious
- rather unhappily married to his wife
- fond of staying in his study as a retreat.

Mary Bennet

Mary is:

- the middle Bennet sister
- described as 'the only plain one in the family'
- said to be the possessor of 'neither genius nor taste'
- eager to show off her accomplishments
- sometimes seen as an embarrassment
- rather strait-laced.

Lydia Bennet

Lydia is:

- the youngest Bennet sister and Mrs Bennet's favourite
- a 'determined flirt'
- pretty but very silly and impulsive
- only 15 years old
- obsessed with officers, whose presence in Meryton have influenced her greatly.

Mrs Bennet

Mrs Bennet is:

- desperately keen for her five daughters to get married to someone rich; she wishes for greater financial stability for them
- fond of being the centre of attention
- melodramatic
- tactless and ill-mannered
- living on the edge of her nerves
- foolish.

Kitty Bennet

Kitty is:

- the next youngest of the Bennet sisters
- often caught in the middle of her family discussions
- influenced by Lydia
- similar to Lydia, though not her mother's favourite.

George Wickham

Mr Wickham is:

- son of the steward of Darcy's father
- one of the officers in the Meryton regiment
- easy-going and charming
- a gambler who has got into debt
- deceitful
- the lover of Lydia Bennet, whom he does eventually marry after a financial settlement.

Mr Collins

Mr Collins is:

- the Bennets' cousin
- a vicar near Rosings (Lady Catherine de Bourgh's estate)
- the legal inheritor of Longfield
- over-formal in his manner and obsequious
- a comical figure due to his social blunders
- keen to marry for the sake of being married
- thoughtless and lacking in Christian charity
- prepared to change the target of his marriage plans when he is turned down.

Caroline Bingley

Caroline is:

- the sister of Mr Bingley
- very snobbish, rude, prejudiced and ill-mannered
- romantically inclined towards Mr Darcy
- jealous of Elizabeth.

Lady Catherine de Bourgh

Lady Catherine is:

- a very wealthy lady
- the aunt of Mr Darcy
- the owner of the Rosings estate
- proud and obsessed with social standing
- haughty, controlling and domineering
- the patron of Mr Collins
- opposed to Darcy's interest in Elizabeth, believing him 'promised' to her sickly daughter.

Charlotte Lucas

Charlotte is:

- Elizabeth's best friend
- neither particularly pretty nor particularly rich
- unmarried at the age of 27 when the novel starts
- 'sensible', but unromantic about marriage
- the wife of Mr Collins after he has been turned down by Elizabeth.

Georgiana Darcy

Georgiana is:

- Darcy's younger sister
- extremely pretty
- very shy
- very musical
- naïvely falls for Wickham's charm and nearly elopes with him
- devoted to her brother.

The Gardiners

The Gardiners are:

- the aunt and uncle of the Bennet girls
- able to offer essential assistance after Lydia elopes
- willing to be seen as having given Wickham money to marry Lydia, to keep Darcy's help a secret
- closely involved in the developing relationship between Darcy and Elizabeth.

Themes

Courtship, proposals and marriage

Austen's interest in the subject of marriage is shown in her study of the relationship between Mr and Mrs Bennet and also in the treatment of Mr Collins and Charlotte Lucas. However, even more of the novel is focused on the processes that take place prior to marriage, and the way in which people set about trying to get married: how and why men propose to women, and how their proposals are responded to. This focus allows her to examine the place of marriage in society and the range of attitudes to marriage that the different characters possess. She contrasts true love matches and romantic attachments (see opposite) with practical, financial or businesslike propositions, such as that of Charlotte Lucas and

Mr Collins. Her attitudes are shown by the sceptical comment: 'Happiness in marriage is entirely a matter of chance'. Charlotte saw marriage as something that she needed to have any status and security and therefore she could not be choosy about her husband.

Love

Just as there are marriages without love, so there is also the scandal of love without marriage, in the case of Lydia and Wickham, although finally the situation is rescued by marriage. Lydia's running off and living with her lover was seen as a terrible disgrace for the family. This contrasts strongly with the two examples in the novel of loving marriages, that between Jane and Bingley, and the central focus of the novel, the eventual triumph of love leading to the marriage of Elizabeth and Darcy.

Pride and prejudice

The fact that Austen chose this title, after originally calling the novel 'First Impressions', shows how important she thought these two undesirable qualities were in the lives of her characters. Pride, closely associated with the arrogance of wealth and class in some cases, is clearly seen in several characters, but none more so than Darcy – although it could be said that Elizabeth's pride is severely wounded by his initial attitude to her. The word 'prejudice' is nowadays associated particularly with discrimination and bias against other people because of matters such as their ethnic background: so-called 'racial prejudice'. The word essentially means 'pre-judging' a person or event, so it is linked to the idea of 'first impressions', Austen's original title. Her idea is clearly that initial impressions can cloud people's judgement and make them unable to see a person's true qualities – and this certainly applies strongly to both central characters in the novel.

Society and social class

Austen wrote at a time when the divisions based on class were seen as vitally important and people largely stayed within their own class. She realised that when the class boundaries were broken things could prove difficult and be, for a novelist, full of interest, particularly if someone from the 'upper class' were to mix with someone from what we might call the 'middle' or even 'upper middle' classes.

The upper classes were so called because they were the richest members of society, and their wealth came from owning a great deal of land, which they had inherited through their families (the aristocracy), at a time before the main impact of the Industrial Revolution, which made many other people rich either through running businesses or through trading. Even the Bingleys were not thought of by some as 'true' upper class, because their fortune was derived from trade, which meant that some of the landed aristocracy could be quite snobbish (and prejudiced) towards them. Lady Catherine De Bourgh particularly represents this traditional sense of her own superiority: she looks down on the Bennets, who clearly do not match up to her social standards. Elizabeth refuses to be overawed by her attitudes, as she is the daughter of a gentleman, but Mr Collins' behaviour shows how the general expectation was that such grand ladies would be treated in a very deferential way by other classes. The novel has numerous examples of how society expected people to behave, and how easy it was to do the 'wrong thing'.

Author's craft

Setting

A feature of Austen's writing is her portrayal of interiors: scenes take place in ballrooms, drawing rooms or other rooms in houses grand or less grand, like that of the Bennets. In a novel with so many female characters, most in the same family, it is inevitable that much of the action and speaking takes place indoors, as the lives of women were mainly conducted indoors. However, the novel is not by any means confined to interiors, and there are notable scenes conducted out of doors. Elizabeth, in particular, is keen on getting out and about, and the incident with the muddy hem of her dress, when she walks to Netherfield to see her sister Jane, who is sick, is of interest not least for the reactions it causes. Elizabeth shows her independence and unwillingness to be trapped by social convention, but this shocks conservative upper-class attitudes. Another way the novel widens its scope is through Jane Austen's use of journeys, either in the nearby area, or the journeys of Elizabeth, which include the fateful one to Darcy's estate, Pemberley, or other characters to other parts of the country. These add interest and variety and prevent it from being a novel entirely trapped in the small local world of Longbourn and Meryton. The elopement of Lydia and Wickham may in part suggest a desire to escape from their small world, and there is also the journey taken to find them once they have eloped.

Figure 2.3 *A large country house, similar to Darcy's estate, Pemberley.*

Observation of people and society

Austen is admired particularly for the accurate and at times ruthless way she observes and portrays her characters and their behaviour. The novel includes many examples of how, either through narrative, her description of characters, or their dialogue, the tone of voice behind the words spoken can be heard. These qualities perhaps help to explain why, some two hundred years after they were written, her novels are still so popular when turned into films and television adaptations. These are often very successful because of the memorable nature of the characters, such as Mrs Bennet, whom Austen observes wickedly and with devastating effect.

Narrative voices

Austen is very much the **omniscient narrator** who controls the events and comments on them, especially indirectly. However, she also employs different ways of moving the action forward, especially through the use of letters at various points to show the characters' reactions and attitudes. She also uses **irony** in her comments and descriptions, right from the start of the novel (see section opposite on humour and irony).

Look at Activity 1 opposite for more on Austen's use of letters as a form of narrative.

Language

Tone of voice

We have seen how important tone of voice is in the words spoken by the characters. This is also true in the narrative of the text.

Humour and irony

The use of irony (which has been defined as 'the contrast between appearance and reality') is one of Austen's main ways of introducing humour, and it is used above all to laugh at the foolish or hypocritical ways of some of the characters she has created. Austen often uses her characters, notably Mr Bennet and Elizabeth, the daughter who shares her father's ironic sense of humour, as her own narrative voice. The reader realises that words cannot be taken at face value – indeed, they often carry the opposite meaning to that which they apparently bear. It is important to look out for examples of irony, especially when they mock characters' weaknesses, and observe how they contribute to an understanding of the novel. The fact that the very first sentence is written with heavy irony should alert the reader to what is to come.

Activity 1: Understanding the text

First, check that you know where the letters appear, what they say, what they tell us about the writers and what their effect is on the characters receiving them. Think about the differences in tone and style. Then choose one letter and write notes about its significance in relation to theme, plot and character. (You may wish to choose Darcy's letter to Elizabeth or the letter from Mr Collins to Mr Bennet before visiting him.) Pick out some key phrases and write a comment on their significance. The first example has been given for you.

Key phrase	Significance
Mr Collins' letter to Mr Bennet: 'I feel it my duty to promote and establish the blessing of peace in all families within the reach of my influence.'	This shows Mr Collins to speak in a very long-winded way, full of himself (self-righteous) and patronising.

Activity 2: Understanding the text

Go through the text and make a record of who goes where and why. Then focus on Elizabeth's journey to Pemberley and write about the way Austen sets up the meeting between Elizabeth and Darcy and its importance for their relationship.

Activity 3: Thinking about the characters

Which characters display 'pride' and how does this affect their actions and relationships with others? List examples of statements by characters who show pride and also what Jane Austen, as narrator, says about them.

Activity 4: Thinking about the characters

It has already been suggested that one of the ways Austen presents her characters is through dialogue. Choose any two characters and, focusing directly on what they say (and how you think they say it), show what aspects of their personality emerge from their words. If working with a partner, take two different characters and compare your findings, checking whether you agree with each other's conclusions.

Some questions to consider

1. Think about the way in which Mr Bennet reacts to his life in a house with so many women. How sympathetic do you think Jane Austen wishes us to be towards him?

2. Look closely at the relationship between Jane and Elizabeth during the course of the novel, and write about its importance in the novel.

3. Does Austen's character of Mr Collins have any redeeming features, or is he there purely to be a figure of fun?

4. Which qualities does Jane Austen seem to admire and which does she dislike in the society she portrays?

R K Narayan: *The English Teacher*

Background and context

R K Narayan was born in India in 1906 and died, aged 94, in 2001. He wrote most of his books in English and is thought of as one of India's finest novelists writing in the English language. His writing career lasted for more than 60 years and he received many honours and awards for his writing. He has said himself that much of *The English Teacher* is autobiographical (based on his own life), in particular the fact that he lost his own wife when he was quite young. In 1939 she died of typhoid, just as Susila does in the novel. Like Krishna, he brought up his daughter, doing so as a single parent, and tried to make spiritual contact with his wife after her death. The novel was published in 1945, the year of the dropping of the first atomic bombs on Japan by the Americans, bringing the Second World War to a rapid end. For years there had been a bitter struggle led by Gandhi for independence from Britain's rule, and at the end of the war Britain let it be known that it would support India's independence, although it took another two years until this was realised.

Plot

Krishna had worked as an English teacher (lecturing at the Albert Mission College) for ten years and had been living on his own at a hostel. At the start of the novel, he feels there is something missing in the routine of his life and he is encouraged by his father-in-law to bring his wife Susila and daughter Leela, who is just seven months old, to live with him. After this, his life becomes more enjoyable and interesting. Susila, however, contracts typhoid from a toilet while viewing a potential new home. This leads to her death, which is devastating for Krishna, who becomes lonely and depressed. All this changes when a stranger contacts him by letter, saying that Susila has been in touch from beyond the grave and wishes to speak to Krishna. This cheers him up greatly and the stranger, someone with psychic powers, leads him on a spiritual journey that brings about his own fulfilment. He becomes friends with a local headmaster, from a school for young children, and decides to work with him because he believes in his inspiring methods. After this, Krishna is for the first time able to communicate with Susila by himself, and this changes his life. This is the event that ends the novel, with Krishna now feeling a great sense of joy that he has become a much more spiritual person.

Figure 2.4 *Gandhi.*

Characters

Krishna

Krishna is:

- the central character in the novel
- based largely on the writer
- married to Susila and the father of a young daughter Leela
- at first, an unfulfilled and frustrated English teacher who lives by set routines
- delighted by the sense of purpose his life gains when Susila and Leela come to live with him
- elated by the news from a psychic who informs him that his wife wishes to contact him after her death
- inspired by the headmaster and his own daughter Leela
- finally able to speak to the spirit of Susila after her death and find fulfilment.

Susila

Susila is:

- the wife of Krishna
- economical and organised, yet spirited and independent
- a positive force in Krishna's life
- a tragically young victim of typhoid, from which she dies
- able, through the help of the psychic, to make spiritual contact with Krishna.

The headmaster

The headmaster:

- is an expert at teaching young children
- is admired and befriended by Krishna who respects his teaching skills
- works with Krishna after Susila's death and his contact with the old man
- is a 'hen-pecked' husband, keen to avoid his wife when he can.

Leela

Leela is:

- the young child of Krishna and Susila
- left motherless by her mother's death
- able to communicate with Susila after her death
- brought up alone by Krishna.

The psychic

The psychic:

- writes to Krishna to tell him that Susila wishes to contact him
- is the means by which Krishna and Susila are 'reunited'
- possessed of psychic powers
- a great and positive influence on Krishna's life after Susila's death, leading him to find a new inner strength and fulfilment.

Themes

The spiritual world

Krishna initially mocks his wife for being a spiritualist. However, as the novel progresses he becomes much more aware of his own (Indian) spiritual traditions, such as meditation, because he realises that he needs greater spirituality to contact Susila after her death. He is delighted with the effect that becoming more in tune with the spiritual dimension has had on him, especially when he is finally able to communicate with her. The presence of the astrologer and his predictions introduces another aspect especially because of the faith the headmaster shows in them, even when he does not in fact die, but is 'reborn'.

Love and marriage

This is an important theme in the novel. At the start of the novel, Krishna is happily married. Susila and their baby Leela still live with Susila's parents, but when they come to live with Krishna they bring him endless pleasure and delight. The strong love that exists is explored fully, together with the change that their arrival brings to his ordered life. Not even Susila's early and untimely death from typhoid can separate them, which brings Krishna a great sense of fulfilment after her death. He also finds great satisfaction from bringing up Leela, doing so as a single parent. Krishna's marriage is contrasted with the unsatisfactory marriage of the headmaster.

Childhood and adulthood

Children are seen in a positive light, compared with adults. This attitude is conveyed especially by the headmaster, who is strongly attracted by the innocence that he sees in the children at his school. The headmaster believes that adults should learn from children. Particularly because of the headmaster's difficult relationship with his wife, he is uneasy in the adult world and seems happier in the company of children. The negative view of being an adult is referred to as the 'curse of adulthood'. The other child who emphasises the difference between the child's world and that of the adult is Leela, who is seen largely through her father's feelings about bringing her up.

The predictable and the unpredictable

This is a major theme in the novel and it is closely linked to Krishna's emotional and spiritual 'journey' and development. The opening of the novel stresses his routine life, working in a college and operating to strict timetables. The arrival of Susila starts to change his attitudes, and the episode with the alarm clock is an important metaphor for unpredictability. First, it is unreliable, and the fact that it goes off at odd times causes Krishna to react angrily. Secondly, Susila's decision to get rid of it shows that she is encouraging him to abandon his former bachelor ways and to become more spontaneous. The fact that they have a long-lasting row about this shows that it is hard for Krishna, who has been very set in his ways, to change. Eventually, he starts to enjoy the unpredictability of Susila's impulsiveness.

Philosophical thinking: Academic and 'real' life

There are 'East versus West' elements in relation to the academic study of philosophy. Western philosophy is represented by the towering figure of the ancient Greek philosopher, Plato, the philosopher of reason and logic. It was written by another Western philosopher that all Western philosophy was 'a series of footnotes to Plato', which suggests how important his influence has been in Western thinking. However, Krishna comes to believe that this kind of abstract philosophical learning cannot help with the big problems of life, especially death. The 'academic' concerns (the word comes from the 'Academy', the school of philosophy founded by Plato) are increasingly seen as irrelevant, and Krishna even teaches his students to think more about real life than the academic.

Eastern and Western culture and education

There are many ways in which East and West are contrasted, but particularly in relation to education and other cultural matters. The opening of the book sees Krishna as operating very much on the Western European (specifically, the British) educational model. This is because the British Raj (the British rule of India) had imposed British ways of life on India, and assumed that the English language and its literature and history should be taught to the Indians. Although Krishna continues to appreciate the quality of English literature, especially that of Shakespeare, he finds the teaching methods he has to use to get his students to learn the English language very unappealing, and he dislikes the influence of the examination system and the rigid rules they have to follow (for instance, with regard to spelling). His dislike of the college and its teaching methods increases as he comes to know the headmaster and his teaching philosophy, which has much more creativity and allows greater space for children's own development.

He notes the British attitude of cultural superiority, especially over language. Then (as now) English people abroad rarely make an effort to learn the local languages, assuming that everyone should and will speak English. Another strong cultural contrast is shown between Eastern and Western medicine, both of which are used in vain when Susila falls ill with typhoid.

Figure 2.5 *Woman placing bindi on her forehead.*

Indian traditions

This is a particular example of the 'East v West' theme, because the Westernised Indians working under the Raj tended to belittle the Indian traditions. It is other characters who show the importance they still attach to these, as when Krishna's own mother adopts the traditional practice of placing the vermilion (orange-red) dye at the entrance to their house, decorating the threshold with mango leaves and the floor and doorway with 'white flour designs', in order to give a proper traditional welcome to her new daughter-in-law. Indian women also traditionally place a vermilion dot (bindi) on their foreheads.

Author's craft

Setting

The novel is set, as many of Narayan's works are, in a southern Indian town called Malgudi, which is his fictional creation. In this town, the homes of Krishna form an important contrast and represent the changes in his life. The dull hostel where he lives initially provides him with security and predictability, yet he has no life beyond the institution and his simply furnished room. Life in the rented house, the one he shares with Susila and Leela, is very different, partly because Susila places her individual stamp on it.

Irony

The main way in which Narayan uses **irony** is what is known as 'situational irony', rather than 'verbal irony' in the mouths of the characters, although both forms can be found in the novel. Some examples of situational irony in the novel would be when Susila protects herself with bindi although this fails to protect her against the typhoid that kills her. There is also irony in the way Krishna mocks Susila's spirituality, as later he comes to discover how important and valuable it is to himself as well. A further example occurs in the fact that the headmaster is seen as an excellent 'father figure' to his schoolchildren, but cannot be an effective father himself.

Foreshadowing

The technique of foreshadowing, used by many writers, gives the readers a taste of what is to come later on in the text. This is used by Narayan especially to foreshadow the spiritual encounters with Susila.

Contrast

Narayan uses contrasts throughout the novel. The main thematic contrasts are linked to Krishna's change of life and his journey of self-discovery. However, Narayan also shows a number of contrasts between his characters, especially those between Krishna and Susila. For example, he contrasts the way in which Krishna panics when he is at the station (Chapter 2) with the calm way Susila acts at that same moment. These contrasts are looked at in Activity 3 on page 68.

Language

Impersonal forms

Krishna's character suggests a lack of warmth and excitement, especially early in the novel, when he lives at the hostel. He does not really know his wife and daughter, who have been living with his father-in-law. Narayan uses a lack of personal words such as 'my', especially when Krishna refers to his daughter as 'the child' and his wife as 'that girl'. Narayan's choice of language suggests that they are not really a part of Krishna's life for which he feels responsible. Later, when he starts bringing up Leela, it is significant that he often calls her 'my child'.

Present tense

As in most novels, past tenses are usually used to describe events, as though the narrator is looking back on past events ('he woke up', 'they met in the market'). However, there is a technique sometimes used to give these events a greater sense of immediacy, which is to switch to describing events in the present tense, even though they have already happened. We sometimes do this when talking to friends, for example, about exciting things that have happened: 'I'm walking down the road, when this guy suddenly comes up to me and starts talking to me'. Narayan does this just after Susila's death, using the device of a diary that Krishna writes to keep Susila's presence alive. It is also used to show his feelings: 'I am blind, dumb, and dazed'. This enables us to identify what he is feeling at this most difficult point in his life. The other effect of this is that it is also a form of foreshadowing, because Krishna eventually comes to believe that Susila really is still with him as a spiritual presence.

Style

Narayan's own way of writing is linked to his views on the contrast between academic and real life (see page 65). Krishna comes to believe that the academic language that he has used in his teaching is too abstract and complicated to be real. The headmaster supports this view by saying 'Children have taught me to speak plainly'. So the simple, uncomplicated style Narayan uses is in tune with his views about the virtue of simplicity.

Spiritual language

Both Narayan's descriptions of Susila in Chapter 3 and his poem use spiritual language, which looks forward to the fact that Susila appears in spiritual form. Activity 1 below asks you to look closely at the way Narayan uses spiritual language, especially in relation to Susila.

Activity 1: Understanding the text

Look first at how Krishna describes Susila in his poem and elsewhere (for example, in his use of a **simile** in Chapter 3). Note down particular words and phrases that suggest that she inhabits a non-physical world. How does this contribute to our understanding of the novel? Look also at the changes that take place in Krishna's attitudes to the spiritual world as the novel progresses. Using the table below, note down examples of positive and negative comments and look at where these occur.

Positive	Negative

Activity 2: Understanding the text

Find references in the book to a Western writer, and comment, using the table below, on the effect of these. One example has been given for you.

Reference	Effect
'The divine creature!, I reflected.'	Narayan links this thought to the Wordsworth quotation 'She was a phantom of delight', to show how perfect and unworldly she was.

Activity 3: Thinking about the characters

Using the table below, write down points that help to build up a picture of the two characters Krishna and Susila and show the contrasts between them: you may use your own impressions, but should give examples of what they say or do, or what other characters say about them, including brief quotations. One example has been given for you.

Krishna	Susila
The alarm clock in the study: 'What have you done with my clock?' Krishna is a creature of habit and wants the clock even though it does not work properly.	The alarm clock in the study: 'How do you like your room? I have cleaned and tidied it up. What a lot of rubbish you gathered there.' Susila just sees the old alarm clock as part of the rubbish that makes the room messy.

Activity 4: Thinking about the characters

Think about how the use of dialogue in the novel helps to bring out the personality of the other characters (that is, everyone except Krishna and Susila, who you have been analysing above). Identify vivid examples of what the characters say and comment on what this tells us about the character of the speaker.

Some questions to consider

1. What do we learn about Narayan's views on education? Look closely at things that he criticises in the teaching of English at his college, and at the evidence of what he dislikes. Compare his views with other ideas in the novel – for example, the way in which children are to be educated in their early years.

2. Think about the way the subject of 'routine' is presented in the novel. List examples of routines that Krishna undertakes. Where in the novel do these occur, and why?

3. What is the significance of the headmaster in the novel? Consider the themes to which he contributes either through his character and personality or through his approach to teaching and to children.

4. The novel is often described as 'Krishna's journey'. This is a metaphor, of course. These days most contestants on reality shows seem to have gone on a 'journey'. What kind of journey does Krishna make, and what does he learn from it?

John Steinbeck: *Of Mice and Men*

Background and context

John Steinbeck was born in 1902 in the Salinas Valley, California, USA, and died in 1968. His birthplace is the setting for his short novel (novella) *Of Mice and Men*. The family he came from was quite well off, but he saw a great deal of the hardships of local people, partly because he himself worked on a ranch for some time. He wrote *Of Mice and Men* in 1936, a time when California was suffering from the effects of the Great Depression, when there was high unemployment and when many people lost everything they had. During this period, many would have been grateful to have a job, even if it was only as a migrant worker, much like Steinbeck's central characters George and Lennie. This would provide a pay packet as well as giving a place to live. It was, however, a time when the government, led by President Franklin D Roosevelt, was trying to create a new sense of hope through political reforms called 'The New Deal', to help the United States out of the Depression.

Figure 2.6 *Gates to a ranch.*

Plot

The two central characters of this novella are close friends; they have known each other for a long time. George Milton is dependable and intelligent, whereas Lennie Small is simple, mentally-impaired and extremely strong. They travel to a ranch near Salinas to work, after receiving an offer of a job. They share a dream that some day they will own a piece of land and be able to settle down. We learn that they have run away from where they were previously working because of accusations of an assault brought about because Lennie stroked and held onto a beautiful garment worn by a girl. Despite the hostility they encounter at the ranch from the son of the boss, Curley, they settle down well on the ranch. They are offered help and support by Slim, who gives one of his puppies to Lennie. The difficulties with Curley do not end here. Later in the story, Curley attacks Lennie who is making fun of him. Lennie does not fight until he receives a signal from George, after which he crushes Curley's hand.

Problems continue when Lennie accidentally kills the puppy. This same lack of awareness of how strong he is leads to even more trouble, when he encounters the flirtatious and lonely wife of Curley in a barn. Things go badly wrong after she allows him to stroke her hair, mostly because of his love of stroking soft objects. When she screams, Lennie panics, and, again without meaning to, kills her by breaking her neck. When George and Candy find the body, they realise that Lennie must have killed her. Soon after this, Curley and his ranch hands come out to 'lynch' him. George realises there is no way out this time for Lennie. George discovers Lennie in the brush by the green pool and tries to calm him down. He talks to him about their dream of owning their own ranch, rabbits and the land, and then, while Lennie is distracted, kills him with a shot from Carlson's gun in the back of his head, just as Candy's dog had been shot. George does this to save Lennie from the lynch mob.

Characters

George

George is:

- sharp-featured, intelligent and loyal
- Lennie's friend and protector
- long-suffering but at times becomes frustrated, impatient and angry
- self-sacrificing and dependable
- the one who feels in the end that he has to kill Lennie to prevent him from suffering further
- a man with a dream of owning his own farm and land, together with Lennie.

Candy

Candy is:

- elderly and physically disabled, with a stumpy wrist
- a swamper (cleaner) on the ranch
- friendly and likes to gossip
- rather a lonely and insecure figure
- attached to his old dog, and does not want him to be put down
- easily intimidated
- hoping to be part of George's and Lennie's dream.

Crooks

Crooks is:

- a black, old and physically disabled man, with a crooked back
- living alone in the harness room because of the colour of his skin
- often blamed by others, because of racial prejudice
- very respectful of Slim
- a man with a reasonable amount of possessions with him, unlike most of the men
- a reader, who has old books that are well used
- 'proud and aloof' – he keeps himself apart from the others
- someone who contemplates, for a short period of time, being part of the dream of George, Lennie and Candy
- cynical about other people's dreams of owning land
- lonely and frustrated.

Lennie

Lennie is:

- the constant companion of George
- large, heavy and slow-moving, with clumsy movements
- simple-minded, slow-witted and childlike, because of his mental impairment
- obsessed by soft, furry creatures, which he wishes to stroke
- a man of great strength, who lacks self-control and the ability to premeditate his actions
- a kind, gentle man, who copies and looks up devotedly to his friend George
- helpless and dependent on George
- someone with a dream of tending the rabbits on the farm he hopes to share with George.

Curley's wife

Curley's wife is:

- beautiful, young and heavily made-up
- the only key female character in the story
- never named, and is referred to only as Curley's wife, being treated very much as a possession
- unhappily married to Curley
- desperate to fulfil her dream of becoming a movie star
- someone who seeks attention and is quite flirtatious
- misunderstood by the men on the ranch, with the exception of Slim
- regarded as being without strong morals, a 'tart'
- impressed by Lennie's strength; this proves in Section 5 to be a fatal mistake.

Carlson

Carlson is:

- a big, strong ranch hand
- pushy and insensitive to the needs of others
- the one who kills Candy's old dog after much persuasion
- the owner of the gun that is used to kill Candy's dog and Lennie.

Curley

Curley is:

- small, well-built and with a head of curly hair
- the boss' son, who has a position of power on the ranch
- an aggressive bully with a temper that he cannot control
- deeply unpopular
- unfriendly to George and Lennie when they arrive
- described as 'calculating' and 'pugnacious'
- newly married; he is jealous and insecure about his wife.

Slim

Slim is:

- a team-leader, liked and respected by all the other men on the ranch
- a tall, distinguished man who wears a Stetson hat
- described as the 'prince of the ranch', a natural leader
- exceptionally skilled at working with the mules
- quiet, modest and thoughtful; people always stop to listen when he starts to speak
- seen as wise, knowledgeable and perceptive
- pleasant and welcoming in his manner.

Themes

Dreams

This is the central theme of the novel, but the dreams rarely, if ever, come true. There is a clue to the book's pessimism in the title, for those who recognise it from the poem by Robert Burns 'To a Mouse', which has the lines: 'The best laid schemes o' mice an' men / Gang aft agley'. This is often translated as 'people's plans – and dreams – often do not work out the way they intend'. The dream of land and a small farm that George and Lennie share is first mentioned near the start of the novel, and is discussed again at a later stage. Finally it recurs, with tragic consequences, just before the mercy-killing of Lennie by George. This dream is a powerful way of keeping them going through their hard lives. Particularly for Lennie, the idea of being able to settle down and keep rabbits (he is obsessively fond of soft, furry creatures) gives him something positive to look forward to. In Section 3, the dream appears to show the beginnings of becoming a reality.

Another character who has dreams is Curley's wife. The occasion when she tells Lennie what she would really like is the first time in the novel that we learn what she thinks and this is shared with Lennie just before she dies. We discover that she would like to escape from her unhappy marriage and be a famous actress and film star in Hollywood, living a life of luxury. This shows that, when she dresses up in what she hopes is a really attractive way, this is linked to how she thinks she must look in order to pursue a dream that she has had since before she married. In a letter to the actress Claire Luce (who was acting the part of Curley's wife on Broadway), Steinbeck indicated that Curley's wife should be perceived sympathetically.

The dreams of the characters in *Of Mice and Men* are also related to the idea of the 'American Dream'. In a book called *The Epic of America* (1931), James Truslow Adams wrote about the idea of a time in the future when all people would be valued and have a fulfilling life. This idea emerged at the time of the Great Depression, and offered people hope of escape from the harsh realities of poverty and even starvation, which the characters in *Of Mice and Men* were struggling to avoid. Many American readers of this story in the 1930s would have been influenced strongly by this dream, but would have been brought up short by the pessimism of Crooks on

Figure 2.8 *'Tell me... about the rabbits.'*

the subject when he said: 'Just like heaven. Ever'body wants a little piece of lan'... Nobody never gets to heaven, and nobody gets no land.'

Loneliness

Most of the characters in the novel are migrant workers, who would feel their isolation and loneliness strongly as they moved from ranch to ranch and found work wherever they could. They therefore had few ties, roots or friends. They saw themselves as undervalued members of the community, with little security and limited sense of identity. When they moved on, they were not really missed.

The lives of lonely characters who lack companionship are shown clearly in the cases of Candy, Crooks and Curley's wife. Candy has company of a kind while his dog is alive, and strongly feels the lack of this after the dog is put down. Crooks makes specific comments on this theme: 'A guy goes nuts if he ain't got nobody. Don't make no difference who the guy is, long's he's with you.' As for Curley's wife, her loneliness comes from the lack of warmth from Curley in her marriage: this emphasises her struggle to overcome loneliness – which the men interpret in very negative ways – and makes the situation worse because they all avoid her, partly from fear of Curley's jealousy. It is worth noting that the name of the town 'Soledad' is Spanish for 'solitude'.

Friendship

In this novel, the theme of such a strong friendship as that which exists between Lennie and George is seen by other characters as striking and unusual. It is explored through the way they relate to each other – they have a mutual dependence. Later, the idea of two men travelling together became a frequent subject of films especially from the 1960s (*Easy Rider* is perhaps the best-known example, and a later female counterpart *Thelma and Louise*). Although in a sense it is obviously Lennie who depends on George, because of his mental limitations, we can see how strongly George's life depends on having Lennie, not least for physical security. So, when George kills Lennie, we feel that George's life is going to be very difficult without him.

In the case of other characters, even where there are no close friendships, there is often an attempt to strike up relationships and have people in whom they can confide, because friendship is highly desirable as a way of overcoming their loneliness. However, the circumstances in which the characters live make it unlikely that many successful relationships will be formed.

Author's craft

Because the text is a novella, the narrative is far less developed than that of many longer works, and there is much dialogue. This emphasises the speed with which events happen, mostly with little time spent on description, although each section opens with details of the setting, rather like a film or play set. (It was also written as a play.) This simplicity of plot and narrative has the following effects:

- It reflects the fact that the novel deals with people who are largely themselves uncomplicated ordinary people.

- The sections of the book are like the Acts of a play, and, like most plays, each section is set in one place, with the following structure:

Sections 1 and 6	The Salinas riverbank and pool
Sections 2 and 3	The bunk house at the ranch
Section 4	The harness room
Section 5	The barn

Note especially that by having the first and last sections set in the same area, the action is cyclical, with the two men together being the only ones on the 'stage'. This helps bind the overall narrative together.

For a closer examination of the settings, look at Activity 1 below.

Language

Use of colloquial language

The characters in this novel speak **colloquially** – that is, they speak how people at that time and in that place would have spoken. Steinbeck clearly understood the local speech patterns, mostly because of his experience of working on a ranch in the same district as the setting of the book. The use of this natural speech makes the words seem 'real' and authentic. They speak simply, naturally and informally. This means the readers can 'hear' the characters very easily – again, as they would if they were watching a play or film. Think further about the use of colloquial language by carrying out Activity 2 on page 74.

Short sentences in the narrative

Just as the speakers often use short sentences, so does the description by the narrator. Look at the following example:

> The silence fell on the room again. A minute passed, and then another minute. Candy lay still, staring at the ceiling.

The effect here is to make the time pass very quickly. This device is used frequently, and you may be able to observe and write down other examples and think about their effect.

Activity 1: Understanding the text

Using the table on page 74, make notes about the settings of each of the six sections, and comment on how Steinbeck's choices of where the events take place contribute to the effect of the novel. Look closely at the 'stage directions', and at things that happen in each scene that add to your understanding. Look at some examples, such as:

- the heron's attack on the water snake in the final scene: 'A silent head and beak lanced down and plucked it out by the head...'

- the objects Steinbeck chooses to include in talking about the places on the ranch: look for instance at the 'apple box' over each bunk.

One example has been completed for you. Add your own comment and find other examples to fill in the table.

Location and time	Example	Comment
1. The Salinas riverbank (Thursday evening)	'Rabbits come out of the brush to sit on the sand in the evening...'	
2. The bunk house (Friday morning, 10 a.m.)		
3. The bunk house (Friday evening, dusk)		
4. The harness room (Saturday night)		
5. The barn (Sunday afternoon)		
6. The Salinas riverbank (late Sunday afternoon)		

Activity 2: Understanding the text

Look closely at the way the characters speak, and notice the examples of colloquial speech. Make a list of what the characters say and write comments on the effect of the language they use. Look for such features as:

- informal, non-standard grammar
- use of 'slang' expressions
- use of unusual spelling to help the reader imagine the right sound
- simple, brief statements and questions, which reflect how people speak
- what these words and phrases say about the characters speaking them.

Activity 3: Thinking about the characters

Use the following as a quick self-test on your knowledge of the characters, by linking up the correct name to the right description. When you have put the right names and characters together, add comments that will help your knowledge of the characters, such as additional physical features, information we learn about them and their lives, and comments on their personalities

George	A black man who works in the stables and lives by himself in the adjoining harness room.
Lennie	A lonely character who has dreams of acting on the stage.
Candy	The one-handed old man whose job is to clean the bunk house.
Curley	A small man who protects and befriends Lennie.
Slim	The very large, strong man who depends on George.
Carlson	The ranch hand who shows the article in the magazine to Slim.
Whit	A man who is admired by everyone because he is wise and skilful at his work.
Crooks	An aggressive but small man, who is feared by some.
Curley's wife	The ranch worker who shoots the old dog belonging to Candy.

Activity 4: Thinking about the characters

Choose two of the characters about whom you have written notes above in Activity 3. Imagine that you have to explain about these characters to someone who does not know the text at all. What would you say to help this person to fully understand how the character looks and acts, and to appreciate his or her importance in the text?

Some questions to consider

1. It has sometimes been suggested that because there is only one key female character, together with some references to the women from the brothel, Steinbeck seems rather anti-women in this novel. Do you feel this is a fair criticism? Make notes about Curley's wife's character – her words and actions – and the way other characters speak about her or treat her. Make sure that you base your response on a close examination of the evidence.

2. Think about the relationship between George and Lennie: how do they depend on each other?

3. Do you understand why George feels he has to kill Lennie? What else could he have done?

4. The novel can be seen as dark and depressing. Why might readers think this? Why do some characters have dreams? Do you think the novel has a message?

5. What impressions do you have about life on the ranch and the community living there?

Figure 2.9 *The colour bar.*

Mildred Taylor: *Roll of Thunder, Hear My Cry*

Background and context

Mildred Taylor was born in 1943, in Jackson, Mississippi, in the Southern states of the United States, but moved north to Toledo, Ohio, with her family. Her father's storytelling gave her the idea that she would like to be a writer. As an adult, she also taught in schools and university. She remembered vividly the journeys that she took with her family back to the South, and the clear discrimination of the road signs put up to show where black people were not allowed to go. Under the so-called 'Jim Crow' laws, there was strict separation (segregation) over housing, schooling and transport. This was meant to create separate but equal communities, but in fact this only confirmed the idea of white superiority, with black people disadvantaged in many ways.

Roll of Thunder, Hear My Cry was published in 1976 and was received very well by readers and critics, winning a prestigious prize the next year. By this time, the campaigns of the civil rights movement had brought changes to the law to prevent racial discrimination, especially the Civil Rights Act of 1964, although political struggles continued for African Americans, through the 'Black Power' movement in the 1970s. The novel looks back to a period before such changes had brought more equality to all citizens, being set in 1933 in Mississippi at the time of the Great Depression, when many people were very poor. This was almost the same time as the setting of *Of Mice and Men*, another American novel in the IGCSE English Literature and Certificate in English Literature specifications, which is interesting to compare with *Roll of Thunder, Hear My Cry*. Both books show how hard the lives of many people working in the country were, though *Of Mice and Men* deals mainly with white Americans and *Roll of Thunder, Hear My Cry* looks at black Americans. The violence which forms an important element in the novel was linked closely to the groups of 'night men' and their attacks on black people. These were from a powerful, racially motivated group called the Ku Klux Klan, which in the 1920s claimed as many as three million members, and was still powerful in states such as Mississippi in the 1930s. The author stated that she 'wanted to show a family united in love and self-respect, and parents, strong and sensitive, attempting to guide their children successfully, without harming their spirits, through the hazardous maze of living in a discriminatory society'.

Plot

The novel is narrated by Cassie Logan, the nine-year-old daughter of the Logan family, members of the black community who were not sharecroppers but owned their own land. Sharecroppers did not own their land, but could work on it provided they gave a share of the crops they harvested to the owner. The novel starts by looking at the lives of the Logan family. This family experiences many incidents of racial discrimination from the white community. Many of the problems are associated with the school bus, which has white children on it; this is deliberately driven close to them in order to cover them with mud. This causes the Logan children to take revenge by digging out a ditch which fills with water and causes the bus to break down. Cassie Logan reports a visit that she makes to Strawberry, a local town. She is confused by the way she is treated, as the white people in the store are served before her. Cassie thinks that the incidents with the bus have caused some of the white community to take violent action. The Wallace boys, whose family own the store, set fire to some members of the Berry family (a local black family), one of whom is badly burned and cannot speak as a result. There is also a fight between Stacey, the Logans' eldest son, and his best friend T.J., at the Wallace store. After this, Mama Logan encourages people not to allow their children to visit the store and not to buy things there (this is known as a boycott of the store). Because there are no real alternatives for the black people, the Logans buy goods in Vicksburg to sell to them.

At Christmas Uncle Hammer and Papa return home for a family gathering, with Uncle Hammer in his new car. Harlan Granger tries unsuccessfully to convince the Logans to stop the boycott of the Wallace store. Things get worse when Mama Logan, a teacher, loses her job because of her beliefs and principles. The families in the community start to drift back to shopping at the Wallace store. During a violent attack, Papa's leg is broken on his way to Vicksburg. The attack is ended by the intervention of the powerful L.T., who offers protection for the Logans' farm.

A further problem for the Logans is that they have to repay a bank loan they had taken out, which forces Uncle Hammer to sell his precious car to help raise the money. Since the fight with Stacey, T.J. has started behaving very badly and is associating with two white teenagers, Melvin and R.W. Simms. He gets into real trouble, however, when they break into a store in Strawberry, stealing a pistol. The Simms brothers frame T.J. after their violent attack on the storekeeper, Mr Barnett. This leads to a crowd coming out for a lynching (where people are hanged illegally, without any kind of trial), which Papa and L.T. try to stop. Suddenly, the cotton field catches alight and starts to burn, which means that everyone, the white lynch mob and the black farm workers, have to band together to stop the fire. Finally, it is learned that Papa had started the fire, because he thought that this would force the mob to stop the lynching. T.J. is imprisoned and the novel ends with Cassie crying 'For T.J. and the land'.

Characters

The book has a large cast of characters, too many to describe here, so those selected are the Logan family and others who play a particularly significant role in the story. See Activity 3 on page 82 for suggestions about dealing with the full cast of characters.

Cassie Logan

Cassie is:

- the narrator and main character
- nine years old and the second eldest of the Logan children
- sister to three brothers, Stacey, Christopher-John and Little Man (Clayton)
- a girl with a strong temper who likes to speak her mind
- intelligent, confident and a tomboy
- at first naïve about the subject of racism, but learns a great deal from what she sees and experiences.

Stacey Logan

Stacey is:

- a 12-year-old boy
- the eldest of the Logan children and their leader, able to boss them around
- shown as being half-way between child and man
- T.J.'s best friend
- brave in trying to help when T.J. gets into trouble.

Christopher-John Logan

Christopher-John is:

- seven years old and the second youngest of the Logan children
- always cheerful
- a rather timid child who tends to follow on behind the others.

Papa (David) Logan

Papa is:

- the father of the four children, of whom he is very protective
- someone who values his independence
- prepared to work on the railroad in Louisiana so that he can keep the Logan land
- a tall, handsome man
- prepared to risk his life over the Wallace boycott.

Big Ma (Caroline Logan)

Big Ma is:

- Papa's mother
- 60 years old but works 'like a woman of twenty in the fields'
- the one who runs the Logan farm
- someone with a strong sense of history, who tells Cassie stories about the past
- very religious
- skilled in the use of medicines.

T.J. Avery

T.J. is:

- at first a close friend of Stacey Logan, with whom he has a fight that has a big impact on events
- very thin and weak in appearance
- from a poor family of sharecroppers on the Granger land
- a show-off; hard-working and intelligent; impulsive
- a cheat in exams
- nearly lynched after his involvement with Melvin and R.W. in a robbery.

Little Man (Clayton Chester Logan)

Little Man is

- six years old and the youngest of the Logan children
- in the first grade at school
- a bright child, who learned to read at the age of four, before he went to school
- a boy who refuses to accept the damaged copies thrown out by the white school
- proud – likes to keep himself tidy.

Uncle Hammer

Uncle Hammer is:

- Papa's brother
- from Chicago
- rather short-tempered and impulsive – likes to show off
- the owner, until he has to sell it, of a shiny new car, a Packard.

Mama (Mary) Logan

Mama is:

- the mother of the four children and wife of Papa
- 33 years old, hard-working and intelligent
- a schoolteacher who loses her job because of her principles about teaching the truth
- sacked because she pasted over the inside cover of the textbooks.

Jeremy Simms

Jeremy is:

- a white boy who likes to go around with and befriend the Logan children
- often in trouble and beaten by his father for this
- the brother of Lillian Jean, who is rude to Cassie and pushes her off the sidewalk
- also brother of two older boys, the trouble-making Melvin and R.W., who pretend to be T.J.'s friends but frame him after the robbery and assault on Mr Barnett at the store in Strawberry
- not racist, unlike others in his family.

Mr Jamison

Mr Jamison is:

- a local white lawyer
- on the side of the black community
- helps the Logans as well as other black people when they are in trouble.

The Wallace family

The Wallace family:

- run the general store, which plays an important part in the community
- are a family noted for violence and cruelty, especially towards the black community.

Themes

Racism

This provides the context and focus of the whole novel, as it is the principal cause of all of the problems faced by the Logans and others in the black community. The novel looks at how there is discrimination against black people in the way in which society is organised legally and politically, but also shows how individuals could be abused, mistreated, and even killed in mob attacks. The novel explores how the children growing up in such a community experienced horrific events caused by racial prejudice. Perhaps there is a hopeful sign in that we can work out that when these children became adults, like Taylor herself, they would see changes for the better in the Southern states and greater equality.

Education

This is a prominent theme partly because Mama is a teacher, one of the few professions really open to most black people at the time, as black children needed educating just as much as white ones. Education was one of the ways in which black children were discriminated against, and was a focus of many of the civil rights movement's struggles for equality. In addition, it is possible to see the lives of the Logan children as representing a more informal kind of learning – they may have learned from books (in very poor condition) at school, but the harsh lessons of life were being learned in the streets and on the land.

Family

The Logans share a belief that family is the most important thing in life, which is something that comes through very strongly in Cassie's narration. The Logan family show the ties between the generations, too, as Big Ma hands down family tradition and values to the rest of the family. There is a contrast with those to whom family matter much less, such as T.J.: the loss of close family relationships contributes to his troubles.

Owning land

The importance of owning their own land is something that the older Logans are constantly emphasising, in the words 'We won't lose the land'. This is what they feel it means to be free and independent. They are no longer slaves, who never owned the land they worked on or sharecroppers who, in terms of land ownership, are not that much better than slaves. This gives the Logans a strong place in the community. The fear of losing this independence is important through the novel, but somehow they manage to keep the land. Uncle Hammer is even prepared to sell his Packard to help pay off the bank loan and secure their ownership of the land.

Time

There is a strong sense of the cycle of time as the four seasons pass. The novel covers a year, starting with one cotton harvest and ending just before the next. The difference between the seasons is underlined by the changes in the weather: each season has its own weather, such as the rainy season of winter. The changing seasons can stand for hope as, however bad it is in winter, we know that it will pass.

Author's craft

Setting

The place and time are chosen to enable Taylor to present her themes. Her own experience had underlined the harsh realities of life for black people in the Southern states during the period of the Great Depression, and she had a strong awareness of the divisions between North and South. Because of discrimination and segregation, there are strong contrasts between the lives of the black and white communities. Contrasts are similarly made between the land-owning Logans and the sharecroppers. Taylor also contrasts the settings of town and country, as when Cassie goes to town and encounters racial abuse, she is told to go back home. The cotton fields of the South were a powerful symbol of the oppression of black people, as millions of slaves had worked on these plantations, and their continuing importance is shown in the novel, not least when there is a fire in the fields. Both the white and black communities knew how much their lives depended on the cotton harvest, so this brought them together to save the cotton.

Narrative voice

The use of a young girl as narrator and central character is something this book shares with another powerful novel about racial prejudice in the South, Harper Lee's *To Kill a Mockingbird*. In both books, we see events through the inexperienced eye of a girl who is coming to terms with the bitter realities of life and who learns and develops through what she undergoes. Through this device, we are able to experience the events vividly, especially as we come face to face with Cassie's own thoughts and emotions. However, **first person narratives** do suffer from the fact that it is harder to deal with events that Cassie has not been present at or seen. Activity 1 on page 82 discusses how Taylor dealt with this potential difficulty.

Use of flashback

The **flashback** technique, which the writer uses to take the story back to earlier times, is often used to give a sense of history and explain why things are as they are today. It is similarly used in the play *Our Town*, discussed earlier in this book, to remind readers of important times in the USA's history, the American Civil War and the ending of slavery. Here, this helps Cassie to understand something of why there is such prejudice, which was shown particularly by the night men from the Ku Klux Klan.

Pathetic fallacy

The term **pathetic fallacy** refers to something that is found in the texts of many writers; it occurs when writers turn inanimate forces, particularly the weather, into beings with powerful feelings. In this way, the weather can take on the character of the people who are experiencing it. In this novel, pathetic fallacy occurs particularly with the descriptions of the rain, mud and dust. These stand for the way in which the black community is beaten down and almost ground into the dust. The rain is like an enemy preventing the black children from getting a proper education. The title includes a reference to a thunderstorm, and the whole novel feels like an approaching storm. Finally, the rain, which has been such a negative force, helps to calm things down as it breaks the tension in the air and serves as a sign that the worst may be over.

Language

Colloquial language

As in *Of Mice and Men* and *To Kill a Mockingbird*, the other 1930s American novels in this book, the **colloquial** language of the characters helps to give a strong sense of the time and place, although here it is particularly the speech patterns and rhythms (sometimes those of song) from the black community that we hear. These are very often in dialect: a simple example is from Chapter 4, where Mr Turner speaks: 'I sho' sorry, Miz Logan... Y'all aint gotta cowtail.' If you look at his whole speech, there are other examples, too, and you will have found many others throughout the novel. Look at Activity 2 on page 82, where you will focus closely on the differences between standard and non-standard forms, and also consider their effect. There is a variety of voices, and the language of children is a particular feature, with much of the action seen through a child's eyes.

Figure 2.10 *The whole novel feels like an approaching storm.*

American language

In places, the language is quite unfamiliar to a 21st-century reader. This can simply be because of American expressions for which British English usually has a different word – 'attorney' for 'lawyer', for example. There are also 'slang' terms such as 'carpetbagger', used by Southerners to refer to people from the North who came South after the Civil War to make money. Some words have simply fallen out of common use, such as 'chignon' for the way the hair was rolled at the back of the neck. It is important to note down words that are not familiar, together with their meaning, as this can aid your understanding.

Imagery

Imagery occurs particularly in the descriptive passages of Cassie's narrative. We have to think of her as a nine-year-old with an unusually vivid imagination and turn of phrase, as when she describes the school bus as: 'spewing clouds of red dust like a huge yellow dragon breathing fire'. This example shows how colourful (in this case, literally so) her language can be, and the images, such as this simile, create strong pictures, almost like cartoons. Another form of imagery Taylor uses, which often links up with the use of pathetic fallacy (see above, pages 80–81) is **personification**: 'the December sun was creeping warily upward' (start of Chapter 5).

Dialogue

Dialogue is important throughout this novel; this tends to be the case in a first person narrative, because otherwise the narrator's voice could easily dominate. As the author is not able to make comments about the characters in the way an omniscient third person narrator would (as happens frequently in another novel in this section, *Pride and Prejudice* by Jane Austen), you often learn a great deal about them by 'hearing' them speak, which helps with this characterisation.

Activity 1: Understanding the text

Think about the times when, for one reason or another, something happens where Cassie was not one of those taking part in the event (this can include events before she was born, as well as ones taking place somewhere else). How does the writer help us (and Cassie) to find out what happened? Use the table below to list examples and comment on how effective the narrative technique seems to you. One example has been given for you.

Reference	Effect
Cassie asks her father to reminisce and explain to her why he had gone to work on the railroad.	The reader learns about key events in the family history at the same time as Cassie, which underlines the importance to the family of staying on the land to pay their tax and mortgage.

Activity 2: Understanding the text

Pick out one example where a character speaks in a colloquial, non-standard way. Rewrite the words as though they were written in **standard English** (for example, 'sho', in the example given on page 81 would be written 'sure' and 'ain't' would become 'do not have to'.) Read your version as though the original speaker was saying the words. What is the effect on the reader? What does this show us about the writer's purpose?

Activity 3: Thinking about the characters

The novel has a very large cast of characters, and the section on pages 77–79 focuses on those with a significant part to play. However, it is a good idea to check that you have the full cast in your head, so make notes of those who are *not* mentioned, together with a brief comment on anything you feel you need to remember about these characters and what they show about life in the community.

Activity 4: Thinking about the characters

Think about the lives of the children in the novel. The author uses their daily lives and attitudes to bring out some of the contrasts explored. Use the table below to list points that show the differences in their lives. One example has been given for you.

White children	Black children
White children go to school by bus.	Black children walk to school.

Some questions to consider

1. Education has been discussed as an important theme in the novel. Why does it seem so important to the Logan family? Make notes about what the different characters, especially the Logans, say about education. How does this help your understanding?

2. Think about the characters in the novel who are violent and those who are non-violent, perhaps placing them in a table with two columns and including notes about what the violent characters actually did. What do you learn from this way of looking at the characters about the place of violence in the novel?

3. One white man who helps the black community is Mr Jamison. Do you find him a realistic character? Pick out examples of his words and actions that support your view about him.

4. Some people have suggested that T.J. is rather like a modern teenager with his attitudes and problems. Discuss this idea: which aspects of his behaviour support your view?

Harper Lee: *To Kill a Mockingbird*

Background and context

Harper Lee was born in 1926, in Monroeville, Alabama – in the 'Deep South' of the United States. The fictional Maycomb, in which the novel is set, is based closely on Monroeville. Although the book is not an autobiography, Lee does draw on her childhood experiences. The events of the novel take place between 1933 and 1935, so the age of the child narrator, the tomboy Scout, corresponds to that of the author. Also, Lee's father was a lawyer, like Scout's father, Atticus. He was also the editor and owner of a newspaper, and this may have influenced Lee's portrayal of the character Mr Underwood. At the heart of the novel is an exposure of the racism that was widespread in the South, and which makes it impossible for the character Tom Robinson to have a fair trial. The novel is set during the Great Depression, a time of economic hardship when poor white families like the Ewells, and the farmers who want to lynch Tom, were having an especially difficult time, contributing to their racism. It was published in 1960, when racism was being strongly challenged by activists like Martin Luther King.

Figure 2.11 *Mockingbird: a symbol of innocence.*

Plot

Scout Finch (age six), and her brother Jem (age ten) live with their father Atticus, a lawyer. Their mother is dead, so they are cared for by the black housekeeper Calpurnia. The children become friends with Dill, an imaginative boy who visits Maycomb to stay with his aunt. All three are fascinated by stories of Boo Radley, a mysterious local loner who has not been seen for years. They fantasise fearfully about him, and play at trying to make him come out of his house. Then they begin to find what they later discover to be presents hidden in a hollow tree outside the Radley home. They try to spy on Boo by sneaking up to the back of the house at night – and narrowly avoid being shot. Shortly after this escapade, the house of the children's friend Miss Maudie burns down. It gradually dawns on Jem that Boo is no monster, and that it was he who he left the presents in the tree, for them.

Atticus is appointed to defend Tom Robinson, a black man accused of raping Mayella Ewell, a young white woman from a poor family. Atticus is determined to do his best, though he knows that the all-white jury will never take Tom's word against that of a white woman. The children have to endure racist taunts from fellow school pupils, and even from a neighbour, Mrs Dubose, but they have new cause to admire their father when he kills a rabid dog with a single shot. On the other hand they have to put up with Aunt Alexandra, who arrives to supervise them until the trial is over. Tension mounts when Atticus, on guard outside the jailhouse, is threatened by a mob intent on lynching Tom Robinson. The mob is shamed into leaving when the children appear and Scout innocently attempts polite conversation with Mr Cunningham, one of the ringleaders.

Against Atticus' wishes, Scout, Jem and Dill watch the trial; they do so from the balcony reserved for black people. Atticus proves that the partially disabled Robinson could not have struck the blows to Mayella's face. There is strong evidence that she and her father, Bob Ewell, are lying, and that she had been making sexual advances to Robinson. Despite this, he is found guilty. The children, especially Jem and Dill, are sickened by the injustice. Worse is to come: Robinson is shot dead while attempting to escape, leaving his wife and children to fend for themselves.

Despite the trial's outcome, Bob Ewell still feels that Atticus's strong defence has humiliated him, and he is therefore bent on revenge. He insults Atticus in public and intimidates Robinson's widow. In a final act of desperate vengeance, he lies in wait for Jem and Scout as they return home in the dark after a Hallowe'en pageant at their school. Jem's arm is broken, and only Scout's wire-reinforced 'ham' costume saves her life. However, their real saviour is Boo Radley, who intervenes and carries Jem home.

Sheriff Tate discovers that Bob Ewell has died in the struggle. Atticus assumes that Jem is responsible and must face trial. Tate doggedly sticks to his version of events: Ewell fell on his own knife. Atticus finally realises that Tate is protecting Boo, not Jem, and accepts this version. Boo asks Scout to take him home, and she shows her new maturity by making it look as if he is escorting her.

Characters

Scout Finch

Scout is:

- the narrator
- intelligent
- a highly competent reader
- a believer in justice
- her brother's greatest admirer
- a loving daughter
- hot-tempered
- a tomboy
- inclined to settle differences with her fists
- well-meaning and generous
- more mature by the end of the novel.

Dill (Charles Baker)

Dill is:

- Scout and Jem's friend
- small for his age
- highly imaginative
- good at making up games
- quick to think of believable excuses
- convinced that his mother and stepfather don't love him
- happy to be with Jem and Scout
- at home in the Finch household
- sickened by the outcome of the trial.

Jem Finch

Jem is:

- Scout's older brother
- good-natured
- thoughtful
- responsible
- respectful towards his father
- anxious to retain his father's respect
- protective towards Scout
- hoping to become a lawyer
- disillusioned and distressed by the outcome of the trial.

Atticus Finch

Atticus is:

- Scout and Jem's father
- convinced of the need for people to understand each other if they are to live in peace
- a believer in equal justice for all, regardless of race or background
- opposed to violence
- opposed to racism
- tolerant
- modest – never tells his children of his shooting talents ('one-shot Finch')
- highly intelligent
- a good lawyer
- a loving though unorthodox father
- a believer in telling children the truth
- good at reaching compromise.

Calpurnia

Calpurnia is:

- Atticus' black housekeeper
- like a mother to Scout and Jem
- the mother of grown-up children of her own
- strict about manners and hospitality
- devoted to the Finch family
- forceful in protecting the children
- respected in the black community.

Boo Radley

Boo is:

- a neighbour of the Finches
- a loner, keeping himself to himself
- assumed for a long time by the children to be a monster
- kept at home by his brother Nathan
- devoted to the children from a distance
- very shy
- responsible for saving them from Bob Ewell.

Bob Ewell

Ewell is:

- a poor white man living near the black part of town
- a widower, like Atticus
- the father of Mayella (19), Burris (in Scout's class at school), and several other children
- lazy, living on state benefits – regarded as 'white trash'
- a drinker
- violent (he beats Mayella and attacks Scout and Jem)
- a liar, even in court
- resentful of Atticus
- probably guilty of abusing Mayella
- killed by Boo Radley.

Aunt Alexandra

Aunt Alexandra is:

- Atticus' sister
- proud of her ancestry
- a snob
- convinced that Atticus over-indulges his children
- overbearing towards Calpurnia
- determined to make Scout behave in a more 'feminine' way
- loyal to Atticus, despite disagreeing with him.

Miss Maudie Atkinson

Miss Maudie is:

- a friend and neighbour of the Finch family
- kind and generous to the children
- honest and straightforward
- a woman with a sense of humour
- sympathetic and tolerant
- opposed to prejudice and hypocrisy
- a keen gardener
- philosophical about her house burning down.

Tom Robinson

Tom is:

- a 25-year-old black man
- married to Helen and the father of three children
- respectable and with a strong moral sense
- partially disabled – his left arm was caught in a machine when he was 12
- a worker for Link Deas
- generous – he helps Mayella and feels sorry for her
- falsely accused of raping Mayella
- killed when trying to escape from prison.

Mr Dolphus Raymond

Mr Dolphus Raymond is:

- a white man who comes from a rich family and lives with a black woman out of town
- the father of mixed-race children
- tolerated by the white community who label him a 'drunk'
- someone who actually only drinks cola
- sympathetic towards Dill and upset by the prejudice shown at the trial.

Themes

Racism

Slavery was abolished in the USA as late as 1865, so at the time when the novel is set – the 1930s – most whites, especially in former slave-owning states like Alabama, still believed themselves to be naturally superior to blacks. In the novel, poor whites like Bob Ewell and the men who form the lynch party headed by Mr Cunningham are brutally racist. They are all too ready to believe that even a respected black man would rape a white woman, and to condemn him without trial. Although Tom Robinson receives a trial, it cannot be a fair one. Atticus knows that he cannot win the case because, whatever the members of the all-white jury privately believe, they will not publicly acknowledge that a black man could be innocent when accused of rape by a white woman. Most of the better-educated, better-off whites are also racist, though less actively so. They think that black people should know their place, speaking respectfully to whites, going only to their own church in the poor part of town, and holding only menial jobs. Only a few whites, like Atticus and Miss Maudie, see racism as an evil. Dolphus Raymond sees it as such, but chooses not to challenge it, preferring to stand outside of mainstream society by pretending to be permanently drunk.

There is considerable irony in the double standards and hypocrisy of some of the better-off whites. For example, the Missionary Circle ladies raise money for the 'saintly' J. Grimes Everett to bring Christian morality to an African tribe, the 'poor Mrunas', but fail to show Christian compassion towards the black community on their doorstep. Scout's teacher, Miss Gates, is opposed to Hitler's persecution of the Jews, but is overheard outside the court-house complaining that the blacks are getting 'above themselves' and should be 'taught a lesson'. Even Scout herself, speaking about Tom Robinson, says, 'After all, he's just a Negro'.

Compassion and empathy

The theme of compassion and **empathy** is closely related to that of racism. When Dolphus Raymond speaks about 'the simple hell people give other people – without even thinking', he is referring to the way in which racial prejudice blinds people to an awareness of what it is like to be its victim. The need for empathy is a guiding principle for Atticus: 'You never really understand a person... until you climb into his skin and walk around in it.' He tries to teach this to his children, for example when he explains to them that the abusive Mrs Dubose deserves their respect

Figure 2.12 *Black people were rarely treated fairly by the law in 1930s' America, especially in the Southern States.*

because she has overcome drug addiction. The Missionary Society ladies' lack of empathy towards the black community is highlighted by Mrs Merriweather's complaint about her servant Sophie after Tom Robinson's trial: she is just being a 'sulky darkie'. Atticus shows his compassion and empathy in many ways. For example, he is understanding towards poor clients like Mr Cunningham, considerate towards Mayella in court, and even partially excuses Ewell himself.

The novel suggests that vulnerable members of society like Boo Radley and Tom Robinson particularly deserve to be treated with compassion. They are like the mockingbirds that Atticus tells the children not to shoot, because they do no harm. It is a telling moment when Jem prevents Scout from squashing an insect (a 'roly poly') for the same reason. Ironically, Tom Robinson's admission of his compassion for Mayella helps to turn the jury against him.

Justice

This theme, too, is linked to that of racism, in that prejudice is *pre-judice* – judging people before knowing what they are really like. Tom Robinson cannot be treated justly in a racist community, but at least the fact that he has been tried in court and that Atticus has actually proved his innocence is, in Miss Maudie's words, a 'baby step' towards a just society. Atticus is a passionate believer in justice, and in the idea that all people should be considered equal in the eyes of the law – so much so that he does not want to bend the law even to protect his own son when he thinks that Jem killed Ewell. Sheriff Tate's version of events is a fabrication, but in protecting Boo Radley it ensures moral justice. To subject him to the public exposure of a trial would only add to the unjust treatment he has already received at the hands of his brother Nathan.

Family life

Atticus' wife died when Scout was two, but Atticus shows no signs of looking for a second wife. However, family life for Scout and Jem seems very secure. They know their father loves them, and he respects their individuality and does not talk down to them. In addition, they are loved and cared for by Calpurnia. For Dill, provided for materially yet unhappy with his mother and stepfather, the Finch family home is a place of security and refuge. When Atticus feels he has to discipline his children, as when Jem destroys Mrs Dubose's camellias and is made to read to her every day for a month, he explains his reasons for the punishment. Aunt Alexandra is a threat to the stability of the Finch family, in that she has very different values from Atticus, wants to dismiss Calpurnia, and wants to turn Scout into a lady. However, Atticus still insists that the children obey her and are polite to her. She seems severe, but despite this she loves and supports her brother. The family life portrayed in the Ewell household is very different. The Ewell children too are motherless, but they are also filthy and neglected. Ewell is a violent drunk living on welfare, and his children have no Calpurnia to care for them – only their eldest sister, Mayella. There is also evidence that Ewell abuses Mayella.

Growing up

The novel spans a period of about three years, during which time the children grow up in many ways. At first they believe that Boo Radley is a drooling monster who eats raw squirrels, but they gradually realise that he is just a very shy and vulnerable man who quietly observes them and wishes them well. It is Jem who first begins to work out that Boo is performing small acts of kindness towards them, and that the reason why he does not leave his home is that he doesn't want to venture out into a cruel world. By the end of the novel, Scout has grown up enough to treat Boo with friendly kindness. Jem learns about self-control and empathy from the incident with Mrs Dubose's camellias, and Scout too gradually learns to exercise self-control, for example when insulted by children at school because Atticus is defending a Negro. But above all the children learn from the injustice of the trial, which is a source of bitter disillusionment to them, especially for Jem.

Author's craft

Narrative voice

The novel is written in the first **person**, from the viewpoint of Scout. This means that we have a very lively and immediate account of her experience and can easily empathise with her, for example in her frustration when Jem seems to be patronising her. However, it presents a technical difficulty in that the author has to find ways to present information to which Scout would not have access. Lee conveys background information about Boo Radley through what Atticus and Miss Maudie tell the children. Occasionally the children hear gossip – of which there is plenty in Maycomb – or overhear adults speaking. This is how they know that Bob Ewell is threatening Atticus. At other times Scout receives information from Jem or Dill, as when Dill reports accompanying Atticus when he goes to tell Helen Robinson that Tom has been shot. Sometimes information is worked in quite naturally as a result of Jem's more mature understanding of events, which he passes on to Scout.

An important feature of this narrative voice, however, is that the young Scout's viewpoint is filtered through the perspective of her own adult self recalling the events. This gives us a child's feelings with an adult's ability to interpret and evaluate. This adult voice comes close to being the voice of Lee herself. Indeed, on rare occasions, Lee's personal views come through more clearly, as when she criticises the school system that actively discourages Scout from reading.

Observation of people and society

Although the novel gives us a vivid impression of its key characters, with particular insight into the thoughts, feelings and development of its narrator, it is also very much a novel about the individuals that make up Maycomb society, and of that society as a whole. Its view is critical – especially of racism and injustice – but it is also very affectionate. The educational system is criticised through Scout's account of her introduction to school, the legal system more severely through the trial, and by the prosecutor Gilmer's lack of respect for Tom Robinson. We also see the self-righteousness of the middle-class white women, including Aunt Alexandra.

On the other hand, we see the virtue of Sheriff Heck Tate, who protects Boo Radley; Mr Underwood, who is ready to defend Atticus from the lynch party and later writes a bitterly critical account of Tom's shooting; and Dolphus Raymond, who sympathises with Dill during the trial. We also see how welcome most of the black churchgoers make Scout and Jem – despite Lula's objections – and the generosity with which they support Helen Robinson. Few characters are shown in a wholly negative light: Mr Avery, for example, is an apparently unpleasant man, disliked by the children – they make a snowman caricaturing him. However, we later see him acting with bravery, rescuing Miss Maudie's furniture from her burning house.

Setting

Most of the novel is set in the town of Maycomb. We are taken outside on one occasion when the children go to swim; another time the family go to Finch's Landing to spend Christmas with Scout's aunt. There are no striking descriptions of landscape, but we do have a strong sense of the town itself, with its wooden houses, its porches on which its residents sit, its tree-lined streets, and its weather – especially its summer heat and humidity, but also, in one chapter, a rare snowfall. We see the squalor of the Ewells' home, relieved only by the flowers that Mayella grows, as if in an attempt to rise above it. There is, in addition, a strong sense of place in the chapter in which Ewell's threats come to a head, appropriately at Hallowe'en, on a warm moonless night that threatens a thunderstorm. He chooses a dark spot beneath a tree, away from the road, to attack the children. Our sense of place here is in a strange way made more marked by the fact that Scout, in her ham costume, has to work hard to know where she is.

Language

Tone of voice

The tone of writing is influenced by the fact that the experience of the young Scout is viewed through the memory of the character as an adult. The language is frequently more sophisticated than that used by even an intelligent and articulate child like Scout, and the tone is often humorously ironic. In effect, the older Scout is affectionately satirising the view of the world that she had as a child. We find this, for example, in the description of her first school teacher, Miss Caroline, and in her strange ideas about Boo Radley. The tone changes subtly as the young Scout grows older, so that by the end of the novel a new maturity has crept into it. We are also made aware of the affection that the adult narrator feels for the Maycomb of her childhood, despite all its faults.

Activity 1: Understanding the text

Read the following passages:

- From the start of the novel to the end of the paragraph beginning 'During his first five years...'

- Chapter 1, the paragraph beginning 'Inside the house lived a malevolent phantom.'

- Chapter 11, to the end of the paragraph beginning 'She was vicious.'

- Chapter 24, from 'I tried pressing my behind against the door...' to the end of the paragraph beginning 'I hadn't meant to be funny.'

Pick out two sentences from each passage that reveal how the experience of the young Scout is seen from her adult viewpoint. This may be because of the sophistication of the language, a use of irony, or an adult understanding of the child's feelings. Using the table below, write down the sentence (or its beginning and end) and comment on its meaning and how it reveals narrative voice. One has been done for you.

Key phrase	Significance
'Mindful of John Wesley's strictures... as the putting on of costly apparel'	Complex sentence; sophisticated formal words like 'strictures' (restrictions); knowledgeable reference to Wesley; ironic use of biblical language that Finch himself might have quoted.

Activity 2: Understanding the text

Go through the text and make a record of what you think are the most important five or six episodes from which Scout and Jem learn about people and life. Then write about what they learn from each. For example, they learn something from how their father deals with a rabid dog.

Activity 3: Thinking about the characters

Some people think that Scout is a tomboy because her mother is dead and she has no strong female role models. Write about how far Calpurnia, Miss Maudie and Aunt Alexandra offer suitable role models for Scout, and what Scout's attitude is towards each of them.

Activity 4: Thinking about the characters

Choose three characters and write about how far you think they are influenced in their outlook and behaviour by the culture of 1930s' Maycomb.

Some questions to consider

1. In what ways are Bob and Mayella Ewell portrayed as being guilty, and what can we say in their defence?

2. What does the novel teach us about race relations in 1930s' Alabama, and about Harper Lee's attitude towards them 30 years later?

3. What passages in the novel do you find funny, and how does humour contribute to the novel?

4. Which qualities does Harper Lee seem to admire and which does she dislike in the society she portrays?

19th-century short stories

General introduction

All of the other texts in this section have been complete novels, and students focus on just one text by a single author. However, for the 19th-century short stories, the approach is different, because you will be reading all of the stories in the collection and in the examination you will answer a question on two of the stories, comparing, for example, the way they deal with characters, a particular subject or theme or writers' methods.

Background and context: The 19th century

The only thing that connects all of these short stories is the period in which they were written. Mostly they are set in Britain or the USA, but there are also stories set in France, Russia and South Africa. The century was a time of great change, much of it affecting Britain particularly.

In the summary of 19th-century history that follows, there is a reference to each of the authors and stories in the Anthology. This is designed to make sure that you can find out some more about the background and context of all of the stories. However, for more on individual authors you should refer back to the introductions in the Anthology.

During this century, the public acquired a great taste for fiction, with many novels being serialised in magazines, almost like episodes of a soap opera so that people would be on the edge of their seats waiting for the next instalment. This led to the rapid increase in the writing of short stories, which began to be seen as a separate **genre** (type of literature). People read all kinds of fiction, with a particular taste developing for the unusual, horrific or mysterious. Examples of such stories include the horror stories of the Americans – Edgar Allen Poe ('Hop-Frog', 1849) and Ambrose Pierce ('An Arrest', date uncertain) – and the writings of the author of the Sherlock Holmes detective stories, Sir Arthur Conan Doyle ('The Adventure of the Speckled Band', 1892).

At the start of the century, Britain and France were locked in battle, during the Napoleonic Wars, which were won finally by Britain. After this, the British Empire continued to expand greatly to include such countries as Australia, Canada and India; in 1876, Queen Victoria became Empress of India. These short stories were written during the last 60 years of the century when Victoria was on the British throne. Part of the reaction against so-called 'Victorian values', which led to censorship and repression of free ideas in literature and art, was the aesthetic movement (which was interested in art and beauty for their own sakes), of which Oscar Wilde ('The Nightingale and the Rose', 1888) was a notable figure.

Although sometimes we think of the Victorian era as a rather serious time, with very strict attitudes, it was also a time of new ideas and new developments. Darwin's book on *The Origin of Species* (1859) revolutionised the study of science. The growth of interest in all forms of science and medicine was reflected in the writings of H G Wells ('The Stolen Bacillus', 1894). Industry made rapid advances, with huge factories and new industrial cities, such as Manchester and Birmingham, springing up to house those who worked in them, often in very poor working conditions. Many people made themselves very rich from industries such as coal, cotton and pottery, which had its centre in the 'five towns' round Stoke-on-

Figure 2.13 *In the examination you will answer a question on two of the stories.*

Trent, of which Arnold Bennett ('News of the Engagement', around 1895) wrote, or from the spoils of running a worldwide empire. However, not everyone shared in the prizes of this success: the poverty of the working classes became an issue that troubled many social commentators of the time. Nobody expressed this concern for the poor as powerfully as Charles Dickens ('The Poor Relation's Story', 1852), for whom the social injustices of society provided a major theme in his writing in such works as *Oliver Twist*. Thomas Hardy ('Tony Kytes, the Arch-Deceiver', 1895) also explored the lives of the 'ordinary person', especially in the rural landscape of southern England (which he called Wessex).

Over the Channel in France, many of the same changes and developments took place, and the struggles of the poor were written about by writers such as Victor Hugo, notably in *Les Miserables*. Guy de Maupassant ('Country Living', 1883) was one of the writers strongly influenced by the social problems and poverty that persisted in France.

Like Britain, France also became a great power, with colonies in Asia, Africa and America, but it suffered from a period of much greater instability after the end of the Revolution. Although many miles from Britain or France, the Russians were also brought into close proximity with Western Europe through the Napoleonic Wars. Napoleon's retreat from Moscow in 1812, after the bitterest of conflicts in which many thousands perished on both sides, gave Russia an ability to control its own destiny, in a vast country that itself became an empire – the USSR. However, its rulers, the Romanoff royal family, became increasingly unpopular, and the rise of communism occurred under the influence of the writings of Marx. His thinking was eventually to lead to the Russian Revolution of 1917, after many internal struggles that had begun in the latter part of the 19th century. The Great Russian writers of this period, especially Dostoevsky, were influenced heavily by the social upheaval: this group included Maxim Gorky ('Twenty-six Men and a Girl', 1899), who often focused in his writing on the lives of the poor and how they could survive poverty.

In the United States, there was a strong sense of an emerging nation. The Californian 'Gold Rush' in the 1840s led to expansion and to the developing of the lands in the south and west of the country. For the pioneers who travelled west, life was often very difficult, as was experienced by Willa Cather ('Lou, the Prophet', 1892). The middle years of the century brought particular political upheaval, with the split opening between the Northern states and the Southern states over the question of slavery. Abolished in Britain and other parts of Europe in the earlier part of the century, slavery was the foundation of the economy of the South, especially through the huge cotton plantations worked by black slaves. (Readers of *Roll of Thunder, Hear My Cry* will be familiar with this part of American history.) Its opponents crusaded for all Americans to have legal rights, especially under President Abraham Lincoln. The dispute led to a bloody civil war between the 'Yankees' of the North and the 'Confederates' of the South, which ended in victory for the North and the ending of slavery. However, the legacy from the conflict would last a hundred years, years of continuing oppression for the black community, largely descended from the African slaves brought over to work in the cotton fields and elsewhere. Contrasts between rich and poor were evident throughout American society, which also saw the growth of industrial cities; Richard Harding Davis ('Van Bibber's Burglar', 1892) explored aspects of these contrasts in his novels and short stories.

In all of these countries, the place of women during the 19th century continued to be far from ideal. Women remained outside the political structures in all of the countries where these stories are set – as they did in effect throughout the 'civilised' world. It was taken for granted by almost everyone that political power, including the vote, should be confined to men. The struggle towards any form of equality was a long and bitter one, and was not won to any appreciable extent until well into the 20th century, although voices for female emancipation and greater independence had begun to be heard in the 19th century, not least through the writings of women themselves in both Britain and the USA, such as Kate Chopin ('The Unexpected', 1895) and Olive Schreiner ('The Woman's Rose', 1880s–90s). The emerging voice of women and focus on their lives and (lack of) opportunities is an important context for a number of the stories in this collection, particularly those written by women themselves, who included the American Charlotte Perkins Gilman ('The Yellow Wallpaper', 1892), who explored negative attitudes to women, and writers such as Mrs Gaskell ('The Half Brothers', 1859), with her observation of women in a domestic situation. If asked to name women writers in Britain or elsewhere before the start of the 19th century, many would find it hard to come up with names. Following the lead of Mary Shelley and Jane Austen at the start of the century, some of the greatest writers of the Victorian era in Britain were women: Emily and Charlotte Brontë ('Napoleon and the Spectre', 1833), Mrs Gaskell and George Eliot. Notice that the last of these felt she had to write under a man's name, as did the famous French writer George Sand.

The comparison of stories

Comparing stories is a central skill, which you need to practise, and in the following pages you will find a number of ways in which you can make such comparisons.

Reading two (or more) stories in a comparative way is a very good way to improve your understanding of each one. Think about being asked, perhaps, to compare a cat and a dog. Having to do this means that you think carefully about the contrasting qualities and characteristics of each: a dog is loyal, a cat is independent; a dog is bouncy while a cat is slinky; a dog's nose is (usually) pointed, while a cat's is much flatter. In these ways, you can end by giving a really clear account of what a dog (or cat) is actually like. You will also note a number of similarities. Both are domestic animals; both are kept as pets by humans; both have four legs and (usually) a tail.

This simple example shows how comparing involves thinking about what is different and what is similar, whether it be in appearance, character, or any other respect. In the case of stories, the obvious point of comparison is the theme or subject-matter. You may say, for example, that two of the stories are similar because they look at the position of women in 19th-century society. However, one may focus on how women are treated by men, while another looks at how women's lives were changing at the time the story was set. It is also possible to compare writers' methods. Obvious points of comparison include:

- the way the story is narrated
- how the story is developed and the atmosphere built up
- the use of dialogue – how the characters speak
- the kinds of description given of the places where the story takes place
- how the characters are presented.

A further, important way of comparing the stories is through how you respond to them. Stories are supposed to give pleasure – to entertain, mystify, tease, satisfy. Many people meet the writing of a particular author first through a short story, and if they like it enough will go on to read other stories and perhaps novels by the same writer. Think about how you might react differently to two stories, as in the following example:

> Story A really scared me and kept me on the edge of my seat and in suspense to find out what happened; however, I did not find Story B as interesting because the characters did not come to life for me and the plot seemed rather thin.

Teachers and examiners encourage a personal response (when it is backed up with analytical comment and close references to the texts); it shows the way in which you are engaging or connecting with the texts and are thinking about the effect the stories are having on you, the reader. It will not surprise anyone that you will prefer some of the stories to others. They were all written over a hundred years ago. You may find some strange or less appealing to you, and if so that is fine; but, where you have a choice of question or of which story to write about, it is generally better to choose to write about stories that you have enjoyed, not least because people generally write better about things they have enjoyed and found interesting – they are likely to find more to write about.

Examples to compare

The following extracts include one from each story, to give an illustration of where a passage may be used for comparison under one of the headings (i)–(vii). Sometimes, they may also be used for one of the other forms of comparison; so cross-references are given where this might apply.

(i)   Comparing openings

The start of a short story has to draw readers in so that they read on. If the readers are not immediately hooked, they can easily just give up and read something else. It is, therefore, important to think carefully about the opening of all the stories you read.

Look at the following examples, how effective are the openings, and why?

> 'She said that she would dance with me if I brought her red roses,' cried the young Student; 'but in all my garden there is no red rose.'
>
> From her nest in the holm-oak tree the Nightingale heard him, and she looked out through the leaves, and wondered.
>
> 'No red rose in all my garden!' he cried, and his beautiful eyes filled with tears. 'Ah, on what little things does happiness depend! I have read all that the wise men have written, and all the secrets of philosophy are mine, yet for want of a red rose is my life made wretched.'
>
> Oscar Wilde, 'The Nightingale and the Rose'

Also useful for (iv).

> I have an old, brown carved box; the lid is broken and tied with a string. In it I keep little squares of paper, with hair inside, and a little picture which hung over my brother's bed when we were children, and other things as small. I have in it a rose. Other women also have such boxes where they keep such trifles, but no one has my rose.
>
> When my eye is dim, and my heart grows faint, and my faith in woman flickers, and her present is an agony to me, and her future a despair, the scent of that dead rose, withered for twelve years, comes back to me. I know there will be spring; as surely as the birds know it when they see above the snow two tiny, quivering green leaves. Spring cannot fail us.
>
> Olive Schreiner, 'The Woman's Rose'

Also useful, with 'The Nightingale and the Rose' for (iii) (the rose as a symbol on the theme of women's lives).

(ii)   Comparing endings

If the opening is important, then so, just as much, is the ending. Readers need to feel satisfied or intrigued by how the story ends, or they will just put it down and think 'So what?' or 'Why did I bother?' Sometimes stories end with the reader not being sure exactly what has happened or what is likely to happen next: this can be frustrating or it can be something readers enjoy, if they like being left with an air of mystery or uncertainty.

Look at the following examples, and think about how effective the endings are, and why.

> Eventually they entered the town, which was all alight, but deserted; only the women and children remained, and they were off the streets. Straight toward the jail the criminal held his way. Straight up to the main entrance he walked, laid his hand upon the knob of the heavy iron door, pushed it open without command, entered and found himself in the presence of a half-dozen armed men. Then he turned. Nobody else entered.
>
> On a table in the corridor lay the dead body of Burton Duff.
>
> Ambrose Bierce, 'An Arrest'

> 'Mon Dieu!' cried the Emperor, 'how is all this come about? Where in the world is Piche?'
>
> 'Piche?' replied the Empress. 'What does your Majesty mean? Had you not better leave the apartment and retire to rest?'
>
> 'Leave the apartment? Why, where am I?'
>
> 'In my private drawing-room, surrounded by a few particular persons of the Court whom I had invited this evening to a ball. You entered a few minutes since in your nightdress with your eyes fixed and wide open. I suppose from the astonishment you now testify that you were walking in your sleep.'
>
> The Emperor immediately fell into a fit of catalepsy, in which he continued during the whole of that night and the greater part of the next day.
>
> Charlotte Brontë, 'Napoleon and the Spectre'

(iii) Comparing themes

The stories you read may have the same theme, treated in a similar way, or the same theme, but with a very different treatment. For example, several of the stories deal with the lives of women, but they focus on quite contrasting aspects of them: their treatment by men; their place in society; their loves and passions.

Look at the following examples on the theme of fear and horror, and think about how effective the different presentations of the same or similar theme are, and why. The extracts chosen give some important aspects, but you will need to look at the texts as a whole to develop your understanding.

> 'It is fear, Mr Holmes. It is terror.' She raised her veil as she spoke, and we could see that she was indeed in a pitiable state of agitation, her face all drawn and grey, with restless frightened eyes, like those of some hunted animal. Her features and figure were those of a woman of thirty, but her hair was shot with premature grey, and her expression was weary and haggard. Sherlock Holmes ran her over with one of his quick, all-comprehensive glances.
>
> 'You must not fear,' said he soothingly, bending forward and patting her forearm. 'We shall soon set matters right, I have no doubt. You have come in by train this morning, I see.'
>
> Sir Arthur Conan Doyle, 'The Adventure of the Speckled Band'

Also useful for (iv) and (v).

> The right path was clear enough in the day-time, although at several points two or three exactly similar diverged from the same place; but when there was a good light, the traveller was guided by the sight of distant objects – a piece of rock – a fall in the ground – which were quite invisible to me now. I plucked up a brave heart, however, and took what seemed to me the right road. It was wrong, nevertheless, and led me whither I knew not, but to some wild boggy moor where the solitude seemed painful, intense, as if never footfall of man had come thither to break the silence. I tried to shout – with the dimmest possible hope of being heard – rather to reassure myself by the sound of my own voice; but my voice came husky and short, and yet it dismayed me; it seemed so weird and strange, in that noiseless expanse of black darkness. Suddenly the air was filled thick with dusky flakes, my face and hands were wet with snow. It cut me off from the slightest knowledge of where I was, for I lost every idea of the direction from which I had come, so that I could not even retrace my steps; it hemmed me in, thicker, thicker, with a darkness that might be felt. The boggy soil on which I stood quaked under me if I remained long in one place, and yet I dared not move far. All my youthful hardiness seemed to leave me at once. I was on the point of crying, and only very shame seemed to keep it down. To save myself from shedding tears, I shouted – terrible, wild shouts for bare life they were. I turned sick as I paused to listen; no answering sound came but the unfeeling echoes.
>
> Elizabeth Gaskell, 'The Half Brothers'

Also useful for (iv) and (v).

(iv) Comparing characterisation

Characters are what give stories their main interest in just about all forms of fiction. Occasionally, as in children's stories, the characters may be animals or birds, who are treated in an anthropomorphic (humanised) way. In short stories, there is a particular challenge for the writers as they have to make their characters interesting in a short space and with little time for the reader to come to know them. Some of the stories in this collection are extremely short, whereas others are closer to a short novel (novella) so the authors have much more scope for describing their characters in detail.

Look at the following examples, and think about how effective the author's characterisation is, and why. You will need to look at the texts as a whole to develop your understanding.

> 'This again,' said the Bacteriologist, slipping a glass slide under the microscope, 'is a preparation of the celebrated Bacillus of cholera – the cholera germ.'
>
> The pale-faced man peered down the microscope. He was evidently not accustomed to that kind of thing, and held a limp white hand over his disengaged eye. 'I see very little,' he said.
>
> 'Touch this screw,' said the Bacteriologist; 'perhaps the microscope is out of focus for you. Eyes vary so much. Just the fraction of a turn this way or that.'
>
> 'Ah! now I see,' said the visitor. 'Not so very much to see after all. Little streaks and shreds of pink. And yet those little particles, those mere atomies, might multiply and devastate a city! Wonderful!'
>
> H G Wells, 'The Bacillus'

Also useful for (i) and for (iii) with 'The Adventure of the Speckled Band', on the theme of medical science.

> But although Hop-Frog, through the distortion of his legs, could move only with great pain and difficulty along a road or floor, the prodigious muscular power which nature seemed to have bestowed upon his arms, by way of compensation for deficiency in the lower limbs, enabled him to perform many feats of wonderful dexterity, where trees or ropes were in question, or any thing else to climb. At such exercises he certainly much more resembled a squirrel, or a small monkey, than a frog.
>
> Edgar Allen Poe, 'Hop-Frog'

Also useful for (v).

(v) Comparing description

Descriptions can of course be of different things, but the main ones are:

- characters (see above): these can be physical descriptions or descriptions of personality
- places: these could be interiors, such as the room where the action takes place, or scenes in the town or country where the weather and setting are important

- events, such as a dramatic scene: a murder, robbery or accident, for example.

When comparing descriptions, you can focus on how authors describe people, or focus on their way of describing particular places – or compare one author's description of a person with another's description of a place, so that you are looking more generally at descriptive powers.

Look at the following examples, and think about how effective the author's descriptions are, and why. Notice in particular the use of verbs, **adjectives** and **adverbs** to carry forward the action or to paint the scene. You will need to look at the texts as a whole to develop your understanding.

Figure 2.14 *'long, inviting shadows about the road'.*

> The country about her grew unfamiliar. She was on a rough, unfrequented road, where the birds in the wayside brooks seemed unafraid. She could perceive no human habitation; an old fallow field, a stretch of wood, great trees bending thick-leaved branches languidly, and flinging long, inviting shadows about the road; the woody smell of summer; the drone of the insects; the sky and the clouds, and the quivering, lambent air. She was alone with nature; her pulses beating in unison with its sensuous throb, as she stopped and stretched herself upon the sward. Every muscle, nerve, fibre abandoned itself to the delicious sensation of rest that overtook and crept tingling through the whole length of her body.
>
> Kate Chopin, 'The Unexpected'

> The rumble of heavy market wagons and the rattle of milk carts told them that it was morning, and as they opened the door the cold fresh air swept into the place and made them wrap their collars around their throats and stamp their feet. The morning wind swept down the cross-street from the East River and the lights of the street lamps and of the saloon looked old and tawdry. Travers and the reporter went off to a Turkish bath, and the gentleman who held the watch, and who had been asleep for the last hour, dropped into a nighthawk and told the man to drive home. It was almost clear now and very cold, and Van Bibber determined to walk. He had the strange feeling one gets when one stays up until the sun rises, of having lost a day somewhere, and the dance he had attended a few hours before seemed to have come off long ago, and the fight in Jersey City was far back in the past.
>
> Richard M Davis, 'Van Kibber's Burglar'

(vi) Comparing dialogue and language

Short stories mostly include a significant amount of **dialogue** – one way in which both the plot and the characterisation are developed. It is often important in giving a sense of place, especially through such devices as regional dialect, or through the kind of language the characters use (vocabulary, register, tone of voice). The other place where language is very important is that of the narration (see page 101).

Look at the following examples, and think about how effective the author's language and use of dialogue are, and why. You will need to look at the texts as a whole to develop your understanding.

'My wife has not made her meaning clear. We wish to adopt him, but he will come back to see you. If he turns out well, as there is every reason to expect, he will be our heir. If we, perchance, should have children, he will share equally with them; but if he should not reward our care, we should give him, when he comes of age, a sum of twenty thousand francs, which shall be deposited immediately in his name, with a lawyer. As we have thought also of you, we should pay you, until your death, a pension of one hundred francs a month. Do you understand me?'

Guy de Maupassant, 'Country Living'

Also useful for (iv).

'No, tell me do – who?'
'Tell you?' the baker turned suddenly to him.
'Well?'
'You know Tanya?'
'Well?'
'Well, there then! Only try.'
'You!'
'Her? Why that's nothing to me – pooh!'
'We shall see!'
'You will see! Ha! ha!'
'She'll –'
'Give me a month!'
'What a braggart you are, soldier!'
'A fortnight! I'll prove it! Who is it? Tanya! Pooh!'
'Well, get out. You're in my way!'
'A fortnight – and it's done! Ah, you –'
'Get out, I say!'

Maxim Gorky, 'Twenty-Six Men and a Girl'

I have no doubt (said the poor relation) that I shall surprise the assembled members of our family, and particularly John our esteemed host to whom we are so much indebted for the great hospitality with which he has this day entertained us, by the confession I am going to make. But, if you do me the honour to be surprised at anything that falls from a person so unimportant in the family as I am, I can only say that I shall be scrupulously accurate in all I relate.

I am not what I am supposed to be. I am quite another thing. Perhaps before I go further, I had better glance at what I AM supposed to be.

Charles Dickens, 'The Poor Relation's Story'

(vii) Comparing narrative voices

There are two main ways in which authors tell their story. The first is the 'third person' narrator, where the writer can describe 'impersonally' what is going on. This is often referred to as the **omniscient** ('knowing everything') **narrator**. The second is the **'first person' narrator**, who is a character taking part in the story and therefore telling it in his or her own words. A variant on these two is to use another of the characters, for example to report events that have taken place elsewhere: this kind of story-telling is derived from the ancient Greek dramas, which often included a messenger speech to give a dramatic account of events.

Look at the following examples, and think about how effective the author's use of narrative voice is, and why. You will need to look at the texts as a whole to develop your understanding.

> I shall never forget Tony's face. It was a little, round, firm, tight face, with a seam here and there left by the small-pox, but not enough to hurt his looks in a woman's eye, though he'd had it baddish when he was a boy. So very serious looking and unsmiling 'a was, that young man, that it really seemed as if he couldn't laugh at all without great pain to his conscience. He looked very hard at a small speck in your eye when talking to 'ee. And there was no more sign of a whisker or beard on Tony Kytes's face than on the palm of my hand.
>
> Thomas Hardy, 'Tony Kytes, the Arch Deceiver'

Also useful for (vi).

> We are a stolid and a taciturn race, we of the Five Towns. It may be because we are geographically so self contained; or it may be because we work in clay and iron; or it may merely be because it is our nature to be stolid and taciturn. But stolid and taciturn we are; and some of the instances of our stolidity and our taciturnity are enough to astound. They do not, of course, astound us natives; we laugh at them, we think they are an immense joke, and what the outer world may think does not trouble our deep conceit of ourselves. I have often wondered what would be the effect, other than an effect of astonishment, on the outer world, of one of these narratives illustrating our Five Towns peculiarities of deportment. And I intend for the first time in history to make such a narrative public property. I have purposely not chosen an extreme example; just an average example. You will see how it strikes you.
>
> Arnold Bennett, 'News of the Engagement'

Also useful for (v).

> Out of one window I can see the garden, those mysterious deepshaded arbors, the riotous old-fashioned flowers, and bushes and gnarly trees. Out of another I get a lovely view of the bay and a little private wharf belonging to the estate. There is a beautiful shaded lane that runs down there from the house. I always fancy I see people walking in these numerous paths and arbors, but John has cautioned me not to give way to fancy in the least. He says that with my imaginative power and habit of story-making, a nervous weakness like mine is sure to lead to all manner of excited fancies, and that I ought to use my will and good sense to check the tendency. So I try.
>
> Charlotte Perkins Gilman, 'The Yellow Wallpaper'

Also useful for (v).

> Perhaps the greatest calamity of all was the threatened loss of his corn crop. He had bought a new corn planter on time that spring, and had intended that his corn should pay for it. Now, it looked as though he would not have corn enough to feed his horses. Unless rain fell within the next two weeks, his entire crop would be ruined; it was half gone now. All these things together were too much for poor Lou, and one morning he felt a strange loathing for the bread and sorghum which he usually ate as mechanically as he slept. He kept thinking about the strawberries he used to gather on the mountains after the snows were gone, and the cold water in the mountain streams. He felt hot someway, and wanted cold water. He had no well, and he hauled his water from a neighbor's well every Sunday, and it got warm in the barrels those hot summer days. He worked at his haying all day; at night, when he was through feeding, he stood a long time by the pig stye with a basket on his arm. When the moon came up, he sighed restlessly and tore the buffalo pea flowers with his bare toes. After a while, he put his basket away, and went into his hot, close, little dugout.
>
> Willa Cather, 'Lou, the Prophet'

Also useful for (iv).

Activity 1: Understanding the text

Look back to (iii) on Comparing themes (page 97), and think about the way in which you could approach the given texts in a comparative way. Reading through the rest of the extracts, see what other themes you can identify. Think about how the stories are grouped in the Anthology, and think about how the stories under these headings can be compared. Make a table of themes with relevant stories listed underneath each, to help you to make links.

Activity 2: Understanding the text

Look back to (v) on Comparing description (pages 98–99), and think about how the authors use different techniques to make their descriptions vivid. Think about the way the writers have used different parts of speech (specifically, verbs, adjectives and adverbs); list some examples, using the table below, that seem to you to be particularly effective, and comment on the choice of word. One example of each has been done for you.

Verb	Adjective	Adverb
'**flinging** long, inviting shadows': this personifies the tree as though it is performing a violent, dramatic action.	'the **quivering, lambent** air': these two adjectives are very unusual in describing the air; they give the impression of a living, breathing creature, moving almost like a snake with flickering ('lambent') tongue.	'**languidly**': this word suggests slow, almost lazy movement.

Activity 3: Thinking about the characters

Look back to (iv) on Comparing characterisation (page 98), and notice the way authors use different techniques to try to make their characters come to life. When you think about the stories you have read, which are the characters that seem most memorable to you and why? Draw up a list of your top five characters in rank order, and add brief comments on why you have chosen these.

Some questions to consider

You will notice that, because the examination may ask you to pair a story of your choice with a named story, the questions may appear rather general, because otherwise not all of the stories would fit them. Looking at the following questions, therefore, you must decide which of the stories you have read will go together best. You will find that the more links you can make, the easier it will be to answer on two stories, whatever the precise question. Having such links in mind will save time and give you confidence.

1. Compare two short stories where the characters face difficult situations.

2. Compare the way two short stories deal with the themes of betrayal and revenge and explain how suspense is created by the authors.

3. Compare the methods used to present a similar theme in two short stories you have studied.

4. Compare and contrast ways in which the writers create suspense, atmosphere and setting in two short stories.

Here are some other questions to consider, which are not in the form of examination questions, but should assist in your preparation. Depending on how many stories you have read, you may wish to make notes on several and then decide which ones seem to give you the best evidence to use when answering the questions.

1. We have seen that, compared with a novel, it is not easy for authors of short stories to develop their characters. Think about the characters in the stories you are studying, and note down any techniques that the authors use. How do they differ? Which methods do you find most successful and why?

2. How important a part do physical descriptions of place play in the short stories you are studying? Is it important that the author gives you a strong picture of the settings?

3. What part do unexpected events or twists in the plot play in the stories you are studying? How do the authors create mystery or suspense?

4. In writing these stories, what do you think really interested the authors and what were they trying to achieve?

Chapter 3: Section C of the Poetry Anthology

Introduction

This chapter deals with all of the 16 poems in Section C of the Anthology, which is the collection of poems that is set for study for Paper 2 for all students preparing for Route 1 of the IGCSE and the Certificate, and for those taking the poetry coursework option (Route 2).

Colour-coding or annotating the poems

In this chapter, the text of each poem is set out, but not as a 'clean text', such as is given in the Anthology for IGCSE and Certificate for English Literature and is available on the ActiveBook. Instead, the text has been annotated in a number of ways, which you should find helpful in supporting your study of the poems. The approach adopted is to highlight the text where there are features of the language that are worth drawing attention to. One standard highlighting is that for repetition, in green, because this is a language feature that all the poems use to some extent. Other features are used in some poems but not in others, and different colours have been used for these, such as the following:

- abstract nouns
- different types of language (for example, religious, industrial)
- **onomatopoeia**
- words that are negative
- use of **caesura**

- **personification**
- words connected with the past or with suffering or death
- use of colour
- compound words.

In addition, the text uses **bold type** and underlining, especially for effects such as alliteration and assonance.

It should be noted that this is not a complete list of all possible features, but an approach you might wish to adopt for other features of the language that occur to you.

The other way the text is marked is by annotations – in particular, explanatory comments and definitions of unusual words and questions to prompt thinking. These are given in text boxes on the left-hand or right-hand side of the page or occasionally underneath the text. Again, you may wish to add additional boxes of your own. It might be possible, for example, to copy the poems onto a large sheet of paper, to give more space for you to annotate the text for yourself.

Thinking about rhythm and meter

The rest of the section on each poem consists of a number of ideas for how you can think further about the poem and its language and ideas. For example, some

Figure 3.1 *You may wish to add your own annotations.*

information is given about looking at the **meter** and **rhythm** of the different poems. Not all poems adopt a set pattern, preferring to use free verse. However, others do have a set formal structure, particularly if they are written in **sonnet** form of 14 lines or, in the case of Dylan Thomas, the villanelle, an unusual19-line form.

When looking at the rhythm of poems, some reference is made to common metrical patterns. Poems in a set rhythm have a meter that consists of a pattern of stressed and unstressed syllables. For example, a common form is the **iambic pentameter**, which has five 'metric feet' called 'iambs', each of which has an unstressed syllable followed by a stressed one, which has been described as 'te-tum'. A famous example of a poem in this meter is 'Gray's Elegy', which starts: 'The *cur*-few *tolls* the *knell* of *part*-ing *day*' – te-tum, te-tum, te-tum, te-tum, te-tum.

The other main meters that you will be likely to come across, some in this collection, are the:

- dactyl: tum-te-te
- trochee: tum-te
- spondee: tum-tum
- anapaest: te-te-tum.

It is important to be aware of poets' use of set forms and meters, because often these have a strong influence on their ideas and use of language. If you have ever tried to write poems that rhyme or have a definite rhythm, you will know that it is often hard to make things fit exactly as you want them to.

Another part of the accompanying material for each poem is a table that invites you to give quotations from the text of words and phrases that you think interesting or important, and to give your reasons for choosing them. In each case, *three* examples have been given, together with a comment on their effect. These are not written by students, but they are intended to give you good examples of the kinds of way in which text can be explored. You are then invited to add further examples of your own, and may wish to try to adopt a similar approach to writing a comment.

Linking more than one poem

You need to remember that in the examination (IGCSE Route 1 and Certificate) you will always have to write about two poems and in the coursework option (IGCSE Route 2) you will need to write about *three poems from Section C of the Anthology and refer briefly to three other related poems to show your wider reading*. So it is always important to:

- look for links between poems, especially on the subject-matter, ideas and themes
- consider links on the form, style or tone of the writing.

When considering links between poems, you may want to draw up a simple grid. The idea of drawing up such a table is to make it easy to see at a glance which poems can be connected to a particular subject, theme or form. You will be able to add to the list, and perhaps think of other poems that can be grouped together for particular purposes.

Remember:

- When making links between poems, you are looking at how different writers can use different (or similar) approaches to dealing with similar themes.
- One poet may treat a subject very seriously, while another poet treats it in a far more light-hearted way.

- You must look at how well they achieve what they set out to do. As you will see in the examination materials in the ActiveBook, students often have to decide how effectively poets achieve their goals, and may be invited to make a judgement: 'Which is more successful at...?'

- When you read the poems, therefore, get used to making critical judgements and evaluations. These should be based on your own response, but informed by reasons and evidence. For example: 'X is more exciting (or powerful or disturbing) than Y because in poem X the language is...'

Questions on the text

Finally, there is a short section with four or five questions for discussion or written response. These can be discussed with your class or in pairs or small groups. However, you may also try to answer them in writing, and if you keep a set of your responses to these questions you will find it a valuable aid to revision.

Reading and listening to poems

When reading poetry, do not be surprised or disappointed if you do not feel you have really understood a poem when you hear or read it for the first time. In the ActiveBook you will be able to hear readings of all of the poems in Section C of the Anthology, to help you with your understanding. Poetry is often hard to grasp because of unusual language, difficult ideas or unfamiliar subject-matter. The important thing is to stick at it. You will find that after a second or third reading things start to become much clearer, especially after discussion with others. We do not necessarily know exactly what the poet had in mind, and we need to make our own interpretations, which will not always be the same as anybody else's. You should have a point of view. Ask yourself why you do or don't like a particular poem and discuss the reasons for your views. Poetry is often meant to make you think hard, as well as to amuse, inspire, disturb or sadden you. Be clear about why you react to some poems in a different way from others.

Summary of key points

The following short summary of key points is intended to help you to analyse the poems in the collection by:
- understanding each poem as you study it
- making effective connections between the different poems
- developing your own engagement with and responses to the poems.

When approaching any poem, there are some central processes that will help you to respond effectively:

- What is the title and what does this suggest to you?

- What is the poem about? What 'central characters' are involved, including any narrator?

- What do you notice about the poet's use of language? Focus on the different techniques and features you can find, and what the effect of these is. This will include:
  - different forms of **imagery** (**simile**, **metaphor**, personification)
  - different sound effects (alliteration, **assonance**, rhyme, rhythm, onomatopoeia).

- How do the form and structure of the poem affect its ideas and your response?

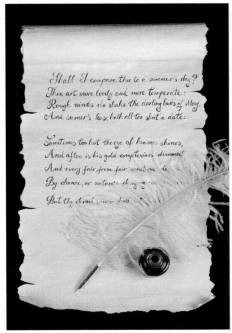

Figure 3.2 *Manuscript of a poem by Shakespeare.*

If –

Background and context

Rudyard Kipling was born in 1865 in India, in the city of Bombay (now known as Mumbai) and died in 1936, having been awarded the Nobel Prize for Literature. He was offered a knighthood but turned it down. Much of his work is based on his knowledge of India and the East, especially the stories in *The Jungle Book*, now best known from the Disney cartoon film. He was known as a very patriotic person, but his attitudes were changed deeply by the loss of his son, John, to whom the poem 'If –' is addressed, in the First World War.

> **Top tip**
>
> You can find out more about Rudyard Kipling and his poetry and other writing from reference books or on the Internet. You could read some more of the poems, which will help you to understand Kipling's attitudes.

If you can keep your head when all about you
    Are losing theirs and blaming it on you,
If you can trust yourself when all men doubt you,
    But make allowance for their doubting too;
If you can wait and not be tired by waiting,
    Or being lied about, don't deal in lies,
Or being hated, don't give way to hating,
    And yet don't look too good, nor talk too wise:

If you can dream — and not make dreams your master;
    If you can think — and not make thoughts your aim;
If you can meet with Triumph and Disaster
    And treat those two impostors just the same;
If you can bear to hear the truth you've spoken
    Twisted by knaves to make a trap for fools,
Or watch the things you gave your life to, broken,
    And stoop and build 'em up with worn-out tools:

If you can make one heap of all your winnings
    And risk it on one turn of pitch-and-toss*,
And lose, and start again at your beginnings
    And never breathe a word about your loss;
If you can force your heart and nerve and sinew
    To serve your turn long after they are gone,
And so hold on when there is nothing in you
    Except the Will which says to them: 'Hold on!'

If you can talk with crowds and keep your virtue,
    Or walk with Kings — nor lose the common touch,
If neither foes nor loving friends can hurt you,
    If all men count with you, but none too much;
If you can fill the unforgiving minute
    With sixty seconds' worth of distance run,
Yours is the Earth and everything that's in it,
    And — which is more — you'll be a Man, my son!

Rudyard Kipling

> Kipling gives two examples of the general principle of not repaying evil with evil.

> *pitch-and-toss*: An old gambling game in which players had to throw coins as close to a wall as possible.

> **Key**:
> Repetition
> Abstract nouns (qualities), written with capital letters

Understanding the text and commenting on the language

'If –' is addressed to the writer's son, John, but is more widely directed at any young boy growing up into adulthood. For most of the poem, the reader is likely to assume it is addressed to people in general, and the words 'my son' come as a shock, as we realise that this is a '**dramatic monologue**' by a father addressing his son. This is where one person speaks directly to another, like a character in a play.

The title and repetition of the word 'if' are important. They show that there is doubt whether the person addressed will be able to achieve all these things, and show how hard they are.

1. Think about the different forms of advice, and whether they seem suitable for talking to a growing boy. Did Kipling think of this as a recipe for life that would apply to anybody?

2. Select some key phrases from the poem, working with a partner if possible. These may:

   ● show the qualities Kipling admires

   ● focus on features of Kipling's language and its effect, such as repetition, personification and metaphor

   ● be words that seem to you striking or unusual and that convey Kipling's powerful ideas.

   Some examples have been given in the table on the right to get you started.

Key ideas for links with other poems

In this course, and in particular in the examination or the coursework essay (Route 2), it is important to think about how different poets deal with similar ideas or themes. Fill in your grid (see pages 106–107), to help you link this poem with other poems.

'If –' is often referred to as an inspirational or motivational poem, with the writer giving encouragement to a young person on how to live. If you think of qualities that Kipling admires, such as courage, self-belief, perseverance, or staying calm under pressure, then you may find links to other poems.

Figure 3.3 *A father and son.*

Language	Comment on meaning/effect
'keep your head…'	He should not panic under pressure.
'talk with crowds and keep your virtue'	He should be able to relate to all people, 'high or low'.
'meet with Triumph and Disaster / And treat those two imposters just the same'	He advises the boy to realise that winning and losing are not really so important, and you should not be too excited by one or depressed by the other, as we all experience both.

Some questions to consider

Thinking about the following questions (and perhaps writing notes or timed short answers) will be helpful when you revise for the examination, because you will have covered the key ideas in this poem.

1. How do you think a teenager would react to being given the advice in this poem?

2. How do the form and structure of the poem help to present the ideas?

3. Why might the attitudes in this poem be described as stoical? (Use a dictionary if necessary for this term.) Do you think this is a good word to use?

4. Why are some of the ideas in the poem linked to sport?

Top tip

You can find out more about MacNeice and his poetry from reference books or on the Internet. You could read some more of his poems, which will help you to understand MacNeice's attitudes and ideas.

Key:

alliteration

repetition

assonance

religious language

dandle: cradle gently

engendered: caused

hector: bully or intimidate

dragoon: to force someone

A lethal automaton is a 'killing machine', with no feelings. It links to the word 'dragoon', as dragoons were heavy-armed soldiers.

Prayer Before Birth

Background and context

Louis MacNeice was born in 1910 and died in 1963. The poem 'Prayer Before Birth' was written in 1944, during the Second World War. At that time, people in Britain were experiencing regular attacks from the 'doodlebug' (V1), a frightening flying bomb that fell silently from the skies. So this is a poem that expresses deep concern about the life that awaited children being born into such a world.

I am not yet born; O hear me.
Let not the **bl**oodsucking **b**at or the rat or the stoat or the
club-footed ghoul come near me.

I am not yet born, console me.
I fear that the human race may **w**ith t**a**ll **w**a**ll**s **w**all me,
with strong **dr**ugs **d**ope me, **w**ith **w**ise **l**ies **l**ure me,
on **bl**ack **r**acks **r**ack me, in **bl**ood-**b**aths roll me.

I am not yet born; provide me
With **w**ater to **d**an**dl**e* me, **gr**ass to **gr**ow for me, **t**rees **t**o **t**alk
to me, **s**ky to **s**ing to me, birds and a **wh**ite **l**ight
in the back of **m**y **m**ind to guide me.

I am not yet born; forgive me
For the sins that in me the world shall commit, my words
when they speak me, my **th**oughts when they **th**ink me,
my **tr**eason engendered* by **tr**aitors beyond me,
my life when they **m**urder by **m**eans of **m**y hands,
my death when they live me.

I am not yet born; rehearse me
In the **p**arts I must **p**lay and the cues I must take when
old men **l**ecture me, bureaucrats hector* me, **m**ountains
fr**ow**n at me, **l**overs **l**augh at me, the **wh**ite
waves **c**all me to **f**olly and the **d**esert **c**alls
me to **d**oom and the beggar refuses
my gift and my children curse me.

I am not yet born; O hear me,
Let not the man who is beast or who thinks he is God
come near me.

I am not yet born; O fill me
With strength against those who would freeze my
humanity, would dragoon* me into a lethal automaton,
would make me a cog in a machine, a thing with
one face, a thing, and against all those
who would dissipate my entirety, would
blow me like thistledown hither and
thither or hither and thither
like water held in the
hands would spill me.

Let them not make me a **s**tone and let them not spill me.
Otherwise k**i**ll me.

Louis MacNeice

Understanding the text and commenting on the language

1. Think about how MacNeice uses the dramatic monologue form in which the speaker is addressing someone else (you will see this in 'If —' and other poems in this section of the Anthology). How does the fact that the narrator of the poem is an unborn child affect the reader's feelings about the monologue? Think also about the form and structure of the poem, including the unusual layout.

2. Select some key phrases from the poem, working with a partner if possible. These may:

   ● show a world full of fears and nightmarish thoughts

   ● focus on features of MacNeice's language and its effect, looking at such aspects as his use of alliteration and assonance/rhyme

   ● be words that seem to you striking or unusual and that convey MacNeice's powerful ideas.

   Some examples have been given to get you started.

Figure 3.4 *Ghouls are one of the images in the poem.*

Key ideas for links with other poems

In this course, and in particular in the examination or the coursework essay (Route 2), it is important to think about how different poets deal with similar ideas or themes. Fill in your grid, to help you link this poem with other poems.

The poem is about birth and death, and also the world of the child (with its hopes of warmth and love but fears of nightmares and terrors, with a background of war and betrayal).

Language	Comment on meaning/effect
'blood sucking bat...club-footed ghoul'	These harsh-sounding words give an immediate impression of a world of vampire and ghost films, with creatures that would terrify a young child.
'With water to dandle me'	There is a strong contrast in this stanza, because the child here would like a comforting and peaceful world.
'Otherwise kill me'	The ending is a very abrupt, strong request. The child does not want to be born into a world of such horrors unless it can be protected.

Some questions to consider

Thinking about these questions (and perhaps writing notes or timed short answers) will be helpful when you revise for the examination, because you will have thought about the key ideas in this poem.

1. Although the poem shows the fears of an unborn child, how far does it also show adult fears?

2. Look at the examples of MacNeice's use of alliteration, assonance and onomatopoeia. Where do these mainly occur in the poem, and why are they used?

3. What kind of person might MacNeice have had in mind when he refers to the 'man who is beast or who thinks he is God'?

4. How would you describe the overall mood and tone of the poem?

Half-past Two

Background and context

U A Fanthorpe, whose full name was Ursula Askham Fanthorpe, was born in 1929 and died just recently, in 2009. She had a number of different jobs, including working for a while as a teacher, and she often wrote about her experience of the world of work: 'Half-past Two' is based on a real or imagined incident in the life of a teacher and child.

Top tip

You can find out more about Fanthorpe and her poetry from reference books or on the Internet. You could read some more of the poems, which will help you to understand Fanthorpe's attitudes.

This is a slight variation on the classic fairytale opening (see the poem 'Once Upon a Time' on page 126 for this idea again). What does this make you think is to come in the poem?

By saying that the boy knows all the important times, it shows that he does not think that proper telling of the time is important. Think about the times that he does think are important.

Silent noise: this is an **oxymoron** – the adjective seems to contradict the noun.

The use of capital letters makes the reader aware that the child thinks it was a terrible thing he had done, but the writer cannot remember what it was. Forgetting is something of a theme.

Once upon a schooltime
He did Something Very Wrong
(I forget what it was).

And She said he'd done
Something Very Wrong, and must
Stay in the school-room till half-past two.

(Being cross, she'd forgotten
She hadn't taught him Time.
He was too scared at being wicked to remind her.)

He knew a lot of time: he knew
Gettinguptime, timeyouwereofftime,
Timetogohomenowtime, TVtime,
Timeformykisstime (that was Grantime).
All the important times he knew,
But not half-past two.

He knew the clockface, the little eyes
And two long legs for walking,
But he couldn't click its language,

So he waited, beyond onceupona,
Out of reach of all the timefors,
And knew he'd escaped for ever

Into the smell of old chrysanthemums on Her desk,
Into the silent noise his hangnail made,
Into the air outside the window, into ever.

And then, *My goodness*, she said,
Scuttling in, *I forgot all about you.*
Run along or you'll be late.

So she slotted him back into schooltime,
And he got home in time for teatime,
Nexttime, notimeforthatnowtime,

But he never forgot how once by not knowing time,
He escaped into the clockless land for ever,
Where time hides tick-less waiting to be born.

U A Fanthorpe

Key:
Repetition
Compound words
Onomatopoeia

Understanding the text and commenting on the language

1. Think about how Fanthorpe shows, through her use of language, the differences between the child's and adult's worlds.

2. Select some key phrases from the poem, working with a partner if possible. These may:

    ● show how Fanthorpe presents the child or the teacher

    ● focus on features of Fanthorpe's language and its effect, including personification, onomatopoeia and repetition

    ● be words that seem to you striking or unusual (such as her use of compound words) and which convey Fanthorpe's ideas.

    Some examples have been given to get you started.

Key ideas for links with other poems

In this course, and in particular in the examination or the coursework essay (Route 2), it is important to think about how different poets deal with similar ideas or themes. Fill in your grid, to help you link this poem with other poems. The poem focuses on the world of the child and how this is affected by the actions of adults. It also looks at how the young child's mind works, with its confusion about things beyond his understanding and the strong use of the imagination.

Figure 3.5 *Half-past two.*

Language	Comment on meaning/effect
'time hides tick-less waiting to be born'	'Time' is personified as someone not yet born, which shows time as set in an eternal world; time was not yet born for the child in the sense that he had not been able to measure it.
'smell of old chrysanthemums'	The child had moved into a world where he was not at all conscious of time, but was very aware of his senses. The 'old chrysanthemums' perhaps provide another example of the teacher's busy, forgetful life, as she had not changed the flowers.
'He knew the clockface, the little eyes'	This shows how the child in his imagination compared the clock to a 'person' with a face and legs, although he did not realise how it told the time.

Some questions to consider

Thinking about these questions (and perhaps writing notes or timed short answers) will be helpful when you revise for the examination, because you will have thought about the key ideas in this poem.

1. How does Fanthorpe's use of 'compound words' (made up for the poem) add to the effect of the poem?

2. When the child 'escaped' into a timeless world, to what extent do you feel that this was a happy experience for him?

3. Does Fanthorpe present the teacher and her actions in a sympathetic way?

4. Is it surprising that the child is supposed to have remembered this incident for a long time? Think about events in your childhood that have had a lasting memory and impact for you.

Top tip

vista: a view – here, the memories he has over the years

insidious: creeping up on you without your realising it

appassionato: an Italian musical term – played with passion

Key:
Repetition
Onomatopeia
Words connected to the past
Alliteration

Piano

Background and context

David Herbert (D H) Lawrence was born in 1885, in Eastwood, a coal-mining town in Nottinghamshire, where his father worked as a miner. He died in 1930, after being ill with tuberculosis for some time. He was devoted to his mother, who died of cancer when he was just 25, which had a deep effect on him. Although he is famous mainly for his novels, he wrote over 800 poems as well.

Softly, in the dusk, a woman is singing to me;
Taking me back down the vista* of years, till I see
A child sitting under the piano, in the boom of the tingling
  strings
And pressing the small, poised feet of a mother who smiles as she
  sings.

In spite of myself, the insidious* mastery of song
Betrays me back, till the heart of me weeps to belong
To the old Sunday evenings at home, with winter outside
And hymns in the cosy parlour, the tinkling piano our guide.

So now it is vain for the singer to burst into clamour
With the great black piano appassionato*. The glamour
Of childish days is upon me, my manhood is cast
Down in the flood of remembrance, I weep like a child for the
  past.

D H Lawrence

Understanding the text and commenting on the language

1. Think of how a particular event (listening as an adult to a solo singer and piano) has reminded the narrator of a memory about the past. You may wish to compare this with something that has taken you back to your own childhood, such as visiting a place you went to on holiday when you were young.

2. Look at the form of the poem, which has twelve lines in three equal length stanzas. Note also the rhythm, which consists mostly of **dactyls** (three syllables, a stressed one followed by two unstressed: tum-te-te) but sometimes **spondees** (two stressed syllables: tum-tum). There is a straightforward rhyme scheme (aa, bb...). Does the fact that this is a poem about memories of childhood make this simple form more appropriate? Look also at the way the content of the poem is set out in the three stanzas.

3. Select some key phrases from the poem, working with a partner if possible. These may:

- show how strong Lawrence's feelings are about his childhood with his mother

- focus on features of his language and its effect, including alliteration, onomatopoeia, metaphor and simile

- be words that seem to you striking or unusual and that convey Lawrence's ideas.

Some examples have been given to get you started.

Key ideas for links with other poems

1. In this course, and in particular in the examination or the coursework essay (Route 2), it is important to think about how different poets deal with similar ideas or themes. Fill in your grid, to help you link this poem with other poems.

2. The themes of this poem are mainly the memory of childhood and the love between a child and mother, and there is also the subject of the power of the senses (in this case, music) to create memories. There are two other poems in Section C of the Anthology (check that you know which they are) that focus on events in people's childhood, and others that look back into the past or that show a parent/child relationship. In 'War Photographer' it is a visual stimulus (a photograph) that evokes memories of a different place: there are some interesting links that could be explored here.

Figure 3.6 *'The tinkling piano'.*

Language	Comment on meaning/effect
'the boom of the tingling strings'	The use of onomatopoeia helps the reader to be able to use the senses to imagine the scene.
'And pressing the small, poised feet of a mother who smiles as she sings'	This tender line helps the reader to visualise the closeness between the child and mother – the young boy presses the mother's feet as she presses on the pedal of the piano.
'insidious mastery of song'	This makes it seem as if the music is like a powerful controller, which traps you into becoming a 'slave', so powerful is the song.

Some questions to consider

Thinking about these questions (and perhaps writing notes or timed short answers) will be helpful when you revise for the examination, because you will have thought about the key ideas in this poem.

1. How would you describe the tone of Lawrence's writing in this poem?

2. What is it about this memory that causes him to 'weep like a child'?

3. In what ways does Lawrence's use of sound reinforce the ideas of the poem? How do the other senses contribute to the overall effect (think especially of sight and touch)?

4. What impression does the poem give of Lawrence's early life? How does the fact that in adult life Lawrence had much unhappiness, especially over the death of his mother, make a difference to our understanding of the poem?

Hide and Seek

Background and context

Vernon Scannell was born in 1922 in Lincolnshire and died in ____ was a soldier in the Second World War, and afterwards did a variety of jobs, including working as a professional boxer, as well as being a well-known writer and poet. He wrote many poems about his wartime experiences.

Top tip

You can find out more about Scannell and his poetry from reference books or on the Internet. You could read some more of his poems, which will help you to understand Scannell's themes and ideas.

Call out. Call loud: 'I'm ready! Come and find me!'
The sacks in the toolshed smell like the seaside.
They'll never find you in this salty dark,
But be careful that your feet aren't sticking out.
Wiser not to risk another shout.
The floor is cold. They'll probably be searching
The bushes near the swing. Whatever happens
You mustn't sneeze when they come prowling in.
And here they are, whispering at the door;
You've never heard them sound so hushed before.
Don't breathe. Don't move. Stay dumb. Hide in your blindness.
They're moving closer, someone stumbles, mutters;
Their words and laughter scuffle, and they're gone.
But don't come out just yet; they'll try the lane
And then the greenhouse and back here again.
They must be thinking that you're very clever,
Getting more puzzled as they search all over.
It seems a long time since they went away.
Your legs are stiff, the cold bites through your coat;
The dark damp smell of sand moves in your throat.
It's time to let them know that you're the winner.
Push off the sacks. Uncurl and stretch. That's better!
Out of the shed and call to them: 'I've won!
Here I am! Come and own up I've caught you!'
The darkening garden watches. Nothing stirs.
The bushes hold their breath; the sun is gone.
Yes, here you are. But where are they who sought you?

Vernon Scannell

Scannell uses the senses, including touch and smell, to create the atmosphere of the child's hiding-place.

The use of personification of the weather perhaps suggests that even natural forces are against the child.

Key:
Repetition
Alliteration
Onomatopoeia
Personification
Commands

Understanding the text and commenting on the language

1. Think about how Scannell uses language to get inside the mind of the child who is hiding, and the stages he goes through. Think in particular about the ending of the poem and its effect.

2. Select some key phrases from the poem, working with a partner if possible. These may:

   ● add to the mounting tension in the poem

   ● focus on features of Scannell's language and its effect, especially his use of the senses

   ● be words that seem to you striking or unusual and that convey Scannell's ideas in an effective way.

   Some examples have been given to get you started.

Language	Comment on meaning/effect
'The bushes hold their breath'	This personification is effective: the natural surroundings are like watchers, waiting to see what happens when the emerging child discovers that he has been left.
'Call out. Call loud: "I'm ready! Come and find me!"'	This opening makes the readers feel they are actually taking part in a childhood game. In the first few words, you can almost hear the child shouting out excitedly.
'They'll never find you in this salty dark'	This gives a good impression of the child's hiding-place, with the senses of sight and taste brought into the description.

Key ideas for links with other poems

In this course, and in particular in the examination or the coursework essay (Route 2), it is important to think about how different poets deal with similar ideas or themes. Fill in your grid, to help you link this poem with other poems.

This poem about a childhood memory has obvious links with others in the collection, but especially perhaps 'Half-past Two' (see page 112), where the child is again isolated and inhabits a timeless world of the imagination. Think about the similarities and differences in how the two writers treat their subject.

Some questions to consider

Thinking about these questions (and perhaps writing notes or timed short answers) will be helpful when you revise for the examination, because you will have thought about the key ideas in this poem.

1. How does Vernon Scannell's language help the reader to see and feel the events that take place?

2. How does the ending come as a surprise – or doesn't it?

3. Why might such an experience have a great effect on the child who is the subject of the poem?

4. How would you describe the overall tone and mood of the poem? Make sure that you note points where these change, and show the different emotions of the child who hides.

Sonnet 116

Background and context

William Shakespeare was born in Stratford-upon-Avon in 1564 and died in 1616. He is Britain's most famous playwright, and his plays are still performed all over the world, having been translated into many languages. Not so many people know his poems, which included 154 sonnets. *The Sonnets* are poems on the theme of love, and some are written to particular people, such as the mysterious 'dark lady'. Sonnet 116 is one of the most popular of all the sonnets, because the ideas are thought by many people to show the strength of true love.

Top tip

You can find out more about Shakespeare and his poetry and plays from reference books or on the Internet. You could read some more of his poems and watch or study some of his plays, which will help you to understand Shakespeare's themes and attitudes, with love being a particularly common subject.

He is both thinking of marriage itself and also of two minds joined together in love.

Let **me** **not** to the **m**arriage of true **m**inds
Admit impediments; love is not love
Which alters when it alteration finds,
Or bends with the remover to remove.
O no, it is an ever-fixèd mark*
That looks on tempests and is never shaken;
It is the star to every wandering bark*,
Whose worth's unknown, although his height be taken.
Love's not Time's fool, though rosy lips and cheeks
Within his bending si**ck**le's **c**ompass **c**ome;
Love alters not with his brief hours and weeks,
But bears it out even to the edge of doom*.
If this be error and upon me proved,
I never writ, nor no man ever loved.

William Shakespeare

ever-fixèd mark: a beacon to guide ships

bark: an old word for a boat

doom: the end of time

Key:
Repetition
Words linked to sea travel
Negative words
Alliteration

Understanding the text and commenting on the language

1. Think about the way Shakespeare uses the sonnet form, of 14 lines. You may be able to do research into the differences between Shakespeare's sonnets and those in the 'Petrarchan' style, from the Italian poet Petrarch. Think about the way this sonnet is divided into three 'quatrains' (four-line stanzas) and ends with a rhyming couplet, which is a summing up of the poem. Notice the tight structure.

Figure 3.8 *'The marriage of true minds'.*

- Quatrain 1: Shakespeare starts by stating that true love will not change, according to his view.
- Quatrain 2: This presents a nautical metaphor for true love, which is seen to steer a path through a stormy sea guided by a fixed beacon or star.
- Quatrain 3: True love cannot be thrown off course by the passage of time or the fading of beauty. It lasts for ever, not changing even if we change physically.
- The final couplet: Shakespeare believes strongly in the truth of what he has written – because, if it is not true, he has never written anything, which, obviously, he has just done, and no one has ever loved, which again many people clearly have done.

2. Select some key phrases from the poem, working with a partner if possible. These may:

- show Shakespeare's thoughts about change and changelessness
- focus on features of his language and its effect, including his use of metaphors and personification
- be words that seem to you striking or unusual, perhaps because they seem old-fashioned; or they may convey Shakespeare's ideas in interesting ways.

Some examples have been given to get you started.

Key ideas for links with other poems

In this course, and in particular in the examination or the coursework essay (Route 2), it is important to think about how different poets deal with similar ideas or themes. Fill in your grid, to help you link this poem with other poems.

The central idea of this poem, that of love, is one that can be found in other poems in the Anthology, but love comes in many different forms and sometimes it does not last (see 'The Last Duchess' on page 132, for example). Other ideas you can find in poems in this section deal with the subject of the passing of time and the subject of change.

Language	Comment on meaning/effect
'Love's not Time's fool'	Love and Time are both personified, and Shakespeare is saying that Time cannot make a fool of Love.
'rosy lips and cheeks…'	These are the outward signs of beauty that are much admired. But they fade with time, unlike true love.
'O no'	This is a strong **exclamation**, which shows that he rejects strongly the idea that has just been stated.

Some questions to consider

Thinking about these questions (and perhaps writing notes or timed short answers) will be helpful when you revise for the examination, because you will have thought about the key ideas in this poem.

1. Think about how Shakespeare writes about changing and unchanging things. Why does he suggest that love is able to resist change?

2. Why do you think Shakespeare chooses to write about a (metaphorical) journey at sea? Think about the following:

- Shakespeare lived at a time of great sea adventures – Sir Francis Drake and Sir Walter Raleigh were his contemporaries.
- Sea travel was extremely dangerous and steering the right course was very difficult, without modern navigational aids.

3. How does Shakespeare use 'negative' language to develop the theme of the poem?

4. Why do you think Shakespeare believes that love can last for ever?

La Belle Dame sans Merci: A Ballad

Background and context

John Keats was born in 1795 and died at the young age of 26 in 1821 from tuberculosis. He trained as a surgeon but later gave up his training to concentrate on his poetry. He was one of the group of romantic poets writing at the same time as Wordsworth and Coleridge. He fell in love with Fanny Brawne but they never married. The ballad form displayed in the following poem was taken from the Middle Ages. Such ballads traditionally contained such themes as love and death. The title of the poem is taken from a French lyrical poem by the writer Alain Chartier, which Keats had read in translation and it means 'the beautiful lady without pity'.

Top tip

You can find out more about Keats and his poetry from reference books or on the Internet. You could read some more of the poems, which will help you to understand Keats and his poetry.

Repeated questions and old-fashioned language are typical of ballads.

*sedge: grasses in the marshland

*granary: a store

The harvest is over: life is fading. In contrast the fairy is 'full beautiful' and blooming.

*zone: belt

The rose, a symbol of beauty, contrasts with the lily, which is associated with death.

*steed: horse

O what can **ail** thee, knight-at-arms,
   Alone and **pal**ely **l**oitering?
The sedge* has withered from the lake,
   And no birds sing.

Oh what can ail thee, knight-at-arms,
   So ha**gg**ard and so woe-be**g**one?
The squirrel's **g**ranary* is full,
   And the harvest's done.

I see a lily on thy brow,
   With anguish moist and **f**ever-dew,
And on thy cheek a fading rose
   Fast withereth too.

I met a lady in the meads,
   Full beautiful — a **f**aery's child,
Her **h**air was long, **h**er **f**oot was light,
   And her eyes were wild.

I made a garland for her head,
   And bracelets too, and fragrant zone*;
She **l**ooked at me as she did **l**ove,
   And made sweet moan.

I set her on my pacing steed*,
   And nothing else **s**aw all day long,
For **s**idelong would she bend, and **s**ing
   A **f**aery's **s**ong.

She found me **r**oots of **r**elish sweet,
   And honey wild, and manna*-dew,
And **s**ure in language **s**trange **s**he **s**aid —
   'I **l**ove thee true'.

She took me to her elfin grot,
   And there she **w**ept and **s**ighed full **s**ore,
And there I shut her wild wild eyes
   With kisses **f**our.

And there she lullèd me asleep
   And there I dreamed — Ah! woe betide! —
The latest dream I ever dreamt
   On the cold hill side.

I saw **p**ale kings, and **p**rinces too,
   Pale warriors, death-**p**ale were they all;
They cried — 'La Belle Dame sans Merci
   Hath thee in thrall!'

I **s**aw their **s**tarved lips in the **g**loam*,
   With horrid warning **g**apèd wide,
And I awoke and found me here,
   On the cold hill's side.

And this is why I sojourn* here
   Alone and pa**l**ely **l**oitering,
Though the sedge is withered from the lake,
   And no birds sing.

John Keats

*manna: food from heaven

Links between the 'strangeness' and 'wildness' of the fairy.

The lack of colour and vibrancy is linked to the absence of bird song and the dying away of the seasons.

*gloam: twilight

*sojourn: remain

Key:
Alliteration
Repetition
Words relating to death or dying

Understanding the text and commenting on the language

1. Think about the near-repetition of the first stanza at the end (what is sometimes called ring composition). You will notice a slight change in the last line, and may feel this is important. You should focus also on the form of the poem, looking at the song-like stanzas with their regular pattern and rhyming of the second and fourth lines, with the short fourth line, where the heavy syllables seem very emphatic (for example, 'And no birds sing'). Note that the poem has the dramatic form of a conversation between an unknown passer-by, who speaks the first three stanzas and asks what is wrong, and the knight, who tells the story of his strange encounter. The poem is said by some readers to be about a 'femme fatale' – a woman whose power over men is fatal. Think about this explanation and see whether you agree.

2. Select some key phrases from the poem, working with a partner if possible. These may:

   - show the character of the knight or of the fairy visitor, and how he is 'enslaved' by her ('in thrall')

   - focus on features of the archaic use of language of Keats and its effect in creating a strange, bygone age

   - be words that seem to you striking or unusual and that convey the poet's ideas about love and death.

   Some examples have been given to get you started.

Key ideas for links with other poems

In this course, and in particular in the examination or the coursework essay (Route 2), it is important to think about how different poets deal with similar ideas or themes. Fill in your grid, to help you link this poem with other poems.

The main theme is that of love, which connects the poem with others in the collection, although the treatment of love is very different from the others. There is also a strong connection with death, which again connects it with some poems in the collection.

Figure 3.9 *'La Belle Dame sans Merci hath thee in thrall!'*

Language	Comment on meaning/effect
'I saw their starved lips in the gloom / With horrid warning gapèd wide'	This haunting image presumably refers to the open mouth of a corpse or skeleton.
'And no birds sing.'	This ending to the poem creates a sense of complete desolation and death. The sound of birds is such a universal, natural occurrence that their absence creates a chilling atmosphere. It was commented on, for example, by soldiers in the battlegrounds of the First World War.
'She found me roots of relish sweet / And honey wild'	The unusual food suggests that he is being put under her spell.

Some questions to consider

Thinking about these questions (and perhaps writing notes or timed short answers) will be helpful when you revise for the examination, because you will have thought about the key ideas in this poem.

1. There is a mystery about this strange lady who appears. What do we find out about her, and why does her appearance to the knight have such a powerful effect on him?

2. The knight admits that he has received warnings about the lady, but he does not seem to have taken heed. Why is this?

3. How do the structure and form of the poem contribute to its effect?

4. Many aspects of the poem seem mysterious, and readers have disagreed over how to interpret it. Comment on what the poem means to you.

Poem at Thirty-Nine

Background and context

Top tip

You can find out more about Alice Walker and her poetry from reference books or on the Internet. You could read some more of her poems, which will help you to understand Walker and her poetry.

Alice Walker is an African-American who was born in 1944. Her writing of poems and novels about her family background especially has been greatly admired. The best known of her works is the novel *The Color Purple,* winner of the Pulitzer Prize for Fiction in 1983 (the year when she was 39, and about seven years after her father's death). This was also made into a very successful film. In the 1960s, she was linked to the civil rights movement in the United States, with its charismatic leader Martin Luther King.

How I miss my father.
I wish he had not been
so tired
when I was
born.
Writing deposit slips and checks
I think of him.

He taught me how.
This is the form,
he must have said:
the way it is done.
I learned to see
bits of paper
as a way
to escape
the life he knew
and even in high school
had a savings
account.

He taught me
that telling the truth
did not always mean
a beating;
though many of my truths
must have grieved him
before the end.

How I miss my father!
He cooked like a person
dancing
in a yoga meditation
and craved the voluptuous
sharing
of good food.

Now I look and cook just like him:
my brain light;
tossing this and that
into the pot;
seasoning none of my life
the same way twice; happy to feed
whoever strays my way.

He would have grown
to admire
the woman I've become:
cooking, writing, chopping wood,
staring into the fire.

Alice Walker

This simile suggests that her father was both excited and at the same time completely absorbed in what he was doing when he cooked.

Because her father had had little education, he was determined that education would be the way out of poverty for Alice.

Key:

Repetition

Words on writing and accounts

Words on cooking

Understanding the text and commenting on the language

1. Find out more about Alice Walker and about the history of African-American people that is so important for her writing. Using this information, think about ways in which the difficulties of her childhood might be relevant to your understanding of this poem.

2. Select some key phrases from the poem, working with a partner if possible. These may:

   - show aspects of her personality and relationship with her father

   - focus on features of Walker's language and its effect, particularly where this has been highlighted in the text

   - pick out the effect of words that seem to you striking or unusual and that convey Walker's ideas.

   Some examples have been given to get you started.

Language	Comment on meaning/effect
'How I miss my father'	This line, which is repeated for emphasis, expresses clearly and simply the idea running through the poem. It is stated without spare words, and this makes the feelings all the more powerful.
'cooked like a person / dancing / in a yoga meditation'	This is an unusual simile, with the one-word line 'dancing' a surprising word in the context; however, this is no ordinary dancing: people in yoga meditations are often completely still.
'the voluptuous / sharing'	The word 'voluptuous' is a word suggesting rich, sensuous pleasures: it comes as a surprise because most of the language is deliberately plain and simple.

Key ideas for links with other poems

In this course, and in particular in the examination or the coursework essay (Route 2), it is important to think about how different poets deal with similar ideas or themes. Fill in your grid, to help you link this poem with other poems.

The main theme explored in this poem is the parent and child relationship, in this case a very personal memory by the daughter of her growing up and learning from her father. Other relationships are focused on in several poems, but perhaps the poem that links most naturally with this one is Dylan Thomas' poem addressed to his own father (see page 136).

Figure 3.10 *'How I miss my father'.*

Some questions to consider

Thinking about these questions (and perhaps writing notes or timed short answers) will be helpful when you revise for the examination, because you will have thought about the key ideas in this poem.

1. Why do you think Alice Walker chose this particular title – does the age of 39 have some significance, perhaps?

2. Discuss the part played in this poem by the ideas of writing, accounts and cooking (look at the words that have been given purple or red highlights); think about what the method of cooking tells us about her and her father's attitudes to life.

3. What do we learn about the relationship between the writer and her father – what signs can you find of problems in their lives and what did she learn from him?

4. What effect has reading this poem had on you? Can you suggest why it has had this effect?

Top tip

You can find out more about Soyinka and his poetry and other writings from reference books or on the Internet. You could read some more of his poems, which will help you to understand Soyinka and his poetry.

It has been suggested that the word 'indifferent' is used as a pun, as it can both mean 'neither very good nor very bad' or 'neutral, not biased' – which turns out to be untrue because it is clearly an area where people can be very prejudiced against different races.

Button A: buttons that had to be pressed when using a telephone in a public booth. Such telephones are no longer in use.

He suggests that the landlady was running through all the different shades (like the colours on a paint chart) in her imagination.

Key:

Repetition

Word connected with colour

Alliteration

Assonance

Telephone Conversation

Background and context

Wole Soyinka was born in 1934 in Western Nigeria, and is still alive. He has written poetry, plays and fiction, and won the Nobel Prize for Literature in 1986. He came to England as a young man in the late 1950s, and the events in 'Telephone Conversation' relate to this period, when there were no laws to prevent landlords from discriminating against different ethnic groups when renting out houses or flats, as there are now.

The price seemed reasonable, location
Indifferent. The landlady swore she lived
Off premises. Nothing remained
But self-confession. "Madam", I warned,
"I hate a wasted journey — I am African."
Silence. Silenced transmission of
Pressurized good-breeding. Voice, when it came,
Lipstick coated, long gold-rolled
Cigarette-holder pipped. Caught I was, foully.
"HOW DARK?"...I had not misheard. ..."ARE YOU LIGHT
OR VERY DARK?" Button B. Button A*. Stench
Of rancid breath of public hide-and-speak.
Red booth. Red pillar-box. Red double-tiered
Omnibus squelching tar. It was real! Shamed
By ill-mannered silence, surrender
Pushed dumbfoundment to beg simplification.
Considerate she was, varying the emphasis —
"ARE YOU DARK? OR VERY LIGHT?" Revelation came.
"You mean — like plain or milk chocolate?"
Her accent was clinical, crushing in its light
Impersonality. Rapidly, wave-length adjusted,
I chose. "West African sepia" — and as afterthought,
"Down in my passport." Silence for spectroscopic
Flight of fancy, till truthfulness changed her accent
Hard on the mouthpiece. "WHAT'S THAT?" conceding
"DON'T KNOW WHAT THAT IS." "Like brunette."
"THAT'S DARK, ISN'T IT?" "Not altogether.
Facially, I am brunette, but madam, you should see
The rest of me. Palm of my hand, soles of my feet
Are a peroxide blond. Friction, caused —
Foolishly madam — by sitting down, has turned
My bottom raven black — One moment madam!" — sensing
Her receiver rearing on the thunderclap
About my ears — "Madam," I pleaded, "wouldn't you rather
See for yourself?"

Wole Soyinka

Understanding the text and commenting on the language

1. Think about the time this poem refers to, over 50 years ago, and about ways in which attitudes to different people have changed in Britain over this period. For example, the law now makes discrimination illegal at work or if you are renting a house, for example.

   You should also ask yourself whether, despite these changes, there are still examples of prejudice in our society – think about any instances you have come across.

2. Think about how poets sometimes use irony as a way of adding humour (words not having their usual meaning, or being used in a mocking way, for example). Find examples of irony in this poem.

3. Select some key phrases from the poem, working with a partner if possible. These may:

   - show how Soyinka portrays the landlady (looking at the contribution of irony)

   - focus on features of Soyinka's language and its effect, especially the language of colour

   - pick out the effect of words that seem to you striking or unusual and which convey Soyinka's ideas about how he feels about being rejected as a tenant.

   Some examples have been given to get you started.

Key ideas for links with other poems

In this course, and in particular in the examination or the coursework essay (Route 2), it is important to think about how different poets deal with similar ideas or themes. Fill in your grid, to help you link this poem with other poems.

The poem is mainly about prejudice and discrimination, but it also about how people sometimes learn hard lessons from their experience.

Figure 3.11 *Old-fashioned telephone box.*

Language	Comment on meaning/effect
'long, gold-rolled / Cigarette holder'	This is very striking language: the writer is imagining, as he speaks on the telephone, what the woman is like from the sound of her voice.
'has turned / My bottom raven black'	This comical exaggeration shows that the woman's reaction has made Soyinka desperate.
'Stench / Of rancid breath of public hide-and-speak'	This is unusual language, partly because of the punning phrase 'hide-and-speak', which may mean that the woman is speaking but hiding her real feelings. The reference to rancid breath may be because a telephone booth may have a bad smell, or he may again imagine that the woman has bad breath, either literally or as a metaphor.

Some questions to consider

Thinking about these questions (and perhaps writing notes or timed short answers) will be helpful when you revise for the examination, because you will have thought about the key ideas in this poem.

1. To what extent do you feel that Soyinka comes across as bitter in this poem? Why?

2. How does the humour in the poem help the reader to explore the poem's themes?

3. Why does the poem concentrate so much on different shades of colour?

4. How much sympathy do you have for (i) the writer and (ii) the character of the landlady? Why?

Once Upon a Time

Background and context

Top tip

You can find out more about Okara and his poetry from reference books or on the Internet. You could read some more of his poems, which will help you to understand Okara and his poetic ideas.

Like Wole Soyinka, Gabriel Okara was born in Nigeria. Okura was born in 1921, and has written both novels and poetry, for which he won the Commonwealth Prize in 1979. He writes about aspects of African society and Western society, and contrasts between his traditional way of life and life in the West provide an important context in 'Once Upon a Time'.

This is a simile in effect: their eyes were as cold as a block of ice.

Once upon a time, son,
they used to laugh with their hearts
and laugh with their eyes;
but now they only laugh with their teeth,
while their ice-block-cold eyes
search behind my shadow.

There was a time indeed
they used to shake hands with their hearts;
but that's gone, son.
Now they shake hands without hearts
while their left hands search
my empty pockets.

'Feel at home'! 'Come again';
they say, and when I come
again and feel
at home, once, twice,
there will be no thrice—
for then I find doors shut on me.

So I have learned many things, son.
I have learned to wear many faces
like dresses—homeface,
officeface, streetface, hostface,
cocktailface, with all their conforming smiles
like a fixed portrait smile.

And I have learned, too,
to laugh with only my teeth
and shake hands without my heart.
I have also learned to say, 'Goodbye',
when I mean 'Good-riddance';
to say 'Glad to meet you',
without being glad; and to say 'It's been
nice talking to you', after being bored.

But believe me, son.
I want to be what I used to be
when I was like you. I want
to unlearn all these muting things.
Most of all, I want to relearn
how to laugh, for my laugh in the mirror
shows only my teeth like a snake's bare fangs!

So show me, son,
how to laugh; show me how
I used to laugh and smile
once upon a time when I was like you.

Gabriel Okara

Because he is used to people saying what they mean, he is not used to the idea that when people in Western countries say 'Come again' they are often only being 'polite' and don't really mean it.

Things that silence his true personality.

The writer regrets that he has found himself adopting the insincere social conventions of the West.

Key:
Repetition
Compound words

Understanding the text and commenting on the language

1. Think about the writer's use of the '**dramatic monologue**' form, and whether this is likely to be a 'real' conversation between father and son. Why does the writer use a simple, one-syllable vocabulary with much repetition? Think about this effect of this. Who are the 'they'?

2. Select some key phrases from the poem, working with a partner if possible. These may:

   ● show what he is really unhappy about in Western society

   ● focus on features of Okara's simple, direct language and its effect (including the use of compound words)

   ● pick out the effect of words that seem to you striking or unusual and that convey Okara's ideas.

   Some examples have been given to get you started.

Language	Comment on meaning/effect
'like a snake's bare fangs'	He chooses a simile that perhaps recalls the dangerous snakes of Africa; the simile shows that he does not like what he sees in the mirror.
'conforming smiles'	These are smiles people wear because they want to fit in with society.
'search / my empty pockets'	He does not trust these people, who he thinks may try to rob him although he is poor.

Key ideas for links with other poems

In this course, and in particular in the examination or the coursework essay (Route 2), it is important to think about how different poets deal with similar ideas or themes. Fill in your grid, to help you link this poem with other poems.

An interesting link is with 'Half-past Two (see page 112)', where the writer also uses compound words; in this poem, they are made up from the word 'face', whereas in 'Half-past Two' they are based on 'time'. The themes of growing older and changing are connected to the father/son relationship, so there are a number of links to other poems in the collection. Think also about the 'clash of cultures' between African society and the West.

Figure 3.12 *'they used to shake hands with their hearts'.*

Some questions to consider

Thinking about these questions (and perhaps writing notes or timed short answers) will be helpful when you revise for the examination, because you will have thought about the key ideas in this poem.

1. What is the importance in the poem of the frequent references to the face and the heart, and the relationship between them? Think about how we call someone 'two-faced' if they are not trustworthy.

2. Think about the title and opening line, which give us the standard opening of a fairytale. Why do you think Okara has chosen these words? Think carefully about the tone.

3. Does this poem make you feel sympathy towards the father? Why?

4. Do you feel that the final four lines are positive, or is there a sense of hopelessness?

Top tip

You can find out more about Duffy and her poetry from reference books or on the Internet. You could read some more of her poems, which will help you to understand Duffy and her poetry.

War Photographer

Background and context

Carol Ann Duffy was born in 1955 and is one of Britain's most celebrated poets. She became the first female Poet Laureate in 2009: this is a post that has been held by many famous poets over the years. A close friend of Duffy was Don McCullin, one of the best known of all war photographers. His pictures have created some powerful images of the suffering that war can cause.

In his darkroom he is finally alone
with spools of suffering set out in ordered rows.
The only light is red and softly glows,
as though this were a church and he
a priest preparing to intone a Mass*.
Belfast. Beirut. Phnom Penh. All flesh is grass.

He has a job to do. Solutions slop in trays
beneath his hands, which did not tremble then
though seem to now. Rural England. Home again
to ordinary pain which simple weather can dispel,
to fields which don't explode beneath the feet
of running children in a nightmare heat.

Something is happening. A stranger's features
faintly start to twist before his eyes,
a half-formed ghost. He remembers the cries
of this man's wife, how he sought approval
without words to do what someone must
and how the blood stained into foreign dust.

A hundred agonies in black-and-white
from which his editor will pick out five or six
for Sunday's supplement*. The reader's eyeballs prick
with tears between the bath and pre-lunch beers.
From the aeroplane he stares impassively* at where
he earns his living and they do not care.

Carol Ann Duffy

These are all capital cities that have suffered greatly from the effects of war.

*Mass: a religious service

These words come from the Bible, so there is a link to the previous line.

There are famous photos from the Vietnam War showing such scenes.

Black-and-white photographs are often thought to be the most powerful for images of war. Also, the phrase is used to mean 'with no room for doubt: clear-cut'.

This phrase recalls the famous war poem by Rupert Brooke, 'The Soldier': 'a corner of some foreign field that is for ever England'.

*Sunday's supplement: a regular additional magazine section placed in a Sunday newspaper

*impassively: without feeling

Key:
Repetition
Alliteration
Words linked to colour
Simile

Understanding the text and commenting on the language

1. Try to find some of Don McCullin's photographs of children running from bomb attacks in the Vietnam War.

2. Think about the idea of people reading the Sunday papers. Does Carol Ann Duffy think that they are affected deeply by what they read and see in them?

   Select some key phrases from the poem, working with a partner if possible. These may:

   ● show how Duffy portrays the scene in the darkroom

   ● focus on features of her language and its effect in creating powerful and disturbing images

   ● pick out the effect of words that seem to you striking or unusual and that convey Duffy's ideas about the work of the photographer or about our reactions to human suffering.

   Some examples have been given to get you started.

Figure 3.13 *A war photographer.*

Key ideas for links with other poems

In this course, and in particular in the examination or the coursework essay (Route 2), it is important to think about how different poets deal with similar ideas or themes. Fill in your grid, to help you link this poem with other poems.

The theme of war is of course central, but there is also the subject of human suffering and how different people respond to it. The poem also makes a strong comment on people's attitudes and uses contrasts and religious imagery.

Language	Comment on meaning/effect
'between the bath and pre-lunch beers'	This phrase gives the idea that people in England have a set routine on Sunday morning (despite the first stanza, going to church does not seem to come into it).
'Solutions slop in trays'	Through the use of alliteration and the onomatopoeic 'slop', you can hear the sound of the liquid used to develop the photos.
'he earns his living and they do not care'	This is a very simple but effective ending. We are left wondering who are the 'they' – his employers or the readers, perhaps? We are also made to think what is it that 'they' don't care about: it could be about the war, or people's suffering or about how he makes his living.

Some questions to consider

Thinking about these questions (and perhaps writing notes or timed short answers) will be helpful when you revise for the examination, because you will have thought about the key ideas in this poem.

1. How does a photograph compare with a 'picture' in words?

2. How do you think the photographer chooses five or six pictures from all those he has taken? What do you think his editor is looking for?

3. How effectively does the writer use contrasts between England and the war zone?

4. How well do you feel that you understand the thoughts and feelings (or lack of them) shown by the photographer?

5. What do you think that the overall message of the poem is? What does Duffy want us to feel about her subject?

Top tip

You can find out more about Blake and his poetry and art from reference books or on the Internet. You could read some more of the poems, which will help you to understand the way Blake thought about his poetry.

The Tyger

Background and context

William Blake was born in London in 1757 and died in 1827, spending most of his life in London, which was the subject of some of his writing. He was an unusual individual and also a talented artist. He produced two sets of poems, which presented strong contrasts: *Songs of Innocence* and *Songs of Experience*. The *Songs of Innocence* include one of his best-loved poems, 'The Lamb', and they show the wonder of childhood. In *Songs of Experience*, the child has grown up into a more suspicious and fearful world, and 'The Tyger' is very different from 'The Lamb', to which Blake actually makes reference in the final line of the next-to-last stanza of 'The Tyger'.

Tyger is simply an old-fashioned spelling of 'tiger'.

Notice how many questions there are. They are addressed, strictly speaking, to the tiger, but may be seen as rhetorical, as no answer is expected.

Did he who made the Lamb make thee?: God

Notice the repetition of the first stanza, with one change. Can you suggest why Blake has done this?

Key:
Repetition
Industrial language
Alliteration

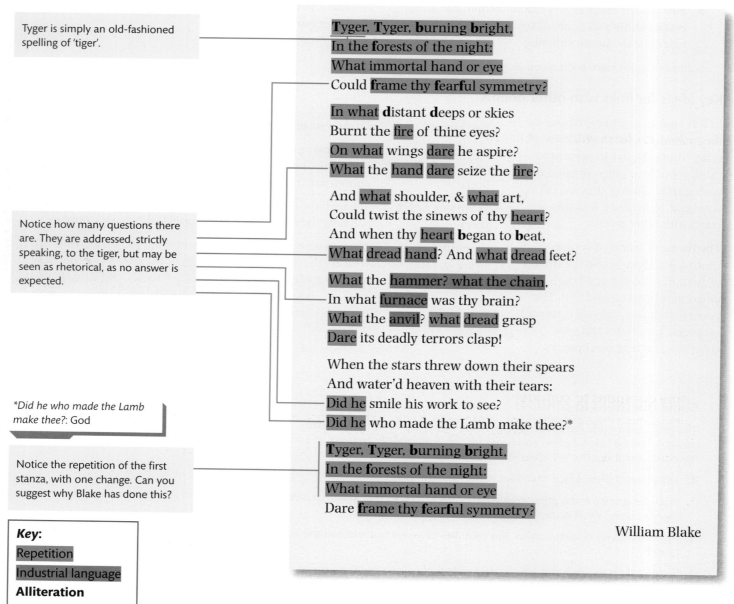

Tyger, Tyger, burning bright,
In the forests of the night:
What immortal hand or eye
Could frame thy fearful symmetry?

In what distant deeps or skies
Burnt the fire of thine eyes?
On what wings dare he aspire?
What the hand dare seize the fire?

And what shoulder, & what art,
Could twist the sinews of thy heart?
And when thy heart began to beat,
What dread hand? And what dread feet?

What the hammer? what the chain,
In what furnace was thy brain?
What the anvil? what dread grasp
Dare its deadly terrors clasp!

When the stars threw down their spears
And water'd heaven with their tears:
Did he smile his work to see?
Did he who made the Lamb make thee?*

Tyger, Tyger, burning bright,
In the forests of the night:
What immortal hand or eye
Dare frame thy fearful symmetry?

William Blake

Understanding the text and commenting on the language

1. You may be able to look at some of Blake's paintings of humans or animals and notice the way in which he focuses closely on the muscles and sinews of his subjects.

2. Think about the idea of creation in this poem and what kind of creator Blake imagines would be capable of making the tiger. Does he seem to believe that the same creator is able to be responsible for both the lamb and the tiger?

3. Select some key phrases from the poem, working with a partner if possible. These may:

   - show the process of creating the tiger

   - focus on features of Blake's language and its effect, such as the use of repetition, questions and alliteration

   - pick out the effect of striking or unusual words to describe the tiger.

   Some examples have been given to get you started.

Figure 3.14 *The Tyger.*

Key ideas for links with other poems

In this course, and in particular in the examination or the coursework essay (Route 2), it is important to think about how different poets deal with similar ideas or themes. Fill in your grid, to help you link this poem with other poems.

The subject-matter of 'The Tyger' is very different from most poems in this section of the Anthology. However, there are other poems that deal with the themes of creation, power and strength, and that describe violent actions. Use these ideas as a basis for making links between poems.

Language	Comment on meaning/effect
'began to beat'	The alliteration seems effective here because the 'b' represents the sound of the beating of the heart.
'What dread hand? And what dread feet?'	The repetition in these two short questions show that the different parts of the creator's body are thought of as inspiring a feeling of fear and dread.
'burning bright / In the forests of the night'	The tiger is shown to be a fiery figure shining through the forests, which are seen as dark.

Some questions to consider

Thinking about these questions (and perhaps writing notes or timed short answers) will be helpful when you revise for the exam, because you will have thought about the key ideas in this poem.

1. How does Blake bring out the idea that creating the tiger must have been a very difficult process?

2. What is the effect of the use of language from industry? (This was the time of the Industrial Revolution in Britain.)

3. Read the poem 'The Lamb', from *Songs of Innocence*, which is paired by Blake with 'The Tyger', and then compare the two poems.

4. Think about the strong rhythm (it is what is known as 'trochaic', with a heavy, stressed beat followed by a light, unstressed one: tum-te, tum-te, tum-te, tum) and the regular rhyme scheme in the poem. How do these help to create the effect of the poem?

5. You have seen how Blake asks a large number of questions in the poem. What do you feel this questioning tone adds to the sense of the poem?

My Last Duchess

Background and context

Robert Browning was born in London in 1812 and died in 1889. Many of his poems were on the theme of love, but if readers expect 'My Last Duchess' to be a conventional love story, they are in for a surprise. Browning started writing poetry when very young but his early efforts did not find a publisher. His many poems include the famous narrative poem 'The Pied Piper of Hamelin' and many of his poems, including 'My Last Duchess', are '**dramatic monologues**' in which one person talks to another. He was married to Elizabeth Barrett Browning, who was herself a famous writer. They lived for a long time in Italy, where 'My Last Duchess' is set, and Browning died in his son's home in Venice.

Top tip

You can find out more about Browning and his poetry from reference books or on the Internet. You could read some more of his poems, which will help you to understand Browning and his poetry.

That's my last Duchess painted on the wall,
Looking as if she were alive. I call
That piece a wonder, now: Frà Pandolf's hands
Worked busily a day, and there she stands.
Will't please you sit and look at her? I said
'Frà Pandolf' by design, for never read
Strangers like you that pictured countenance,
The depth and passion of its earnest glance,
But to myself they turned (since none puts by
The curtain I have drawn for you, but I)
And seemed as they would ask me, if they durst,
How such a glance came there; so, not the first
Are you to turn and ask thus. Sir, 'twas not
Her husband's presence only, called that spot
of joy into the Duchess' cheek: perhaps
Frà Pandolf chanced to say 'Her mantle laps
Over my lady's wrist too much,' or 'Paint
Must never hope to reproduce the faint
Half-flush that dies along her throat': such stuff
Was courtesy, she thought, and cause enough
For calling up that spot of joy. She had
A heart — how shall I say? — too soon made glad,
Too easily impressed; she liked whate'er
She looked on, and her looks went everywhere.
Sir, 'twas all one! My favour* at her breast,
The dropping of the daylight in the West,
The bough of cherries some officious fool
Broke in the orchard for her, the white mule

She rode with round the terrace — all and each
Would draw from her alike the approving speech,
Or blush, at least. She thanked men, — good! but thanked
Somehow — I know not how — as if she ranked
My gift of a nine-hundred-years-old name
With anybody's gift. Who'd stoop to blame
This sort of trifling? Even had you skill
In speech — (which I have not) — to make your will
Quite clear to such an one, and say, 'Just this
Or that in you disgusts me; here you miss,
Or there exceed the mark' — and if she let
Herself be lessoned so, nor plainly set
Her wits to yours, forsooth*, and made excuse,
— E'en then would be some stooping; and I choose
Never to stoop. Oh sir, she smiled, no doubt,
Whene'er I passed her; but who passed without
Much the same smile? This grew; I gave commands;
Then all smiles stopped together. There she stands
As if alive. Will't please you rise? We'll meet
The company below, then. I repeat,
The Count your master's known munificence
Is ample warrant that no just pretence
Of mine for dowry will be disallowed;
Though his fair daughter's self, as I avowed
At starting, is my object. Nay, we'll go
Together down, sir. Notice Neptune, though,
Taming a sea-horse, thought a rarity,
Which Claus of Innsbruck cast in bronze for me!

Robert Browning

Annotations:

He calls the painting 'a wonder'; think about whether he also thought the real woman was a 'wonder'.

Not a real painter, it is thought. 'Fra' suggests a Friar in the Catholic Church.

Note how Browning describes the colour on her face in the painting and as she was in real life. What does he think about this colour?

What might the Duke be trying to say here about what the Duchess 'looked on'?

*favour: a gift, such as a jewel, perhaps

Notice the Duke's pride in his long family history.

*forsooth: in truth (archaic)

Again, probably not a real sculptor; the name is meant to sound impressive.

Neptune: the Roman god of the sea. Does the Duke see himself as a god, taming his wives?

He will never 'stoop'; he expects her always to bend to his will and defer to him – it has to be that way round: this is perhaps her worst 'offence'.

Key:
Repetition
Use of caesura
colour/painting words

Understanding the text and commenting on the language

1. Think about the way in which the 'dramatic monologue' is used in this poem. You should consider both the speaker and the man being spoken to. The speaker is Alfonso II d'Este, the fifth Duke of the Italian city of Ferrara and he is speaking to a representative from the Count of Tyrol. The 'last duchess' is the daughter of Cosimo I de' Medici, Lucrezia de' Medici. The Medicis were a powerful, rich family, but lacked a 'nine-hundred-years-old name' (line 33). The poem is set in the period between 1561 (when Lucrezia died) and 1565 (the Duke's second marriage).

2. Select some key phrases from the poem, working with a partner if possible. These may:

   - show aspects of the Duke's character or give his views about the 'Last Duchess'

   - focus on features of Browning's language and its effect, including his use of archaic (old-fashioned) words or phrases

   - pick out the effect of words that seem to you striking or unusual and that show Browning's ideas about his characters effectively.

   Some examples have been given to get you started.

Key ideas for links with other poems

In this course, and in particular in the examination or the coursework essay (Route 2), it is important to think about how different poets deal with similar ideas or themes. Fill in your grid, to help you link this poem with other poems.

Language	Comment on meaning/effect
'a nine-hundred-years-old name'	This shows how much importance the Duke put on coming from a long-established family, which he thinks the Duchess needed to respect much more, compared with everyone else.
'I gave commands'	This phrase seems deliberately vague – we don't even know who he gave the commands to, but it does sound ominous, especially with the pause (caesura) after it.
'The Count your master's known munificence...'	The language here seems very pompous and formal, emphasising that he is thinking of this marriage entirely as a business contract.

This is a poem that focuses on the marriage of a Duke and Duchess, and on the theme of marriage more generally, as the Duke is now looking to arrange another marriage, to the Count's daughter. There is reference to the idea of men seeing women as objects or possessions. It also explores a number of aspects of character, in his case the ideas of jealousy, selfishness and pride. You may be able to compare the way Browning uses the dramatic monologue form with other poems from Section C of the Anthology.

Some questions to consider

Thinking about these questions (and perhaps writing notes or timed short answers) will be helpful when you revise for the examination, because you will have thought about the key ideas in this poem.

1. What is the effect on the reader of the opening line? Does it suggest that the Duke had warm feelings towards the Duchess?

2. It is said that part of Browning's skill is to make the Duke reveal much more about himself than he intends. Can you find places in the poem where this happens?

3. What do you notice about the tone of the last ten lines of the poem (47–56)? What is the effect of the ending?

4. Look at the ways Browning uses the rhyme (rhyming couplets) and rhythm (iambic pentameter). Consider also how he uses **enjambement** in this poem, with very few end-stopped lines. (You can tell this immediately by the lack of punctuation at the end of most lines, which flow into each other.)

5. Do you think that Browning wanted us to believe that the Duke had his wife murdered? Find evidence for your view.

Top tip

You can find out more about Achebe and his poetry and novels from reference books or on the Internet. You could read some more of his poems or try his books, which will help you to understand how Achebe thinks about society and its problems.

A Mother in a Refugee Camp

Background and context

Chinua Achebe was born in 1930 in Nigeria and is still alive. He is most famous for his novel *Things Fall Apart*, and is one of a number of Nigerian poets whose work features in this collection. Nigeria suffered a particularly violent civil war between different tribal groups in the 1960s, and this had a great effect on many of these writers. The scene from the refugee camp is clearly in Africa, but it could be found in many countries and different times. For example, the famine in Ethiopia in the 1990s came to the attention of people in the West particularly through the LiveAid campaign.

The Madonna and Child are Mary and her son Jesus, who are represented in many religious paintings, and are seen as a symbol of love and peace.

This refers to the condition of babies whose stomachs are blown out from their bodies, not because of being overweight, but because they are starving.

This shows her care and tenderness.

Note the musical use of 'humming', suggesting the burning vibration of tears in her eyes. This gentle action is the emotional centre of the poem.

Key:
Repetition
Alliteration
Words connected to suffering
Words connected to feeling

No Madonna and Child could touch
Her tenderness for a son
She soon would have to forget. . . .
The air was heavy with odors of diarrhea,
Of unwashed children with washed-out ribs
And dried-up bottoms waddling in labored steps
Behind blown-empty bellies. Other mothers there
Had long ceased to care, but not this one:
She held a ghost-smile between her teeth,
And in her eyes the memory
Of a mother's pride. . . . She had bathed him
And rubbed him down with bare palms.
She took from their bundle of possessions
A broken comb and combed
The rust-colored hair left on his skull
And then—humming in her eyes—began carefully to part it.
In their former life this was perhaps
A little daily act of no consequence
Before his breakfast and school; now she did it
Like putting flowers on a tiny grave.

Chinua Achebe

Note the American spelling of 'odors' 'diarrhea' 'labored' and 'colored'. (English spellings: odours, diarrhoea, laboured and coloured.)

Understanding the text and commenting on the language

1. Think about the way Achebe begins with a powerful religious idea. It may be helpful to study some images of the Madonna and Child like that on the right and reflect on what ideas these images create for you.

2. Select some key phrases from the poem, working with a partner if possible. These may:

   - show Achebe's feelings towards the mother and child

   - focus on features of his language and its effect in creating physical description and the mother's love

   - be words that seem to you striking or unusual and that convey Achebe's ideas about the conditions he had witnessed at the camp.

   Some examples have been given to get you started.

Figure 3.15 *Madonna and Child.*

Language	Comment on meaning/effect
'rust-colored hair'	The word 'rust' is effective because it combines a clear visual image of reddish-brown hair with the idea of 'decay', as in rusty metal.
'Like putting flowers on a tiny grave'	The simile is a powerful one, because it brings the idea of death into sharp focus at the end of the poem.
'She held a ghost-smile between her teeth'	This is another place where the idea of death cannot be avoided; the smile is faint as the child is close to death, with the 'ghost-smile' bringing to mind the idea of a skull, perhaps.

Key ideas for links with other poems

In this course, and in particular in the examination or the coursework essay (Route 2), it is important to think about how different poets deal with similar ideas or themes. Fill in your grid, to help you link this poem with other poems.

This is another of the poems in the Anthology that focuses on a parent and child relationship. It also fits into a group of poems that deal with pain, suffering and death.

Some questions to consider

Thinking about these questions (and perhaps writing notes or timed short answers) will be helpful when you revise for the examination, because you will have thought about the key ideas in this poem.

1. How does Achebe build up a strong picture of the scene at the camp?

2. How does the imagery used by Achebe contribute to the tone and mood of the poem?

3. What is the significance of the references to washing in the poem?

4. What impression does the reader receive of the refugee camp and those in it?

5. How did reading this poem affect you?

Do not go gentle into that good night

Background and context

Dylan Thomas was born in Swansea, South Wales in 1914, just after the start of the First World War, and died in New York, in November 1953, aged just 39. He was buried in Wales. Although he is considered a great Welsh poet, he wrote almost all of his works in English; he had a love of words and sounds, and wrote in a very musical way, enjoying such devices as rhythm, alliteration and assonance.

Top tip

You can find out more about Thomas and his poetry and other writing from reference books or on the Internet. You could read some more of his poems, which will help you to understand Thomas and his poetry.

Do not go gentle into that good night,
Old age should burn and rave at close of day;
Rage, rage against the dying of the light.

Though wise men at their end know dark is right,
Because their words had forked no lightning they
Do not go gentle into that good night.

Good men, the last wave by, crying how bright
Their frail deeds might have danced in a green bay,
Rage, rage against the dying of the light.

Wild men who caught and sang the sun in flight,
And learn, too late, they grieved it on its way,
Do not go gentle into that good night.

Grave men, near death, who see with blinding sight
Blind eyes could blaze like meteors and be gay,
Rage, rage against the dying of the light.

And you, my father, there on the sad height,
Curse, bless, me now with your fierce tears, I pray.
Do not go gentle into that good night.
Rage, rage against the dying of the light.

Dylan Thomas

The wise men may feel that they have not said or written things that have a dramatic impact, but they should not abandon hope of doing so.

Notice the pun on 'grave men' – men who are serious and are going to the grave.

Key:
Repetition
Personification
Alliteration
Rhyme

Understanding the text and commenting on the language

1. Think about the form of the poem, which is a villanelle, a form that always has nineteen lines, with a fixed rhythm (iambic pentameter: five metrical 'feet', each te-tum) and rhyme scheme. There are five groups of three lines (tercets) with a final quatrain (four lines – an extra line after the sixth tercet, which rhymes with the previous line. The scheme is: a, b, a; a, b, a; a, b, a; a, b, a; a, b, a; a, b, a, a. Note that the pattern is based on the idea of alternating night and day.

When Dylan Thomas' father was in his eighties, he became blind and weak. The poet is therefore trying to persuade him to remain strong and fight against death, keeping an energetic hold on life.

2. Select some key phrases from the poem, working with a partner if possible. These may:

- be taken from the repeated lines, analysing the effect of the repetition

- focus on features of Thomas' language and its effect in presenting his 'advice' to his dying father

- pick out the effect of words that seem to you striking or unusual and that convey Thomas' ideas about approaching death.

Some examples have been given to get you started.

Key ideas for links with other poems

In this course, and in particular in the examination or the coursework essay (Route 2), it is important to think about how different poets deal with similar ideas or themes. Fill in your grid, to help you link this poem with other poems.

Language	Comment on meaning/effect
'Blind eyes could blaze like meteors'	This is a striking simile because normally you would not expect blind eyes to be 'fiery' in this way: 'meteors' suggest objects that have a really powerful impact.
'there on the sad height'	His father is placed by Thomas in a high place, perhaps his deathbed, showing him being separated from the world of the living. Note that it is the poet who is really sad, not the place where his father is dying.
'frail deeds might have danced in a green bay'	This use of personification of the deeds suggests that, even though physically frail, it is possible, metaphorically, to dance. The green of the sea is suggested by 'in a green bay', but also green is the colour of life and youth.

The main themes of the poem are the approach of death and the father and son relationship – there are other poems in the collection that have clear thematic links to this. Some of the poet's emotions – anger and defiance, for example – may also suggest connections with other poems. You may feel that the attitude to death in Thomas' poem is very different from others in the collection.

Some questions to consider

Thinking about these questions (and perhaps writing notes or timed short answers) will be helpful when you revise for the examination, because you will have thought about the key ideas in this poem.

1. What different types of man does Dylan Thomas think about, and what is the effect of his reference to these differences?

2. Why does the writer think that people should fight against the approach of death? Is it that he does not want to lose his father, or are there other reasons to do with his attitude to life and death?

3. How do the different forms of imagery, including personification and metaphor, add to the presentation of the ideas in the poem?

4. In what ways do the very set form and structure of the poem contribute to its effect on the reader? (Think especially of rhyme, rhythm and use of repetition.)

5. Look carefully at the tone of the poem. How does this help your understanding of the poet's feelings?

Remember

Background and context

Christina Rossetti was born in London in 1830 and died in 1894. She was part of a family of writers and artists, the best known of whom was her brother, Dante Gabriel Rossetti, a leading figure of the Pre-Raphaelites. She suffered frequently from illnesses, including depression, and the poem 'Remember' suggests that she wrote it when she was convinced she was about to die, although she lived many years after it was written (in 1849) and after its publication, in the collection called *Goblin Market* in 1862. She never married, but was engaged, breaking it off when her fiancé, James Collinson, became a Catholic. It is not known for sure if the poem is addressed to Collinson, but this is thought by many to be the most likely person for her to write to in this way, as there are references to plans for a future life together.

Top tip

You can find out more about Rossetti and her poetry from reference books or on the Internet. You could read some more of the poems, which will help you to understand Rossetti and the attitudes shown in her poetry.

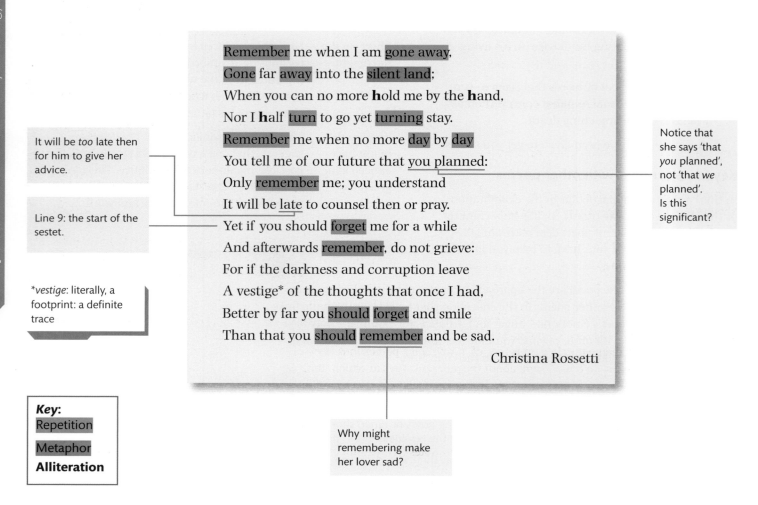

Remember me when I am gone away,
Gone far away into the silent land;
When you can no more **h**old me by the **h**and,
Nor I **h**alf turn to go yet turning stay.
Remember me when no more day by day
You tell me of our future that you planned:
Only remember me; you understand
It will be late to counsel then or pray.
Yet if you should forget me for a while
And afterwards remember, do not grieve:
For if the darkness and corruption leave
A vestige* of the thoughts that once I had,
Better by far you should forget and smile
Than that you should remember and be sad.

Christina Rossetti

It will be *too* late then for him to give her advice.

Line 9: the start of the sestet.

vestige: literally, a footprint: a definite trace

Notice that she says 'that *you* planned', not 'that *we* planned'. Is this significant?

Why might remembering make her lover sad?

Key:
- Repetition
- Metaphor
- **Alliteration**

Understanding the text and commenting on the language

1. Think about the way Rossetti uses the sonnet form. This is the Petrarchan or Italian sonnet, rather than the Shakespearean sonnet, which you have met in studying 'Sonnet 116'. Both types of sonnet have fourteen lines and the iambic pentameter rhythm (ten syllables, with each unstressed syllable followed by a stressed one: te-tum. 'Remember' has an eight-line section (the octave) followed by a six-line section, the sestet. It does not have any rhyming couplets, but there is a carefully structured rhyme scheme, different in the octave and in the sestet. There is a definite change in the ideas when the octave ends: the first eight lines are all asking the lover to remember her, but in the sestet the idea that it might actually be better in some ways to forget, at least 'for a while', is introduced.

2. Select some key phrases from the poem, working with a partner if possible. These may:

   - show how Rossetti thinks he should act after her death

   - focus on features of her language and its effect

   - pick out the effect of words that seem to you striking or unusual and that convey Rossetti's ideas.

   Some examples have been given to get you started.

Key ideas for links with other poems

In this course, and in particular in the examination or the coursework essay (Route 2), it is important to think about how different poets deal with similar ideas or themes. Fill in your grid, to help you link this poem with other poems.

The themes of love and death are, as we have seen, found in various ways in a number of the poems, and there are interesting contrasts between their handling in this poem and in, for example, 'Poem at Thirty-Nine' (page 122) and 'Do not go gentle...' (page 136). Another theme touched on is that of 'time': some poems look back, some look forward, some do both. Think about the different ways in which 'time' is discussed in the different poems.

Figure 3.16 *'Remember me when I am gone away'.*

Language	Comment on meaning/effect
'Nor I half turn to go yet turning stay'	This is a line that is interesting because it seems to switch from talking definitely about the journey into the metaphorical land of death to a 'real' situation.
'darkness and corruption'	These words themselves suggest death (the decaying of the body), but here they also seem to suggest bad thoughts in his mind that she does not want him to have.
'Remember me when I am gone away'	The start is a very direct and clear request, but the reader does not yet know that she is referring to death rather than going away on a journey.

Some questions to consider

Thinking about these questions (and perhaps writing notes or timed short answers) will be helpful when you revise for the examination, because you will have thought about the key ideas in this poem.

1. Why do you think Rossetti refers to the 'silent land'? Does this seem to you a positive or negative image? Why? How do you think the writer felt about dying?

2. Give your thoughts on how a lover (perhaps a fiancé) might have reacted to the poem.

3. Discuss the way the writer uses the ideas of remembering and forgetting in this poem.

4. Explain the change that takes place from the octave to the sestet, and how this affects your overall reading of the poem.

Chapter 4: Responding to unseen poems

Introduction

The Unseen Poem is offered as an optional question in Section A of Paper 2 for those taking IGCSE Route 1 and the Certificate. The skills of responding to a poem that you have never seen before, understanding its meaning, and commenting on its subject-matter and language, are demanding ones, and require just as careful practice as responding to prepared poems.

Because there is no set body of text to study, the way in which you study poetry in preparation for this part of Paper 2 (Question 1) is very much up to the individual student and school or college. Preparing for the unseen poem does mean that a good number of poems have to be studied, though in a slightly different way. This is because all students will become better at reading and responding to unfamiliar poems of different kinds the more practice they have. Examples are given in the examination practice section for 'The Unseen Poem' in the ActiveBook. As, in one sense, the whole of the course can be seen as practising for the examination, it is important to look at:

- different poems
- different styles of writing
- poems written in English but from different countries
- poems from the late 19th and early 20th century (for example, First World War poems) as well as more recent poems from the second half of the 20th century or even the first decade of the 21st.

The more you become used to a wide range of poetry, the more likely it is that you will appreciate the kind of poem that you are faced with, and will be able to respond accordingly.

Figure 4.1 *You need to get used to a wide range of poetry.*

What to look for when reading poems

It is important to keep in mind that there are common elements in reading poems, so the skills you will need when answering on the unseen poem in Section A are the same as those needed for Section B on the Anthology poems.

Seeing the poem as a whole

Concentrating on commenting on individual points (some of which are set out on page 141) can sometimes mean that you miss the real point of a poem. This is a reminder *not* to do that. Poems are meant to be experienced as a whole, and so thinking about the complete poems, their overall *shape* (structure, form), *purpose* and *meaning* is particularly important. Briefly summarising in your notes/plan to make sure that the *content and direction* of the poem are understood can be a way on focusing on the subtle shifts that poems often include.

How poets use language

The same kind of point applies with language. It is very tempting to pick out individual examples of such things as *imagery, use of the senses* or *sound effects* – all of which are very important for understanding how poets use language. However, the risk is that some students tend to pick out examples, and say nothing about their purpose or effect. This is known as '*feature-spotting*', and examiners (and teachers) really hate it. They are always saying that you get no marks for naming a feature ('this is an example of alliteration'), and they are right. Think about *how* and *why* writers use particular words and phrases.

Looking in detail at the poem

You should appreciate how important the overall response to poets' *ideas, language* and *structure* are, and never lose sight of the overall ideas. However, it is equally important to examine the detail. In the chapter on the Anthology (pages 105–139), a number of these elements are discussed, and this guidance is therefore included here as well. Moreover, the Anthology itself can be used for close study, using blank texts at first and then looking at the relevant section of this book to see how the poems are discussed. Some ways of following up an initial reading are suggested (and remember, it is always good to read, or listen, to a poem at least twice before starting to talk or write about it).

Colour-coding or annotating the poem

In the chapter introducing the poems from Section C of the Anthology, detailed advice and examples are given for colour-coding and annotating a poem (page 105). You may wish to reread this section and apply the suggestions to the unseen poem below. It is not a complete list of all possible features, but an approach you might wish to adopt for other features of the language that occur to you when you study an unseen poem.

It might be possible, when you are practising approaches for an unseen poem, to copy the poem onto a large sheet of paper, to give more space for you to annotate the text for yourself.

For the unseen poem, you should be able to use this way of annotating techniques, and follow the checklist that is given to make sure that you have thought about as many ways of thinking about the poem as possible.

Thinking about rhythm and meter

Please reread the 'Thinking about rhythm and meter' section in Section C of the Poetry Anthology Introduction (pages 105–106) and apply the advice to the unseen poems where appropriate. Examiners often comment that students tend not to write very well about metrical effects, so it is worth devoting a good amount of time to preparing this aspect of your study.

Looking at examples

The suggestion has been made that you might use, for your study, poems from the Anthology and the examples in the examination practice section in the ActiveBook. Three more poems are given on pages 142–144, and these are meant to be ones you can work on by yourself, with a partner or in a group.

When you have finished your response to the poems, you can go to the ActiveBook to see some detailed annotations, so that you can test how your own understanding matches with that given there. A few prompts for things to consider are given after each poem.

Example 1

Blackberry Picking

Late August, given heavy rain and sun
For a full week, the blackberries would ripen.
At first, just one, a glossy purple clot
Among others, red, green, hard as a knot.
You ate that first one and its flesh was sweet
Like thickened wine: summer's blood was in it
Leaving stains upon the tongue and lust for
Picking. Then red ones inked up and that hunger
Sent us out with milk cans, pea tins, jam-pots
Where briars scratched and wet grass bleached our boots.
Round hayfields, cornfields and potato-drills
We trekked and picked until the cans were full,
Until the tinkling bottom had been covered
With green ones, and on top big dark blobs burned
Like a plate of eyes. Our hands were peppered
With thorn pricks, our palms sticky as Bluebeard's.

We hoarded the fresh berries in the byre.
But when the bath was filled we found a fur,
A rat-grey fungus, glutting on our cache.
The juice was stinking too. Once off the bush
The fruit fermented, the sweet flesh would turn sour.
I always felt like crying. It wasn't fair
That all the lovely canfuls smelt of rot.
Each year I hoped they'd keep, knew they would not.

Seamus Heaney

Figure 4.2 *'summer's blood was in it'.*

1. Overall interpretation: is this a poem about blackberries or something else?

2. It has been suggested that the ripeness of Heaney's language reflects the ripeness of the fruit. What do you think of this idea?

3. How do Heaney's similes and metaphors enrich the texture of the poem?

4. Think about the use of the five senses (taste, touch, sight, sound, smell) and the focus on colour.

5. What is the importance of the way in which the poem ends?

Example 2

Patrolling Barnegat*

Wild, wild the storm, and the sea high running,
Steady the roar of the gale, with incessant undertone muttering,
Shouts of demoniac laughter fitfully piercing and pealing,
Waves, air, midnight, their savagest trinity lashing,
Out in the shadows their milk-white combs careering,
On beachy slush and sand sprits of snow fierce slanting,
Where through the murk the easterly death-wind breasting,
Through cutting swirl and spray watchful and firm advancing,
(That in the distance! Is that a wreck? Is the red signal flaring?)
Slush and sand of the beach tireless till daylight wending,
Steadily, slowly, through hoarse roar never remitting,
Along the midnight edge by those milk-white combs careering,
A group of dim, weird forms, struggling, the night confronting,
That savage trinity warily watching.

Walt Whitman

*Barnegat: a town in America situated on the Atlantic coast

Figure 4.3 'Wild, wild the storm'.

1. What happens in this poem?

2. Why is the rhythm so important in this poem? (Think about the rhythm and how this contributes to the pace of the poem.)

3. What repetition can you find in the poem, and what effect does this have on the reader?

4. Is the alliteration here simply a sound effect or is it more than this?

5. What do you think the poet means by the 'savage trinity'?

6. How effective do you find Whitman's use of the language of the sea?

7. How are human emotions presented in the poem?

Example 3

Afternoons

Summer is fading:
The leaves fall in ones and twos
From trees bordering
The new recreation ground.
In the hollows of afternoons
Young mothers assemble
At swing and sandpit
Setting free their children.

Behind them, at intervals,
Stand husbands in skilled trades,
An estateful of washing,
And the albums, lettered
Our Wedding, lying
Near the television:
Before them, the wind
Is ruining their courting-places

That are still courting-places
(But the lovers are all in school),
And their children, so intent on
Finding more unripe acorns,
Expect to be taken home.
Their beauty has thickened.
Something is pushing them
To the side of their own lives.

Philip Larkin

Figure 4.4 *'The leaves fall in ones and twos'.*

1. What do you think Larkin was mainly focusing on in this poem?

2. How does Larkin handle the theme of the different generations?

3. The poem starts with reference to the seasons – think about how Larkin uses time and place to contribute to his ideas.

4. Is this a love poem?

5. How do you interpret the words 'But the lovers are all in school'?

6. The poem has quite a set structure. What is the effect of this?

Chapter 5: Responding to unseen prose texts

Introduction

In Section A of Paper 2, you must answer *either* one question set on an unseen poem *or* one question set on an unseen prose extract from a novel or short story. The skills of responding to a passage of prose that you have never seen before, understanding its meaning, and commenting on the writer's skills, the subject-matter, the structure, form and language, are demanding ones, which require just as careful practice as responding to prepared texts.

You will become better at reading and responding to unfamiliar passages of different kinds the more practice you have. Further examples are given in the examination practice section for 'The Unseen Prose Passage' on the ActiveBook. As, in one sense, the whole of the course can be seen as practising for the examination, it is important to look at:

- passages from novels and short stories
- passages from different periods
- passages written in English but from different countries.

The more you become used to a wide range of prose, the more likely it is that you will appreciate the kind of passage that you are faced with, and will be able to respond accordingly.

What to look for when reading prose

It is important to keep in mind that there are common elements in reading all kinds of prose. In particular, the work that you do in preparation for Paper 1, on the prose texts that you will be studying, will also be very useful in thinking about the unseen prose, as you will be considering such key points as:

- how writers achieve their aims
- structure and form
- the writers' use of language.

How writers use language

When commenting on language, it is very tempting to pick out individual examples of such things as *imagery*, *use of the senses* or *sound effects* – all of which are very important for understanding how writers use language. However, it is also important to look at its purpose and effect, not just to notice examples, which is known as '*feature-spotting*', as has been discussed in the section on the unseen poem (pages 140–141).

Figure 5.1 *Novels and short stories*

Looking in detail at the passage

You should appreciate how important the overall response to writers' *ideas*, *language* and *structure* is, and never lose sight of the central ideas. However, it is equally important to examine the detail. In extracts from novels or short stories, it is not possible to look at the overall pattern of events that takes place over the whole work. Hence it is necessary to focus closely on the way in which events and characters are presented within the selected passage, and at the variety of narrative and descriptive techniques employed.

Colour-coding or annotating the passage

As with the study of unseen poems, the use of colour-coding and annotation can be a helpful way to focus on particular effects or language features in the text. Different codes or colours can be used to show connected ideas or images, for example. It is worth looking especially at the use of contrast, which is a powerful feature of many passages of prose, and comparisons. Also:

- use of descriptive adjectives, which can give insight into a character, place or activity

- adverbs linked to verbs, which show how an action was performed: for example, 'he talked loudly, quickly, incoherently, illogically, excitedly, distractedly'

- the use of dramatic or precisely chosen verbs, such as jostled, meandered, exploded, snapped, hovered

- contrasts in colour (light and dark), texture (rough and smooth), taste (bitter and sweet) or sound (shrieked, whispered)

- variation in paragraph, sentence or phrase length

- indicators of time (for example, 'passing rapidly' or 'slowed to a standstill')

- thematic words or ideas, linked to a central focus of the text (love, loneliness, disappointment, fear)

- use of direct speech – exclamations, conversations, commands, arguments.

Looking at examples

When you have finished your response to this passage, you can go to the ActiveBook to see some detailed annotations and test how your own understanding matches that given there. A few prompts to consider are given after each passage.

Example 1

This is the opening of a short story by Alison Randall about the arrival of the first public telephone in a town in the United States, and how a young girl and her twin brother Frank were desperately keen to be able to use it.

End of the Line

When Frank and I stepped through the post office doors, there was a crowd gathered, gawking at the new fixture on the wall like a chorus of wide-mouthed frogs. I had to get closer, and that was where being a girl that's scrawnier than a wire fence came in handy. Fortunately, Frank, my twin of eleven years, was just the same.

"Come on." I said, grabbing his hand, and we slid through the cracks between people until we spilled out in front.

Finally I got a good look. It was fixed to the plaster next to the postmaster's window, the place of honor usually reserved for the Wanted posters. Beady-eyed Zedekiah Smith, the bank robber, still hung there, but even he had been pushed aside for something more important.

A telephone. The first one in town.

"How's it work?" Noah Crawford called out. Noah's the best fix-it man around, and I could tell he was itching to get his fingers on those shiny knobs.

"Don't rightly know," answered the postmaster, and he tugged at his goatee as if it might tell him. "I do know the sound of your voice moves along wires strung on poles. It's sort of like the telegraph, only you hear words instead of dots and dashes."

"Ah," the crowd murmured, and I felt my own mouth move along.

Figure 5.2 *'your voice moves along wires strung on poles'.*

I gazed at that gleaming wood box and something happened inside me. Something — I can only guess — that might be like falling in love. The thought of talking into that box — of making my voice sail through wires in the sky — it took over my brain. I couldn't get it out.

"Frank," I whispered to my twin. "I have to use that telephone."

Five minutes later, Frank towed me up Main Street, toward home. "Liza — " he began, but I cut him off. We two thought so much alike, I had Frank's questions answered before he even asked.

1. How do people react in general to the arrival of the telephone?

2. What do we discover from the way people speak?

3. What do we learn about the wall of the post office?

4. Think about the way the children and their thoughts and actions are described.

5. What do you learn about the twins from the way the extract ends?

Example 2

This is the opening of a short story by William Carlos Williams, who draws on his experience as a doctor dealing with patients.

The Use of Force

They were new patients to me, all I had was the name, Olson. Please come down as soon as you can, my daughter is very sick.

When I arrived I was met by the mother, a big startled looking woman, very clean and apologetic who merely said, Is this the doctor? and let me in. In the back, she added. You must excuse us, doctor, we have her in the kitchen where it is warm. It is very damp here sometimes.

The child was fully dressed and sitting on her father's lap near the kitchen table. He tried to get up, but I motioned for him not to bother, took off my overcoat and started to look things over. I could see that they were all very nervous, eyeing me up and down distrustfully. As often, in such cases, they weren't telling me more than they had to, it was up to me to tell them; that's why they were spending three dollars on me.

The child was fairly eating me up with her cold, steady eyes, and no expression to her face whatever. She did not move and seemed, inwardly, quiet; an unusually attractive little thing, and as strong as

Figure 5.3 *William Carlos Williams was a doctor.*

a heifer in appearance. But her face was flushed, she was breathing rapidly, and I realized that she had a high fever. She had magnificent blonde hair, in profusion. One of those picture children often reproduced in advertising leaflets.

She's had a fever for three days, began the father and we don't know what it comes from. My wife has given her things, you know, like people do, but it don't do no good. And there's been a lot of sickness around. So we tho't you'd better look her over and tell us what is the matter.

As doctors often do I took a trial shot at it as a point of departure. Has she had a sore throat?

Both parents answered me together, No . . . No, she says her throat don't hurt her.

Does your throat hurt you? added the mother to the child. But the little girl's expression didn't change nor did she move her eyes from my face.

Have you looked?

I tried to, said the mother, but I couldn't see.

William Carlos Williams

1. What impression do you have of the doctor and his work from this extract?

2. What do we discover about the thoughts and feelings of the family?

3. How does the writer describe the place where the scene takes place?

4. How does the writer's use of direct speech add to the effect of the passage?

5. In what ways does the writer make the little girl the central focus?

Example 3

In this extract from *The Child in Time*, by Ian McEwan, the writer describes how, one sunny Saturday at a supermarket in South London, Stephen Lewis and his three-year old daughter Kate are routinely doing the shopping when there is a sudden crisis.

The Child in Time

Fifteen minutes later they were at the checkout. There were eight parallel counters. He joined a small queue nearest the door because he knew the girl at the till worked fast. There were three people ahead of him when he stopped the trolley and there was no one behind him when he turned to lift Kate from her seat. She was enjoying herself and was reluctant to be disturbed. She whined and hooked her foot into her seat. He had to lift her high to get her clear. He noted her irritability with absent-minded satisfaction – it was a sure sign of tiredness. By the time this little struggle was over, there were two people ahead of them, one of whom was about to leave. He came round to the front of the trolley to unload it on to the conveyor belt. Kate was holding on to the wide bar at the other end of the trolley, pretending to push. There was no one behind her. Now the person immediately ahead of Stephen, a man with a curved back, was about to pay for several tins of dog food. Stephen lifted the first items on to the belt. When he straightened he might have been conscious of a figure in a dark coat behind Kate. But it was hardly an awareness at all, it was the weakest suspicion brought to life by a desperate memory. The coat could have been a dress or a shopping bag or his own invention. He was barely a conscious being at all.

Figure 5.4 *A father and a daughter in a supermarket.*

The man with the dog food was leaving. The checkout was already at work, the fingers of one hand flickering over the keypad while the other drew Stephen's items towards her. As he took the salmon from the trolley he glanced down at Kate and winked. She copied him, but clumsily, wrinkling her nose and closing both eyes. He set the fish down and asked the girl for a carrier bag. She reached under a shelf and pulled one out. He took it and turned. Kate had gone.

Ian McEwan

1. What impression do you have of the father who is doing the shopping?

2. What do learn about the relationship between the father and his daughter, Kate?

3. How does the writer describe the place where the scene takes place?

4. In what ways does the writer make Kate the central focus?

5. How does the writer use suspense as this extract develops?

Chapter 6: The poetry coursework option

Poetry coursework (Paper 3)

Section C of the Poetry Anthology on pages 105–139 should be studied in detail when preparing for this option.

The coursework option is part of Route 2, which is available *only* to IGCSE students. For this option, a poetry essay is completed as part of coursework instead of the examination paper, Paper 2.

What do I have to do?

You are required to write *one* essay on at least *six* poems. You need to:

- write critically and sensitively on *three* poems in detail from Section C of the Anthology and refer to at least *three* other poems

- show understanding of how meanings and ideas are conveyed through language, structure and form

- make sure that the three poems from the Anthology form the main part of your writing

- make connections between poems, referring to details to support your view

- make sure that the three poems for wider reading are published texts.

Where do the other poems have to come from?

The other poems may also come from the Anthology or they may be chosen from anywhere but they must be published poems. They may be other poems written by the same poets who have written the 'central poems', or they may be drawn from a wider group of poems, writing on the same chosen theme or topic that you have covered in class. As students, you may make the choices yourselves (with guidance from the teacher about suitability) or the topic or topics may be suggested by the teacher.

If the extra three poems are chosen from a wider group that has been studied, you may choose which poems to refer to from this selection. The three central poems from Section C of the Anthology should be analysed in detail. The other three poems are included to show evidence of wider reading and so are referred to only briefly through a few related points, with brief quotations. You are certainly not expected to offer a full analysis of all six poems.

How long should the essay be?

The guidance offered suggests a range of between 1,000 and 1,500 words for the essay, but this is not an absolutely set limit. There is no penalty for writing more

Figure 6.1 *You are required to write one essay on at least six poems.*

than this, but essays much shorter than 1000 words will be unlikely to have sufficient coverage of the poems.

How must it be produced?

You may either write the essay by hand or use a word-processor.

What topics can I choose for this assignment?

- The choice of topic may be decided by the teacher or in some cases left to students.

- You should think about assignments that have scope for development, comparisons and personal interpretation.

- Some topics may be centred on themes.

Activity 1: The thematic approach

Having studied the poems in Section C of the Anthology, make lists of categories, putting the poems under different headings. Suggested areas/ groupings include:

- childhood
- love and loss
- rejection
- parents and children
- relationships
- memories
- suffering
- places
- conflict

- love
- possessiveness
- death
- families
- women
- time
- prejudice
- friendship

Note that these are some possible ideas, but you may have other headings to add. You may list poems under more than one heading.

Other assignment topics could be related to the *writer's technique* or to *poetic form* – for example, a:

- strong *narrative* element
- distinctive *voice*
- particular *poetic form*.

You could also focus on:

- *imagery*
- *vivid description* or an *appeal to the senses*
- *reflective thoughts*
- strong *ideals* or the poem's '*message*'.

There are endless possibilities for topics, allowing scope for individual interpretations and preferences.

Activity 2: The thematic approach

Make a table under the headings as shown:

Narrative	Voice	Form	Imagery	Description/ appeal to senses	Reflection	Ideals/ message

This table may be useful if you are trying to choose a focus or topic. (N.B. If an area or focus has already been decided, you can limit some of these tasks.)

Activity 3: The thematic approach

When you have a closer focus, think about how to make effective connections. You should try to:

- find links for the three central poems from Section C of the Anthology

- highlight differences. or similarities between the poems

- see where you can include your references from the three additional poems, to show your wider reading

- write a plan to incorporate your references and develop your argument.

The following illustrate how to embed quotations:

> **Top tip**
>
> Always look for brief quotations to support ideas and embed these in clear critical statements.

Lawrence remembers her while she 'smiles as she sings', which demonstrates the bond the two of them shared and the happiness of the memory.

D H Lawrence, 'The Piano'

The situation is made even more grim by the juxtaposition of 'Madonna and child', giving an image of holy purity, with the description of the refugee mother and her 'ghost smile' together with the child with 'rust-coloured hair on his skull'.

Chinua Achebe, 'A Mother in a Refugee Camp'

What kind of titles work best?

Remember that your title should allow you to be analytical. It is better to include words such as 'explore', 'analyse' or 'discuss' than to have a title such as 'Write about...' or 'Explain'.

When thinking about the scope of the assignment, you may find it helpful to ask yourself such questions as:

- How far are the poems successful...?
- How far is it true to say...?
- How far do you agree that...?

What kinds of selection of poems work well?

You may have been guided by your teacher towards a particular choice, but if you are making the choice for yourself, think about ways of linking poems clearly. The following examples, under some of the headings listed on page 151, offer a few possible suggestions, but these are not meant to limit your own choices, and you may wish to add other poems instead of those suggested.

Suffering

It is natural to think of war poems, but you may find it helpful to analyse different types of suffering explored in Section C of the Anthology with a wider group of poems about different types of conflict and the results of such conflict.

Three from Section C of the Anthology

These might be chosen from: 'A Mother in a Refugee Camp', 'War Photographer'. 'Once Upon a Time' or 'Telephone Conversation'.

Additional three (from any source)

Think about poems such as the following:

'Disabled' (Wildfred Owen, from Section B of the Anthology); 'Dulce et Decorum Est' and 'Exposure' (both Wilfred Owen); 'Refugee Blues' (W H Auden, from Section B of the Anthology); 'Mid-Term Break' (Seamus Heaney); 'Old Man, Old Man' (U A Fanthorpe); 'Suicide in the Trenches' (Siegfried Sassoon).

Love

It can be a good idea to look at poems that show different forms of love, such as young love, love within a family or married love, for example.

Three from Section C of the Anthology

'Sonnet 116', 'La Belle Dame Sans Merci', 'Poem at Thirty-Nine'.

Additional three (from any source)

Think about poems such as the following:

'To His Coy Mistress' (Andrew Marvell); 'Valediction forbidding Mourning (John Donne); 'Valentine' (Carol Ann Duffy); one of the 'Lucy' poems (William Wordsworth); one of the 'Emma' poems (Thomas Hardy); Sonnet 18 (William Shakespeare 'Shall I compare thee...?'); 'Song for Last Year's Wife' (Brian Patten); 'Our Love Now' (Martyn Lowery).

Chapter 7: Preparing for examinations

Successful revision

There is much advice around on revision, and one thing that is certain is that the same things don't work for everyone. Each person has particular ways of revising and habits of working. Look at all the advice and try out the different suggestions. Decide clearly what knowledge, skills and techniques you need to develop, consolidate or revisit. It is important to study examples of student responses and practise your own answers; please look at examples in the ActiveBook.

Figure 7.1 *Each person has particular ways of revising and habits of working.*

How to plan a schedule

- Draw up a table to show the days and weeks before the examination.
- Decide how much time to give to the subject in each week or day.
- Work out a timetable with reasonable blocks of time.
- Think about the need for variety and breaks.
- Make sure that your schedule is building towards a 'peak' at the right time.

How to improve

- Test yourself.
- Test a friend.
- Practise examination questions.
- Write answers within the time limits of questions in the actual examination.
- Check your understanding of all texts, looking at words, meaning, plot and character, as well as themes and poetic devices.
- Revise literary terms, using a glossary.
- Be sure that you can apply these properly, spell them properly, give examples and explain how and why they are used.

Aids to learning

Write short, clear notes. Use such aids as:

- postcards
- diagrams
- flowcharts
- mnemonics (aids to memory, such as rhymes)
- computer programs
- audio tapes.

Other people

Do not try to go it alone. Ask others to check your progress including:

- teachers
- parents, aunts or uncles
- elder or younger brothers/sisters
- classmates/friends.

Approaching the exams

The whole of this book is designed to help you to approach the IGCSE or the Edexcel Certificate in English Literature with as much confidence as possible. Everyone knows that examination grades are seen as very important. Many courses of study and jobs require particular grades.

Good preparation

Good preparation is one of the main elements affecting how people perform in examinations. This includes both attitude of mind and physical preparation.

Attitude of mind:

- be positive
- be ready
- be calm.

Physical preparation:

- be fit
- be alert
- be awake.

In the examination room

- Come well-equipped.
- Bring pens, pencils, rubbers and rulers.
- Arrive in plenty of time.

Prepare and plan:

- Check how long the examination lasts and use your time properly.
- Look at the details below for your route.
- Don't be tempted to rush the initial reading of passages, poems or questions. It is surprising how many examination candidates make basic mistakes because they did not read through the text in front of them properly.

Using your time effectively in the examinations

Note that the time allocations are intended to include time to check instructions and read the paper carefully. Decide how much time you need to allocate to each question, dividing time sensibly: but remember that you need to include your planning and checking time. You may wish to plan your time for each paper in the following way:

Paper 1: Drama and Prose (both routes)

Reading the question paper	Section A (Drama)	Section B (Prose)	Final checking
5 minutes	Planning – 5 minutes Writing – 40 minutes	Planning – 5 minutes Writing – 40 minutes	5–10 minutes
105 minutes (One hour 45 minutes)			

Paper 2: Poetry (Route 1)

Reading the question paper	Section A (Unseen Text)	Section B (Poetry Anthology)	Final checking
5 minutes	Planning – 5 minutes Writing – 35 minutes	Planning – 5 minutes Writing – 35 minutes	5 minutes
90 minutes (One hour 30 minutes)			

For both Paper 1 and Paper 2:

- Write a brief plan for each answer (approximately 5 minutes).

- Look at any *key words* in the question.

- The most important things of all are to: *answer the question and support your points.*

Check your work. Check that you are keeping to your planned timings. Keep thinking throughout about:

- relevance

- presentation

- accuracy

- evidence.

With your time at the end:

- Make sure that you have answered all questions fully and appropriately.

- Check for accuracy.

- Be certain that everything can be read clearly and that you have used quotations and close reference.

Planning your answers

Answer the question

Do *not* just write down everything you know: this is the most common mistake made by examination candidates.

Planning consists of the following elements:

- reading the question carefully and deciding what are the key words in it

- deciding the main points you wish to make (what the question is looking for and how you intend to tackle it); you should use notes at the planning stage and not write in full sentences until you write your response

- making sure what you wish to include in the answer; a simple diagram or 'map' of your ideas can be very helpful

Figure 7.2 *Make sure that you answer the question asked!*

- giving your answer a structure: introduction, main section(s) and conclusion

- choosing examples or quotations.

Thinking about the question

Be sure that you really understand what the question means. You may find it useful to turn it into your own words and make sure that all the *key words* in the question have been understood. Identifying these can help to show:

- what the question is looking for

- how you need to tackle it.

The content of the answer

The examiner *does* want to know what you think: your own *ideas* and *opinions*. But a series of unsupported statements that start with the words 'I think' is *not* enough, as the examiner also needs to know what these ideas are based on: the analysis of language and content, the understanding of the subject-matter, and the evidence on which your views are based.

Deciding the structure: Introduction, main section(s) and conclusion

- **Introduction:** A clear, brief introductory paragraph can make a very good initial impression, showing the examiner that you are thinking about the actual question.

- **Main section(s):** Decide how many paragraphs or sections you wish your answer to contain. (Four or five paragraphs, each with a clear point, evidence and explanation, would be a good number for a timed examination essay.)

- **Conclusion:** This may be quite a brief paragraph. It should sum up clearly and logically the argument that has gone before. Above all, it should show the examiner that you have *answered the question*!

Top tip

As soon as you know what the question is asking, jot down one or two key quotations, to make sure that you do not forget to include them.

Using quotations

When writing about English Literature texts, whether prose, drama or poetry, one of the most important things is to use quotations. Using quotations effectively is a skill that has to be practised. Over-use of quotations is as much of a mistake as not using enough. You should use quotations especially for the following reasons:

● to illustrate or give an example; such as of a simile or an instance of alliteration

● to explain why you believe something, to support an opinion or argument or to prove a point.

Quotations should be short (one word to a line or two at the most), relevant and effective. Introduce quotations fluently into your sentence structure, *embedding* them in what you are saying, with the use of quotation marks. Look at the following example from an answer about *Romeo and Juliet*:

> *The fact that the play begins with the words 'two households' gives an immediate idea of what the subject of the play will be, and prepares us for the introduction of the 'star-cross'd lovers' who come from these rival households.*

Remember

All students have their own methods for planning and revision, but always take time to remember these three things:

● Practise planning and writing answers to *time*.

● Divide *time* sensibly.

● Finish the exam in *time*, with *time* to check.

Adjective: a word that describes a noun (a person, place or thing), such as 'blue', 'huge', 'cold', etc. Adjectives (and adverbs) can have **comparative** and **superlative** forms such as cold – colder – coldest; great – greater – greatest.

Adverb: a word that gives extra meaning to a verb, an adjective, another adverb or a whole sentence. Adverbs sometimes give us additional detail about how, where, when or how often something occurs.

Alliteration: adjacent or closely connected words beginning with the same sound of a consonant.

Assonance: use of the same or similar vowel sounds close together.

Audience: the person or people for whom a text is intended. They may be defined by age, interest, existing knowledge, gender or any other linking characteristic.

Blank verse: a line of five iambs (unstressed/stressed) feet, the **iambic pentameter**, without a rhyme (as opposed to rhyming couplets), favoured by Shakespeare and other poets.

Caesura: a break or pause in the middle of a line of poetry.

Character: an individual whose personality can be deduced from their actions, what they say and what others say about them. Physical description and dress can give additional clues about character.

Cliché: a hackneyed or over-used phrase such as 'a close shave'. These may also be idiomatic.

Colloquial: relating to conversation/language used in familiar, informal contexts. Contrasted with formal or literary language.

Dialogue: in a play or novel/short story, a conversation between two or more people (where one person is alone and speaking, this is a **soliloquy**).

Didactic language: the language of teaching, when a speaker is trying to impart a message or lesson.

Dramatic irony: a convention whereby the reader or audience is aware of what is going to happen while the main characters are unaware of it.

Dramatic monologue: where a single person (first person narrator) tells the events, especially in a poem, either to a single listener or to the reader.

Empathy: the ability to identify with a person or thing and so understand how he or she feels.

Enjambement (or enjambment): the technique of running the sense on from one line or stanza of poetry to the next without a break. Its opposite is an end-stopped line, usually shown by a punctuation mark – a comma, semi-colon, colon or full-stop.

Epigram: a brief, witty statement, often involving a play on words or a twist to a common saying. Oscar Wilde was the supreme epigrammatist: plays such as *The Importance of Being Earnest* abound in epigrams.

Exclamation: a word or words that are suddenly uttered, perhaps in joy, pain, sadness or surprise. Indicated by the use of the exclamation mark – !

Figurative language: language used to create vivid and dramatic effects where the meaning of words is not the same as their literal meaning, Will tend to make use of metaphor and simile; for example, 'As a tailor, he was a cut above the rest.'

First person narrative: where the person telling the story or recounting events does so as one of the characters, using 'I'; contrasted with the third person, or omniscient narrator.

Flashback: when the time of the action in a novel or play flashes back to an earlier time (often to help explain why the present is as it is).

Form: the kind and style of writing required for a particular purpose.

Genre and generic structure: different text types conform to certain conventions of language, layout and purpose. Texts that share the same conventions are said to be in the same genre, Readers often recognise these patterns and use them to shape their expectations about what may be in a certain text and how it will be written.

Iambic pentameter: a line with five metric feet consisting of two syllables, one unstressed and the second stressed – te-tum – used in **blank verse** and often in **rhyming couplets**.

Imagery: the use of language to create pictures in the minds of the readers, often by using simile and metaphor.

Irony: a situation (situational irony) or statement (verbal irony) where what appears to be the case is not, but perhaps has the opposite effect or sense.

Metaphor: a way of describing something by saying that it is another thing, rather than merely being like another thing. 'The sprinter was an express train, hurtling towards the finishing line.'

Meter: the regular rhythmic pattern of a poem, with a fixed sequence of stressed and unstressed syllables (see **iambic pentameter**, for example). The basic unit of meter is the metrical foot; those commonly found in the poems in this book are: iamb (te-tum), spondee (tum-tum), dactyl (tum-te-te), trochee (tum-te) and anapest (te-te-tum).

Mime: the use of silent movements of the body, such as hand gestures, to convey meaning, with no words spoken.

Narrative text: a text that seeks to retell a story or event, and as such may often be prose fiction. Will tend to use temporal connectives and stress sequence and chronology of events.

Omniscient narrator: a 'third person' narrator who can stand apart from events with a complete knowledge (from the Latin for 'knowing everything').

Onomatopoeia: words that imitate or suggest what they stand for, such as 'cuckoo', 'bang', 'pop'.

Opinion: a belief or a judgement, which may be strongly held, but for which there is no strong evidence or proof.

Oxymoron: an expression made up of two contrasting ideas, such as 'loving hate' in *Romeo and Juliet*.

Pantomime: a performance where everything is carried out through **mime** – movement without words.

Paradox: something said or done that appears to be impossible or self-contradictory.

Pathetic fallacy: attributing human feelings or qualities to nature or to inanimate objects, as in phrases like: 'cruel weather'; 'angry winds'.

Person: in speech and writing we distinguish who we are referring to by using the *first*, *second* and *third* person: the *first* person refers to oneself (I/we); the second person refers to one's listener or reader (you); and the third person when referring to somebody or something else (he/she/it/they).

Persona: the character assumed by a writer or actor; poems often have a persona that we should not assume is identical to the poet – though, in autobiographical poems, it often is.

Personification: a way of giving things or ideas human characteristics; for example, 'Death hovered over the battlefield.'

Platitude: like a **cliché**; something that has been said so often that it has lost its freshness.

Pun: a playful use of language suggesting another word that sounds the same as that used; for example, 'a grave man' (spoken by Mercutio in *Romeo and Juliet*).

Rhetorical question: a question that is for effect rather than to seek an answer; for example, 'Who cares?'

Rhythm: the movement of the meter through the pattern of stressed and unstressed syllables.

Simile: an image created by describing something by saying it is like something else; for example, 'She sang as sweetly as a bird.'

Slang: words or phrases that are very informal/**colloquial** and are used to be vivid or to show association with a particular group of people or part of the country.

Soliloquy: a speech by one person to an **audience**.

Sonnet: a 14-line poem with a formal structure, consisting of a set pattern of lines. The Shakespearean sonnet has three quatrains and a couplet (four and two lines respectively); the Petrarchan sonnet has an octave and a sestet (eight lines and six).

Standard English: Standard English is that which is most widely used and is considered the usual or accepted form of grammar and expression. It is not specific to any region and has no connection with accent.

Symbol: a word to describe one thing that also suggests or embodies other characteristics; for example, the lion is the symbol of courage.

Theme: the subject about which a person speaks or writes. The theme may not be explicitly stated but will be a linking idea that connects the events and ideas in a piece of writing.

Vendetta: a long-standing quarrel, particularly between families.

Witticism: clever humour, often involving word-play.

Please note that while resources are correct at the time of publication, they may be updated or withdrawn from circulation. Website addresses may change at any time.

Anthology

The *Edexcel Anthology for IGCSE and Certificate Qualifications in English Language and Literature* is available to download free of charge from the Edexcel website.

Many English course books used in schools contain sections that relate to literature. Additional guidance can be found in the books/series listed below.

Textbooks

Gill, R. *Mastering English Literature* (Palgrave, 2006) ISBN 9781403944887.

Taylor, P.; Addison, R.; Foster, D. *Edexcel IGCSE English A & B* ISBN 9780435991265. This text includes analysis of poetry and prose.

Study guides

Letts Literature Guides (study guides on specific individual texts)
York Notes (study guides on specific individual texts)

Websites

The Internet offers sites with background information on selected texts and authors. Teachers may also find relevant teaching material on these sites. A selection of websites is listed below.

www.bbc.co.uk/schools/gcsebitesize/english_literature	GCSE revision site for English Literature
www.novelguide.com	Free online literary guides to texts
www.teachit.co.uk	Teaching and revision resources for teachers

CD-ROMs

Romeo and Juliet Longman School Shakespeare ISBN 9781405816526
Much Ado About Nothing Longman School Shakespeare ISBN 9781405856416
Of Mice and Men Heinemann ActiveTeach ISBN 9780435016692
An Inspector Calls Heinemann ActiveTeach ISBN 9780435016593